The Quest for God

The Quest for God

A Personal Pilgrimage

Paul Johnson

HarperCollins*Publishers*

This book is dedicated to
my philosophy tutor, Dr Sophie Botros
and
my parish priest, Father Michael Hollings

This book was originally published in Great Britain in 1996 by Weidenfeld & Nicolson, Orion House.

HarperCollins books may be purchased for educational, business, or sales promotional use. For information please write: Special Markets Department, HarperCollins Publishers, Inc., 10 East 53rd Street, New York, NY 10022.

FIRST U.S. EDITION

Library of Congress Catalog-in-Publication Data

Johnson, Paul, 1928-
    The quest for God : a personal pilgrimage / Paul Johnson. — 1st ed.
      p.   cm.
    Includes index.
    ISBN 0-06-017344-0
    1. Apologetics. 2.Christianity—20th century. 3. Johnson, Paul,
    1928-   . I. Title.
BT1102.J65 1996
239—dc20   96-10721

96 97 98 99 00 RRD 10 9 8 7 6 5 4 3 2 1

Contents

CHAPTER 1

Why I am writing this book

Why am I writing this book? The answer is: partly to help myself, partly to help other people. The existence or non-existence of God is the most important question we humans are ever called to answer. If God does exist, and if in consequence we are called to another life when this one ends, a momentous set of consequences follows, which should affect every day, every moment almost, of our earthly existence. Our life then becomes a mere preparation for eternity and must be conducted throughout with our future in view. If, on the other hand, God does not exist, another momentous set of consequences follows. This life then becomes the only one we have, we have no duties or obligations except to ourselves, and we need weigh no other considerations except our own interests and pleasures. There are no commands to follow except what society imposes upon us, and even these we may evade if we can get away with it. In a Godless world, there is no obvious basis for altruism of any kind, moral anarchy takes over and the rule of the self prevails.

Yet all of us know that the logic of Godlessness would not prevail in our own case. Even if we have no belief whatever in a God, even if we are certain no afterlife will follow and that there is no eternal system of rewards and punishments to regulate our behaviour in the world, we know that we are incapable of pursuing a purely selfish existence. Try as we will, total self-regard, let alone total wickedness, is beyond us. Even the worst of us has redeeming qualities, often positive virtues. Selfishness may be our policy, the pursuit of pleasure our sole aim, but altruism keeps creeping in. It is as though we are morally incapable of conducting our lives without some element of morality.

That human beings have a certain propensity to evil, which

Christians call Original Sin, is obvious to all, and explains much
of the misery of the world. But that we also have a propensity to
good is pretty clear too. It is the existence of these competing
instincts – or whatever they are – struggling for paramountcy in
the same individual at any one time, which makes men and
women so endlessly fascinating, so elusive of final judgments, so
worthy of study. We are not so virtuous as the angels, or so
beautiful or powerful, but we are much more interesting.

The fact that we have the altruistic urge – as well as the evil
one – is the great safeguard of the well-meaning atheists. The
propensity to do good, they argue, makes God and his commandments, his rewards and punishments, unnecessary. Men and
women pursue righteousness for its own sake. The human race is
morally autonomous and, properly led and instructed, will strive
for perfectibility or at least steady improvement, without any
intervention of the supernatural. We want to be good, and the
only problem, in a Godless world, is how to make that altruistic
will prevail over the temptations of the self and the cravings of
the flesh. And that problem can be solved by the right kind of
moral education.

Yet it is a fact that those who hold such views have never been
numerous. Atheism as a positive set of beliefs, including a code of
moral behaviour, has failed to flourish. It may be that fewer and
fewer people in Western countries practise their religion, but the
number of those prepared to state their disbelief in God openly
and specifically is minute. Except to a small minority – probably
no greater today than it was in the time of Percy Bysshe Shelley,
expelled from Oxford University for atheism – denial of God has
no human appeal. We shrink from it. The vast majority are, and
probably always will be, believers or agnostics – and agnosticism
has every degree of doubt and bewilderment, ranging from near-
belief to total confusion.

I suspect the reason why atheism has so little attraction is
precisely our awareness of a desire in ourselves to do good. All of
us have a conscience, whatever we may call it. We know we have
this thing inside us, this nagging inner voice which tells us not to
be so selfish or to help those in need or to prefer right to wrong.
We may suppress it, but it is made of psychic indiarubber and
springs back, however unwanted or unheeded, to wag a finger at

us. The conscience can never quite be killed. And because it exists and we know it exists, we are periodically driven to ponder – or half-ponder – the question: how did it get there? Who put it there? Darwinism may be everywhere the received wisdom, and the process of Natural Selection may be unthinkingly accepted as scientific truth. But these scientific explanations cannot tell us why humanity became uniquely self-conscious. Nor can they explain why an ineradicable part of that self-consciousness is, precisely, our conscience, this moral mentor, instructor and castigator, whose sinewy limbs constantly seek to restrain our animal urges, just as the Old Man of the Sea wrapped his legs tightly round the neck of Sinbad the Sailor. The agnostic cannot shake off conscience as easily as he shakes off positive belief in God, and because conscience remains, there is always in the background of the agnostic's mind the suspicion that some agency put it there. What other explanation can there be? So the shadow of God is never quite dispelled.

There is another force, in addition to conscience, which militates against atheism in the human mind. That force is fear. The Bible says, 'The fear of the Lord is the beginning of wisdom.' One might add, 'The fear of the unknown is the beginning of belief.' For an intellectually self-confident man or woman, with a healthy body and reasonably contented mind, and a job and a sufficient income, atheism is a possible philosophy. But when misfortunes, pain and sorrows arrive, bringing with them fear, and fear not just of present ills but of future, unknown ones to come, then atheism is not enough. A human spirit must indeed be resolute to face adversity utterly alone. In chronic pain and in distress without apparent end, even the confirmed atheist longs for a God, and placed thus *in extremis* the agnostic is an agnostic no more. Fear and pain drive out human self-confidence, and faith returns to fill the vacuum thus left. In hospices for the dying, in the emergency wards of hospitals, in operating theatres, among soldiers on the eve of battle, or sailors in a storm or travellers in a stricken aircraft or ship, there are few atheists and, for the moment at least, no agnostics. The more stricken or terrified the human being is, the more God is needed – and called for. Doubts may return later but, at this moment of terror, fear and belief walk hand in hand.

What, then, is this God who places a conscience in our minds and whose existence – doubted at most other times – comes to our rescue when we are scared? There have been human beings of a sort for perhaps 250,000 years, and during this time the vast majority of them have believed in God or gods. Most of that time their beliefs have been astonishingly specific and detailed, and the gods which have regulated their lives have been clearly portrayed divinities, with biographies, known strengths and weaknesses, likes and dislikes, favourites and enemies. Even with the advent of monotheism, and an omnipotent God who, almost by definition, is less knowable than the pagan pantheons, the scriptures of the Jewish, Christian and Islamic faiths provide a great mass of information about what God does, says and requires.

Yet, in the world today, where our knowledge of the material world increases faster than we can take it in, our ignorance of God also tends to increase. We are less sure about what God is, or what he means to us, than our parents were, just as they were less clear and confident about God than their parents. If I ask someone today, 'Do you believe in God?', the answer is likely to be 'Well, yes, I do in a way, I suppose.' But if I press him or her further and ask, 'What exactly do you mean by God?', the answer is less forthcoming. 'That is a difficult question', they reply, or 'These are deep waters, Dr Watson.' Moderns are not used to questioning themselves about God. Often, they do not wish to inquire – the answers might be disquieting – or, if they are not afraid of the answers, they do not know how to put the questions. These are no-go areas to the modern mind, unexplored territory. Many say to themselves – or rather, they do not exactly say so, but it goes unsaid – 'Let sleeping gods lie.'

But God does not sleep, and will not lie, and sooner or later these questions have to be faced and answered. Better, perhaps, to face and answer them now, than on our bed of sickness, or our deathbeds. For a long time I have been thinking about conducting, on my own behalf, a systematic inquiry into what I understand by God, and what that understanding and its consequences mean in my life and future hopes. I have been a Christian – a Roman Catholic – since birth. From earliest childhood I have been well instructed in my faith. My parents and my elder sisters were devoted Catholics and gave me the best possible family grounding in my religion, and their efforts were supplemented by the Sisters of St Dominic, at my infant school, by the Christian Brothers, at my preparatory school, and by the Jesuits, at my public school. Since then I have written a history of Christianity and a history of the Jews, a study of ancient Palestine, biographies of two modern popes, and countless articles dealing with matters of faith and religion. I have been in Rome for every papal conclave since the war, and for the Second Vatican Council, and I have visited shrines and centres of religious life and thought all over the world. Yet there are many *lacunae* in my knowledge and many unresolved doubts, many questions I have failed to answer or have not sought to examine earnestly enough. For one who has had the best of religious educations, I am disturbingly ignorant and uninstructed, insufficiently curious and persistent in inquiry. I have many things to think about and a lot to learn.

Hence I have begun this book, to resolve many doubts in my own mind, to clarify my thoughts and to try to define what God means to me and my life. I write it in the expectation that, by straightening out my own beliefs, it may help others to straighten out theirs. It is in no sense a manual of religious instruction. Still less is it an attempt to proselytise. It is a meditation, or a series of meditations, on religious subjects, by one who has imperfect knowledge and often ill-defined beliefs, but who has an absolutely genuine anxiety to explore the truth and convey it. I trust it will arouse interest and discussion, disagreement and responses, and thereby intensify debate about the questions which matter more than any others. And, in its own way, I pray it will provide a degree of comfort for those, like me, who wish to move from obscurity to daylight, from doubt to certitude, from infidelity to faith – or from faith to greater faith – and from apprehension, even despair, to hope.

CHAPTER 2

The God who would not die

Sometimes, even more remarkable than historical events are historical non-events. What matters in history is not always what does happen, but what obstinately fails to happen. The twentieth century is a case in point. Immense events took place during it, events to make us marvel – and shudder. But from one perspective – the perspective of human spirituality – the most extraordinary thing about the twentieth century was the failure of God to die. The collapse of mass religious belief, especially among the educated and prosperous, had been widely and confidently predicted. It did not take place. Somehow, God survived, flourished even. At the end of the twentieth century, the idea of a personal, living God is as lively and real as ever, in the minds and hearts of countless millions of men and women throughout our planet.

This curious non-event is worth examining in a little detail. To begin with, we have to appreciate that belief in God has always been strong in the human breast. Until quite modern times, it is impossible to point to any society anywhere, however primitive or advanced, where belief in a god or gods – of some kind – was not general, and as a rule universal. Atheism was remarkably late in making its appearance in human societies. There was, to be sure, talk of atheists in the sixteenth century. Sir Walter Ralegh and his circle of scientific friends, such as Dr John Dee, were accused of atheism in the 1580s. But, closely investigated, their ideas turn out to be no more than a repudiation of the Christian Trinity. Ralegh certainly believed in a divine providence: his *History of the World*, indeed, is impregnated with the notion of a benign, determining hand in history. The world view of Sir Francis Bacon, another man suspected of atheism, turns out to be similar.

It is a remarkable fact that the first well-known European figure who not only proclaimed himself a genuine atheist in life, but died an atheist, was David Hume, the great Scottish historian and philosopher. Hume's death in 1776, as an unrepentant atheist, aroused awed comment on both sides of the Atlantic. Benjamin Franklin thought it a portent – rightly so. Dr Samuel Johnson could not be convinced of the seriousness of Hume's atheism – 'He lies, Sir', he told Boswell. Johnson found it difficult to believe the assurance of Boswell, who had visited Hume on his deathbed, that the philosopher felt no pain at the thought of complete annihilation, a descent into nothingness.

> It was not so, Sir. He had a vanity in being thought easy. It is more probable that he should assume an appearance of ease, than that so very improbable a thing should be, as a man not afraid of going (as, in spite of his delusive theory, he cannot be sure but he may go) into an unknown state, and not being uneasy at leaving all he knew. And you are to consider, that upon his own principle of annihilation he had no motive to speak the truth.

The death of the first confirmed atheist, then, was so remarkable as to seem almost incredible. But in the quarter-century that followed, events moved fast. Five years after Hume died, Immanuel Kant published his *Critique of Pure Reason*, in which he seemed to deal a mortal blow to traditional metaphysics. Metaphysics, as taught in the schools for the best part of a millennium, had been the means by which most Christian intellectuals, especially the clergy, had demonstrated belief in God to be a reasonable proposition, as well as an emotional conviction. Even more destructive of belief, especially among educated people, was the work of Friedrich Hegel. Hegel was not exactly a non-believer himself, though he certainly came close to it in his revolutionary youth. In his maturity, when he was Professor of Philosophy at Berlin University, and conscious of the beginnings of the nineteenth-century religious revival which swept through Europe in the years after 1815, he found it convenient to assert his religious orthodoxy. But his work as a whole pointed in quite a different direction. Hegel presented the entire history of humanity as an inexorable progression from lower to higher forms, from ignorance to knowledge, from unreason to reason. In this process religion had its

place: an important place, indeed, because in its higher manifestations, such as monotheism and then Christianity, it established and then disseminated important aspects of knowledge.
But it was no more than part of the continuing process and,
having fulfilled its role, would yield to higher forms of human
consciousness.

The assumptions behind Hegel's philosophy took a tremendous
hold on the Western mind. They penetrated every aspect of intellectual life, from the physical sciences to the burgeoning social
sciences such as philology, economics, sociology and history, and
even to biblical studies. Almost every radical thinker in the nineteenth century was a Hegelian of sorts. Marxism, for instance,
would have been inconceivable without Hegel's notion of progression. In economic terms, Marx presented human progress as
an advance from primitive to feudal to bourgeois to Communist
societies. Just as pagan forms of belief were projections of the
way in which the means of production were organised in tribal
communities, so Christianity was a function of capitalism. When
capitalism disappeared, as it soon would, Christianity – and
Judaism, its fount of origin – would disappear too. The very notion
of a personal God would vanish from the minds of men and
women, except as a historical curiosity, like the weird crocodile-
and dog-gods of ancient Egypt.

The notion that belief in God was a mere phase in human
development was reinforced by the hammer-blows of scientific
discovery. First came the total recasting of the world's geology, in
the 1820s and 1830s. The traditional chronology and historicity
of the Old Testament were fatally undermined, or so it seemed.
This demolition of the Book of Genesis was a more potent source
of disbelief in Victorian times than the Darwinian Revolution
which followed, in the 1840s and 1850s. Indeed Charles Darwin
himself professed belief and was at pains to emphasise that his
work had no direct bearing on arguments for or against the existence of God. Nonetheless his work was used by the atheists, now
organised and vocal, to assault belief frontally. His most articulate
and forceful follower, T. H. Huxley, virtually declared intellectual
war on Christianity at the 1860 Oxford meeting of the British
Association for the Advancement of Science – and was widely held
to have got the better of Samuel Wilberforce, the Bishop of Oxford,

on that exciting occasion. Thereafter it became almost a commonplace, in intellectual circles, to assume that religious belief was a receding force in human spirituality, and this applied whether you valued it or despised it. Ernest Renan's *Vie de Jésus* (1863) betrayed a sentimental attachment to Christ's ideas but presented him as a purely historical and human figure. Friedrich Nietzsche, on the other hand, declared the death of God to be not merely a fact but a liberation for humanity: he appeared to hate God so much as almost to bring him back to life as a malevolent monster. Probably the most accurate presentation of the prevailing sentiment, on both sides of the Atlantic, was provided by Matthew Arnold's haunting poem, *Dover Beach* (1867), which stressed the almost unbearable sadness among sensitive and righteous men which the loss of faith occasioned. 'The Sea· of Faith', Arnold writes,

> Was once too, at the full, and round earth's shore
> Lay like the folds of a bright girdle furl'd.
> But now I only hear
> Its melancholy, long, withdrawing roar,
> Retreating, to the breath
> Of the night-wind, down the vast edges drear
> And naked shingles of the world.

This slowly became, and has remained, Arnold's best-known and most quoted poem, because so many intelligent and sensitive people exactly shared its awareness of the decline of faith, and regretted the loss of certitude. But there are problems with the poem. The image, though memorable, is not well suited to the loss of faith, if that loss is indeed irrecoverable. Tides do not merely ebb, they flow. The sea does not just withdraw and retreat, it returns and advances. If we pursue Arnold's metaphor, we can expect faith not just to decline but in time to recover. Alternatively, if Arnold was using the metaphor to portray a once-and-for-all disappearance of the sea of faith from mankind's Dover Beach, his forecast has been belied by the events of the twentieth century. The sea has not vanished leaving a naked shingle. What Arnold saw as a continuing event, in a Hegelian sense – he was much influenced by Hegel's ideas – until faith had disappeared completely and yielded to a higher form, has not continued. The withdrawal has halted. There may be no more positive atheists than in Arnold's time. There are without doubt many more agnostics. But equally there are many more believers. It is impossible to say whether the percentage of believers in the world is higher now than it was in the second half of the nineteenth century, partly because it is so difficult to define what we mean by belief, among Western populations let alone among Asian and African ones. But clearly, the event which Arnold thought would in time be completed, and which he tried to depict metaphorically, has not occurred. We still live in a world where the great majority believe in something, in some way or another. Indeed, many more than a billion human beings are Christians – more than there were in the 1860s, when Arnold wrote the poem.

So Arnold was wrong. He was needlessly pessimistic. We can see too that Hegel was wrong because we have had demonstrated, before our eyes, the catastrophic failure of the system based on the ideas of his most influential follower, Karl Marx. The collapse of the Communist empire, or realised Marxism, in total and unqualified ruin, has been a vivid and costly and utterly persuasive demonstration that Hegel's central proposition, translated by Marx into political and economic terms, that human beings progress from lower to higher forms, is false. Humankind may improve and learn to behave better, at any rate up to a point, but it does not change in fundamentals, and Utopian visions are dangerous fallacies. And one way in which men and women do not fundamentally change is that they continue to hanker for a supreme being, above and outside themselves.

I was much struck by a story I read in the newspaper in 1979, and I have often thought about it since. During the early summer of that year, near Luxor in Upper Egypt, the local police found the bones of a 35-year-old Canadian woman, who had disappeared two years before without trace. It appeared that, while wandering alone over an ancient burial site, nearly 4,000 years old, she had stumbled into a deep labyrinth of abandoned archaeological diggings, sixteen feet deep. Unable to climb up its crumbling sides of earth and sand, she had died a lonely and horrible death, of hunger and thirst. She had with her a picture-postcard, and on it she described what had happened. She knew, she said, that escape was impossible and rescue almost hopeless, and concluded: 'I am preparing myself for death.' She did not say to which, if any, of the formidable secular philosophies of her time she had turned in her last days and hours; or whether, like most ordinary people of all ages and races throughout history, she had placed her trust in a deity. But she knew that death was coming to her, and that she must prepare for it. The instinct to prepare for death, to anticipate it and in some way to confront it, is absolutely fundamental in mankind. I believe the woman felt she was to meet, if not her maker, then someone or something, and that she must get ready for this encounter. It is significant that, only a few hundred yards from where this heart-sickening little tragedy occurred, the theologians of ancient Egypt, around 2000 BC, had first clarified the concept of individual death and judgment – a concept which, however confusedly, was in the stricken woman's mind, is with us still, and is likely to remain with us, indeed, as long as the human race endures.

Why has belief in God – or belief in something beyond us – endured in the twentieth century? There seem to be many reasons. Let us look at them in turn. First, it seems as though science, which once upset the certitudes of so many Victorian believers, has lost its power to shake faith. Scientific knowledge has marched on in the twentieth century, faster and more formidably than ever. Yet, as Darwin himself first pointed out, what science tells us does not necessarily have any relevance to what we feel in our minds and hearts about God. The physical and the metaphysical can be seen to exist on different planes. The great scientific discoveries and engineering events of the twentieth century are primarily statements not about God but about man, and the state of his knowledge. The theologians of the eighteenth century found no difficulty in reconciling Newtonian physics with God's universe. But when Albert Einstein first published his General Theory of Relativity in 1915, which turned Newton's straight lines into curves, and presented space-time as a continuum rather than separate dimensions, and when the General Theory was verified in 1919, there was no convulsion in the religious world, no attempt to challenge or deny the change in our view of cosmology. It is as though the world of religion had long since learned to absorb all the shocks of science. When human beings split the atom, and then created nuclear energy; when they built rockets and landed on the moon, and sent other rockets to distant space; when they discovered the double helix and began to decode the genetic basis of creation, and learned to splice genes and make entirely new living substances – when all these dramatic events took place, human belief or disbelief in a prime mover or a first cause or a divine creation remained unaffected. Science and the religious life continued alongside each other throughout our century. Often they overlapped. It is significant that the great majority of those who work in the scientific world – perhaps as many as 80 per cent – profess some kind of religious belief.

It is, therefore, a notable fact about the twentieth century that, during it, science and religion ceased to be enemies. In some modest ways they became friends. Looking back on them, the great rows between the clergy and the scientists in the nineteenth century seem childish. Hard to say, now, who cut a more absurd figure in 1860, Bishop Wilberforce or Professor Huxley. The great evolutionary and geological discoveries of the 1820s, 1830s, 1840s and 1850s upset the traditional religious chronologies. So what? These chronologies were gimcrack schemes worked out by pious men who took the biblical patriarch-lists literally or, rather, assumed they were as comprehensive as they claimed. Such clues were useless to determine prescriptive history, as is obvious to all now. But it does not mean that the patriarch-lists are mere myth, any more than the king-lists of Ancient Egypt.

In fact, the science of modern archaeology and historical philology actually provides verification of the most ancient biblical texts. Whereas, from the time of Spinoza, throughout the nineteenth century and almost up to the Second World War, systematic criticism of the Old Testament texts tended to destroy their historicity, and to reduce the Pentateuch, in particular, to mere myth or tribal legend, the trend over the last half-century has been quite in the opposite direction. The Flood, for instance, has been restored to history. Archaeological discovery provides now a firm historical background to the patriarchal society described in the Book of Genesis. Such names as Abraham, Isaac and Jacob, far from being later eponyms, attached to collective groups or tribes or nations, were in fact common in the Ancient Near East during the first half of the second millennium BC. The French excavations at the ancient palace of Mari, and still more the American excavations at Yorgan Tepe (ancient Nuzu) 100 miles north of Kirkuk in Iraq, have produced an enormous number of cuneiform documents – over 20,000 clay tablets, dating from the fifteenth century BC, in Nuzu alone – which illuminate the background to the patriarchal narratives. Many of these tablets are from private archives, recording exactly the kind of legal transactions, so puzzling to us, in the patriarchal stories. The proposal for the adoption of Eliezir as heir-presumptive to Abraham, the latter's negotiations with Sarah, the transfer of a birthright from Esau to Jacob, the binding power of a deathbed blessing and disposition of property, Rachel's theft of her father's teraphim or household gods and Jacob's tortuous legal relations with Laban – all of these were in accordance with standard legal practice as illustrated repeatedly in the Mari and Nuzu tablets.

Thus science, having once appeared to destroy the historicity of the Bible, now seems more likely, on the whole, to corroborate it. I could give many other examples – most of the cities mentioned in the Old Testament, for instance, have now been identified and their remains explored. Of course, none of this proves God exists, only that the ancient people of the Hebrews believed he did. However, another science, astrophysics, does have an inherent tendency to bring us closer to the creator, or a creator. The universe is so vast that information from its distant corners, albeit travelling at the speed of light, may take millions of years to reach us. In theory, then, it is possible for us to study very ancient history in distant stars. All we need, in fact, is the physical instrumentation to look far enough. What we do know confirms the biblical notion of a specific moment of creation. Some years ago, I remember listening, or half-listening, to a talk on the radio about the Big Bang which set the entire universe in motion. I suddenly sprang into consciousness and exclaimed, 'But this is the first chapter of Genesis, told in scientific terminology!' The Big Bang theory of the origins of the universe is now accepted by virtually all astrophysicists. It has yet to be verified for certain, though all recent discoveries tend in that direction. However, the day on which we will be able to see, by study of distant space, the actual moment of first creation may not be far distant. It is a matter of money, rather than technology. We have the physical means, even now, of erecting a giant telescope on the moon, which for a variety of reasons could function far more effectively than on earth. Images of such a telescope, radioed back to earth, could distinctly show us two people tossing a coin in the streets of New York or London, and could tell us whether it landed heads or tails. The same telescope, directed into the far peripheries of the universe, could take us so far back in time as to approach the moment of creation itself.

At that stage we would know *how* the universe came into being. Of course, that does not automatically tell us *who* did it. But it was a famous maxim of Dorothy L. Sayers' fictional detective, Lord Peter Wimsey, that 'If you know *how*, you know *who*.' What applies to murder investigations does not necessarily apply to cosmogony. But the point is worth thinking about. If we can see the moment of creation, how long will it be before we can apprehend the creator too?

Of course, these are wild speculations and I do not put too much stress on the ability of science to teach us theology. All the same, it would have astonished Bishop Wilberforce to see science suddenly emerge as theology's strong right arm, even in theory. And yet – why not? Medieval intellectuals, like St Thomas Aquinas, did not see them as enemies – on the contrary, he called theology 'the Queen of the Sciences'. Aristotle would have taken the same view: to know about God was the highest of all forms of know-ledge, and it was only natural for all the sciences, humble and sublime, to pursue that end. So what might be called the friendly neutrality, or the benevolent objectivity, of science in the twen-tieth century is one reason why God has stayed in men's minds.

Another is the actual events of our dreadful century. The evil done in our times is beyond computation and almost beyond the imaginations of our forebears. There is nothing in the previous history of the world to compare with the scale and intensity of destruction of the two world wars, with the indiscriminate slaugh-ter of the bombing of European and Japanese cities – even before the use of the A-bomb – and with the colossal cruelty of the Nazi death-camps and Soviet Gulag. More than 150 million people have been killed by state violence in our century. One might expect most people to ask: how can God allow such things? Or, how can there *be* a God if such complete moral anarchy reigns? Yet experience shows that only a tiny minority ask these questions.

Most people react to the horrors of war by turning to God for protection, solace and comfort.

Again, a few critics of religion point out scornfully that in both world wars, Catholic and Protestant chaplains administered to the troops on both sides, bade them fight courageously in a righteous cause, and prayed with them for victory. In the United States and Britain on the one hand, in Germany on the other, the churches were packed with worshippers praying for mutually incompatible views of justice. How, the critics ask, could God preside over this moral confusion? But such arguments cut no ice with most people. It is worth remembering that, during the American Civil War, the Protestant churches (the Catholic authorities did their best to stay out of the controversy) were right to the forefront in backing the cause of States' Rights on the one hand, and Emancipation on the other, that they were among the most vehement in urging both sides to fight to the finish, and that, without them, the war would have been less ferocious, and would have ended sooner. All that may be so, but it is an undeniable historical fact that most of the churches concerned emerged stronger from the war. The Southern churches, in particular, having separated themselves from their Northern brethren, and acquired separate identities, entered on a long period of growth and militancy, characteristics which endure to this day. America's Bible Belt, the heartland of Protestant fundamentalism in the United States, is in many ways the product of the Civil War. Some of America's most God-fearing institutions – universities, colleges, churches, charities, missionary and revivalist centres – are the products of that fearful conflict.

So it has been in the twentieth century. Its horrors were instrumental in turning men and women towards God rather than against him. Most people saw the wars as themselves the products of Godlessness, materialism and sin, and their perpetrators as those who had banished God from their hearts. And it is undeniable that the two greatest institutional tyrannies of the century – indeed of all time – the Nazi Reich and the Soviet Union, were Godless constructs: modern paganism in the first case and openly proclaimed atheist materialism in the second. The death-camps and the slave-camps were products not of God but of anti-God. Hitler was born and brought up a Roman Catholic and Stalin was once a Russian Orthodox apprentice-monk, but it is hard to

imagine any two men in history who were more bereft of basic
Christian instincts or more systematically committed to the
destruction of Christian values.

Both these regimes persecuted Christians, the Soviet Union
more thoroughly but in some respects less viciously than the Nazi
Reich. Both these attempts to damage or crush Christianity failed
utterly. The churches were, if anything, revitalised by Nazi and
Communist hostility, and emerged stronger. Oppression, torture
and executions of Christians who protested against these regimes
produced a rich crop of saints and martyrs, Protestant, Catholic
and Orthodox, whose sufferings and example have nourished the
faith all over Europe.

The outstanding collective example of the way in which the
horrors of the twentieth century promoted organised religion and
belief in God has been Poland. Poland is a morally ambivalent
country in some ways. It has been both a persecutor of Jews and
a refuge for them. Like the Jews, it has been an egregious victim
and, in a paradoxical way, it has flourished as a result of the
experience. Wedged between the pagan and the atheist *colossi*,
occupied by both, plundered and ravaged by both and, above all,
religiously persecuted by both – for both saw the Catholic Church
as the very essence of the Polish spirit of resistance – God-fearing
and God-praising Poland emerged stronger from this searing
experience. The Polish church is now the strongest Christian
church in Europe, perhaps in the world. Even on weekdays, in the
early hours of the morning, churches in Poland are thronged
with worshippers and communicants. There are more priests and
seminarians, more monks, friars and nuns, than ever before. No
one saw more clearly than the Poles that their religious faith, their
belief in God, and their adherence to his commands was the best
defence – usually their only defence – to the Nazi and Communist
attempts to crush them out of existence. Hence, in the post-war
period, it was Poland which began the process of undermining,
then overthrowing, the Communist tyranny in Eastern Europe. It
was Poland which made available to the Catholic Church thousands of priests, missionaries, teachers, theologians and evangelists to strengthen the Christian faith throughout the world.
Finally it was Poland which produced the greatest of the twentieth-
century popes, John Paul II, who has treated the entire globe as

his parish and has carried the Christian message, as he sees it, to every corner of all five continents. You may or may not agree with what John Paul II teaches in some areas. But it cannot be denied, even by his critics, that he presents Roman Catholic Christianity, pure and undefiled, in its most uncompromising and rigorous form, that he makes no concessions whatever to the twentieth century and its hedonism, and that despite this – almost certainly because of this, too – he is listened to and heeded by hundreds of millions throughout the world. That unwillingness to compromise in the face of evil springs directly from the Polish experience, and that in turn is the fruit of a twentieth century which set out to banish God and ended by confirming him in many hearts.

There is a third reason why belief in God has survived the twentieth century. That is the total, and in many cases abject, failure of the alternatives to God. This phenomenon is so striking that it merits separate treatment.

CHAPTER 3

Is there an alternative to God?

It is a striking fact that, at the end of the twentieth century, the vast majority of people in the world still believe in a god, and this is true even of those who live in the 'enlightened' West. But it cannot be denied, also, that the Promethean spirit, the spirit of those who believe they can do without God – or that they can find substitutes for God – is also strong today, perhaps stronger than ever before. This Promethean spirit, proud of man's progress and seemingly limitless potential, unwilling to submit to the subordination which the notion of God demands, driving itself first to resistance, then to denial that God exists at all, has been growing with dramatic speed over the past 250 years. It is presented as the voice of modernity, the creed of rationalism, the march of progress. It preaches the absurdity of belief in God, the fatuity of religious doctrine, and the positive evil of much of the teachings and practices of the organised faiths. In the Western world today, it is possible that a majority of the people who consider themselves well educated – that is, who have attended university, read books regularly and regard themselves as people who think seriously about the public issues of the day, and the meaning of life – would range themselves in the Promethean camp, with varying degrees of consciousness and enthusiasm. Scepticism towards or denial of the existence of God is the hallmark of modern *homo sapiens* – Thinking Man.

One characteristic of the Protheans has always been, and is still today, to mock at the beliefs of religious people, especially Christians. Voltaire began the practice. It is fashionable even now, notably in the polemics of Professor Richard Dawkins of New College, Oxford, a biologist and author of *The Selfish Gene*, who has put himself at the head of the Protheans in Britain and is probably today the world's best-known atheist evangelist. To such people, Christianity is an absurdity, not just because it subscribes to an impossible belief in God – who does not exist – not only because it is an anti-social force in the world – for instance, by opposing artificial birth control – but also and above all because it teaches a whole series of ridiculous doctrines. These range from the resurrection of the dead to transubstantiation (consubstantiation is scarcely more credible), from belief in miracles to Papal Infallibility. To the Prometheans, religion would be a joke, were it not so serious, and destructive. And, certainly, if you look back at some of the things which religious men have taught and believed in over the long centuries of Christianity, it is hard not to smile.

However, it is a moot point whether to preach and believe in the manifestly incredible is a characteristic of Christians or of *homo sapiens* as a whole. For what is most remarkable about the Promethean movement is not its castigation of Christianity but the absurdity of its own alternative explanations of life. I find that one of the many advantages of being a historian is that you are constantly obliged to refer to the exact *data*, to what precisely happened at any one time, and what people actually said then. The record of the Prometheans, to judge by their utterances, is no more impressive than that of the benighted and obscurantist Christian clergy they denounced. Here, taken almost as random, are some of them. For instance in 1764, by which time the Prometheans were already powerful in educated society, their leader, Voltaire, wrote: 'Theological religion is the enemy of mankind.' Note: not *an* enemy, but *the* enemy. There are many enemies of mankind today, many more than in Voltaire's time, I fear, but no one in his senses would put 'theological religion' high on his list. Or again, here is Winwood Reade, whose powerful tract *The Martyrdom of Man* was a bible of many atheists in the late nineteenth century: 'The destruction of Christianity is *essential* to the interests of civilisation.' Note again, the tone of extremism: not 'desirable' but 'essential'. Today, our civilisation, or what is left of it, seems far more fragile than in Reade's fortunate lifetime, and were he to return to earth today I do not believe he would find a solitary soul, agnostic, atheist or anything else, who would agree that the destruction of Christianity is essential to keep civilisation going. Quite the reverse. The vast majority see it as a prop, however feeble.

Other central propositions of the Promethean faction, or what at the end of the nineteenth century became known as the humanists, seem equally ridiculous with the passage of time. Ernest Renan, the French popular historian and seer, was foolish enough to write: 'History proves beyond possibility of contradiction that Christianity is not a supernatural fact.' Poor Renan! So plausible and sure of himself in his day, when his agnostic *Vie de Jésus* was one of the top best-sellers of the entire nineteenth century, and now no more convincing than Bishop Usher, who worked out from the Old Testament the exact day and year the world began. Both now raise only smiles of compassion.

Actually, Renan, by the standards of most nineteenth-century anti-religious intellectuals, survives comparatively well. The ones who appear most absurd are precisely those who tried to apply the principles of contemporary science – the frontiers of knowledge – to explain the world in non-religious terms. The French lexicographer Émile Littré defined 'soul' as 'anatomically the sum of functions of the neck and spinal column, physiologically the sum of function of the power of perception in the brain'. Not exactly helpful, is it? The German follower of Darwin, Ernst Haeckel, by contrast, wrote: 'We now know that ... the soul [is] a sum of plasma-movements in the ganglion cells.' In England, Professor John Tyndall thought 'all life' was 'once latent in a fiery cloud'. In France, the philosopher-historian Hyppolite Taine stated: 'Man is a spiritual automaton ... Vice and virtue are products like sugar and vitriol.' Late nineteenth-century atheists were particularly positive, though contradictory, on the process of thought. Karl Vogt laid down: 'Thoughts come out of the brain as gall from the liver or urine from the kidneys.' Jacob Moleshott was even more certain: 'No thought [can emerge] without phosphorus.'

The twentieth-century Prometheans do not survive with much more credit and their *obiter dicta* are already acquiring the same fusty whiff of absurdity. H. G. Wells, world-famous in his day, not least in America, was a marvellous writer of science fiction, but it is now almost impossible to point to a single pronouncement of his on society in his own day which carries the ring of truth or even mere plausibility. He ended his life (in 1945) in despair, having painted a strange mural on the walls of his London house, of horned devils and an image of Man, accompanied by the slogan: 'Time to Go'. Bertrand Russell, whom I knew – he figures prominently in my book *Intellectuals* – was perhaps the leading evangelist of anti-God rationalism of the century. But it is hard to find a subject – and he wrote on most subjects, including those of the highest importance – on which he did not change his mind fundamentally, often more than once, and usually without explanation or apology; indeed his rule was to deny that any change of position had taken place. His immense output, supposedly offering an alternative philosophy of life and morals to one based on belief in God, thus leaves the reader who struggles through it – and there cannot be many these days – with an impression of total confusion. The truth is, Russell could not devise a Promethean alternative to God which convinced even himself for more than a few years; his secular faith was in a state of constant osmosis, like that of Auguste Comte, who occupied the same position of intellectual eminence in the mid-nineteenth century as Russell did in the twentieth and is now simply a joke, if a pathetic one.

Russell's most passionate disciple was the late Sir Alfred Ayer (A. J. Ayer), an engaging man, like Russell a tremendous egoist and an unconsciously comic figure, in whose company I delighted. We used to meet at the Beefsteak Club, where I enjoyed teasing him. 'Freddie, I suppose it would be a correct statement to say you are the most intelligent man in Britain.' 'Oh, no, no, no, my dear fellow,' he would begin modestly, 'don't be so absurd.' Then, intellectual rigour and his love of truth would assert themselves. 'Well, if one looks at the statement seriously – if one considers – if, in short, one wishes to be strictly honest, I suppose – indeed I *must* – conclude you are right; you are, in fact, *absolutely right!*' My other tease was to threaten to visit him on his deathbed, accompanied by a Jesuit of powerful intellect, who would convert him to Roman Catholicism at the eleventh hour. I soon realised this genuinely frightened him, so I dropped it. In fact, Ayer's end was a little mysterious, because he had a physical experience which convinced him he had died and come to life again, and his final writings on the subject are so unclear to me that I am not sure whether he met his God in a state of disbelief, belief or genuine doubt. At all events, as with Russell himself, there was evidence of instability and confusion in Ayer's thought.

A third leading Promethean I knew, Jean-Paul Sartre, died I think in a state of disbelief, but his life and writings are no better an advertisement for the secular, humanistic, alternative to religious faith than Russell's. Sartre was not a bad fellow in some ways. He was, for instance, one of the very few progressive intellectuals I have ever met who was really generous about money. But the heroic secular morality he preached, derived largely from Heidegger and christened by the media 'existentialism', was belied by the extraordinary squalor, selfishness, confusion, cruelty and not least cowardice of his own life. His final years, in fact, were squalid bordering on the horrific. Moreover, there was in his writings – his output, like Russell's, was enormous – a degree not so much of inconsistency, though there was certainly that too, as of incoherence, so that in the end one was not clear what, if anything, he did believe, and what, if anything, he advised humanity to do. Sartre, I feel, bewildered even his intellectual followers, who were once numerous. What then had he, classified in his heyday in the late 1940s as the world's leading philosopher, to offer to the great mass of ordinary people? Yet if there is to be a truly secular, humanist alternative to God, it must speak clearly to the masses, as Christianity has always done.

Humanism, in our time, has been a dismaying failure, and my impression is that, at any rate as a substantial body of thought, it is in decline. It is interesting to note that, in Europe, membership of organised atheist and humanist societies, as a proportion of the population, reached its peak in the 1880s, at roughly the same time as the maximum percentage of those regularly attending church. But while Christianity has survived, and in many places flourishes and renews itself, no one could now conceivably believe that humanism is the spiritual force of the future, or indeed anything at all except a faint impress in the minds of a small minority. A more interesting and difficult question is the degree of harm it has done, particularly in our century. I believe that the political teachings of Sartre, for instance, were immensely pernicious among the French-educated leaders of Third World countries in South-East Asia and North Africa. The genocidal leaders of the Pol Pot regime were in a sense Sartre's children. In general, however, the humanist impact was ephemeral and in many respects superficial. Millions read Wells and saw the plays of George Bernard Shaw, found them clever, were impressed for a time, then laughed, as the absurdities and misjudgments – and essential frivolity – of both became manifest, and went their ordinary, humble ways as before. Russell, like Sartre, retained a small, fanatical following to the end; but had neither man existed, such grotesque disciples would have found equally irritational and eccentric masters to serve.

Far more dangerous than the humanist impact have been the twentieth-century attempts to find substitutes for God – attempts both conscious and unconscious – which appeal not so much to the intellectual pretensions as to much deeper, darker and stronger instincts in mankind. The detonator of the modern tragedy of humankind was the First World War, which began in Europe in 1914 and which America joined three years later. Its destructive impact on established and improving notions of human behaviour and international morality was immeasurable and we are still suffering from its consequences. This war was not merely without reason, it was plainly avoidable. What caused it? I suggest it was, above all, the worship of money and still more power which already, by 1914, was becoming for many people a substitute for the worship of God. We have already noted that in Europe the percentage of the population attending church regularly began to decline, for the first time, from the end of the 1880s. Now church attendance is not a key, certainly not *the* key, to social and individual morality. But history suggests that the regular practice of a structured religion does impose restraints on human appetites, both individual and collective, which are difficult to achieve by any other means.

In the United States church attendance continued to rise until the end of the 1950s, but in Europe its fall around the beginning of the twentieth century was accompanied by a marked and progressive increase in materialism, at all levels of society. What is materialism? It is the belief that the object of life is to satisfy instinctual human desires to possess, use, consume and control. At all levels of society, the growth of materialism leads to forms of moral squalor which make the heart sick and destroy decency and happiness. At the highest levels it leads to war, and to war on a scale and of a savagery hitherto inconceivable. The growth of gross national products in the years 1890–1914, especially in the United States, Russia, Germany and Japan, was truly prodigious. This led to greedy competition and, not least, fear. One primary cause of the First World War was terror among Germany's rulers that Russian industrial growth was now so rapid, and must inevitably be reflected in such growing military power, that Germany, with her weaker ally Austria, had a duty to provoke the Russian bear into conflict while they were still strong enough to overwhelm the monster. The courts of central and eastern Europe were still nominally Christian but riddled with superstition and Erastianism. Russian Orthodoxy was a state church of the most craven kind. Prussian Lutheranism was an enthusiastic bedfellow of a largely militarised society. Austrian Catholicism was a formal palace creed which had long since cut itself off from spiritual roots of any kind. In France the militant secularists won an overwhelming political victory in the aftermath of the Dreyfus Affair and had systematically tried to purge the state, the schools and the armed forces of Christian influences. In all four states, the spiritual vacuum thus created was increasingly filled by adoration of power, above all military power. Guns replaced altars, and barracks churches. Thus the stage for catastrophe was set.

The war was fought with a degree of unscrupulousness and high technology – and thus violence – never before experienced in world history. It reversed the increasing civility of the nineteenth century and introduced an era of extremism in thought and action which itself bred systematic attempts to create totalitarian alternatives to religion. These produced formulae for horrors yet unimagined by man. The first, the Soviet Communism imposed on Russia from 1917, specifically denied the existence of God, whom its ideological mentor, Karl Marx, described as an imaginative superstructure on the capitalist system of production. Change the system, and the notion of religion itself would gradually fade from people's minds. The system was certainly changed, but it was nonetheless found necessary to close down by force thousands of churches, synagogues and mosques, add compulsory atheism to the school curriculum, and slaughter thousands of practising Christians, Jews and Muslims – policies which continued unremittingly until the late 1980s. Grotesque secular alternatives to traditional Christian practices were devised. Baptism and confirmation were replaced by induction into the *komsomol* youth movement. Elaborate but lifeless secular marriage-services were conducted in Moscow's Hall of Weddings. The founder Lenin, once dead, was installed in a patriarchal tomb and worshipped. His successor Stalin was adored while yet alive and, like the savage gods of Aztec Mexico, demanded and received worship by hecatombs of sacrificial victims.

Other living gods sprang up from the diseased bowels of this alternative religion: petty but nonetheless bloodthirsty deities like Hoxha of Albania and Ceauşescu of Romania, and self-proclaimed supergods like China's Mao, who wrote and forced his entire nation to learn by heart his catechism or Little Red Book, and who performed 'miracles', such as swimming 20 miles in the Yangtze at the age of 75. When the entire worldwide system of murder, mendacity and fraud began to collapse at the end of the 1980s, evidence of every form of corruption known to man began to emerge from this system based on 'reason' and 'idealism' – rather as, when the triumphant Christians first took over pagan Alexandria, they discovered that wooden idols which miraculously spoke oracles had hidden recesses in which the devil-priests had concealed themselves while oraculating, and from which now sprang forth swarms of mice and rats and other vermin.

This first totalitarian alternative to God, founded in 1917, bred others. Mussolini, himself originally an orthodox Marxist, praised by Lenin, then branded a heretic, founded a new political church. He adopted the symbols of ancient, pagan Rome, but his Fascist movement was never quite sure whether to deny the existence of God, or subvert and utilise it, whether to persecute the church or exploit it. Mussolini himself oscillated between atheist braggadocio and the craven superstition typical of the most primitive forms of Italian Catholicism, but it was still unclear whether he was a Christian when, in 1945, summarily executed, he was hung, naked and upside down, alongside his mistress on the shores of Lake Como. Hitler's Nazism, based on both the Soviet and Italian models, but with many characteristics drawn from southern Germany and Austria, was more deliberately and consciously an attack on Christianity, and an alternative to it. It preached various forms of purity, including race-purity. Hitler spoke of 'the higher morality of the Party' to justify mass-murder, just as Lenin used the excuse of what he called 'the Revolutionary Conscience'. The Nazis devised elaborate quasi-religious services, ranging from mass parades with sacred torches, to private wedding ceremonies between party members, who had to prove their Aryan ancestry. Both involved ancient pagan practices, such as sacrificial fires, sprinkling of salt, incense and other substances, the swearing of vows and blood-pledges, and millenarian hymns. The striking characteristic of Hitler's alternative to God is that, while in theory appealing to the highest human ideals, it exploited in practice the basest human instincts – cruelty, greed, corruption and the desire to tyrannise over the weak. It also combined a yearning for a primitive past, the pagan forest culture of the *Nibelungenlied*, with the rapid acquisition and use of the most modern methods of warfare, torture and mass-slaughter. Hitler's own end illustrated this sinister paradox, he being immolated on a pagan funeral pyre inflamed by *ersatz* gasoline.

Such totalitarian substitutes for religion spread rapidly in the 1960s, following the withdrawal of the colonial powers, to Africa and parts of Asia. Voltaire's dictum that religion was the enemy of mankind rang particularly hollow in South-East Asia (as well as China), where the missionary Catholicism of the French was replaced by the totalitarian poverty and militarism of Ho Chi Minh, who soon had the largest armed forces, in relation to population, in the world, and by the genocide of Pol Pot. Missionaries had been accused of many 'crimes' in Africa and the East – of trying to stamp out human sacrifice, polygamy and cannibalism, for instance, of forcing local women to cover their nakedness, and their husbands to make love to them in the orthodox 'missionary position'. What a golden age it now seemed, as large parts of Africa embraced the Communist alternative to God, and so plunged themselves into civil and internecine wars, perpetrated man-made famines, as had Stalin in Russia, and acquired huge armies and modern weapons at the cost of everything else. The martyrdom of Ethiopia – a Christian state, if an elementary and rough-hewn one, since the fourth century – has been of particular poignancy, as its noble-looking and God-fearing people were decimated by endless civil war, famine and disease. And, in many parts of black Africa, where missionaries had tried to introduce Western standards of moral behaviour along with their altars, self-made chieftains, now calling themselves generals and presidents, reverted to mass-slaughter on a colossal scale and in some cases to cannibalism too. The witch-doctor and the commissar walked hand in hand to assist in this continental tragedy.

In the minds of almost all intelligent people in the West, these totalitarian alternatives to God, whether sophisticated or primitive, have now been demonstrated to be incorrigibly destructive and evil. Belief in them lingers on, only in that home of lost causes – though even there fitfully now – the university campus. There are still Marxist dons, just as, if Hitler had won the war, there would still be Nazi dons. But the intellectual consensus has now belatedly joined the commensense consensus, that totalitarianism is the negation of morality. However, that does not mean that the search for Godless solutions has been abandoned. Quite the contrary. Even Marxism itself, though conclusively and repeatedly demonstrated to be a system of thought without the smallest merit, created by an intellectual crook who constantly invented and manipulated his so-called 'scientific evidence', has reappeared in a quasi-religious form in the teachings known as Liberation Theology. This is plainly and simply an anti-Christian heresy, without any moral basis, and indeed, as experience in Latin America has shown, a source of violence and great moral evil.

Even more worrying are the non-Marxist alternatives to God now being canvassed, because some at least of them contain elements of rationality and even of justice and therefore exercise a genuine appeal. An acquaintance of mine, whom I think I should now term a former Marxist, not so long ago expressed himself undaunted by the intellectual collapse of Communism as a system for promoting prosperity combined with equality. Marxist economic theory, he argued, and its stress on the industrial aspects of materialism, had always been a handicap. 'What we can now turn to,' he said, 'are far more attractive and exciting forms of action – race politics, sexual politics, environmental politics, health politics. There are other forms of action which will emerge in due course whereby we will transform and overthrow existing society.'

We are here concerned not with the overthrow or defence of

existing society, but with the alternatives to God men have proposed in our times. But to some extent the two topics are the
same. The radical agenda my acquaintance listed, with its strong
appeal to the idealistic, as well as the materialistic, instincts of
mankind, especially among young people, does constitute an
alternative religion. Like any other form of humanism, it replaces
God by man, and the welfare – or supposed welfare – of man, rather
than the worship of God and obedience to his commandments, as
the object of human existence and the purpose of society. That,
of course, is its radical defect. The Jesuit theologian Karl Rahner
once argued that it is the consciousness of God, the acceptance
that there is a power outside and above ourselves, to whom
we owe allegiance and whose guidance we must follow, which
essentially distinguishes mankind from other creatures. If belief
in God were ever to fade completely from the human mind, we
would not, Promethean-like, become masters of our fate; on the
contrary, we would descend to the status of very clever animals,
and our ultimate destiny would be too horrible to contemplate.

I believe this argument to be profoundly true, and corroborated
by history, and what worries me about the new radical agenda is
the danger that it will dehumanise man just as the totalitarian
alternatives did, though no doubt in rather different ways. But
there are further, related objections. All the items on the agenda
lend themselves to extremism. Take, for instance, the issue of
homosexuality, an important part of the sexual politics item.
There were many of us, in the 1960s, who felt that there were
grave practical and moral objections to the criminalisation of
homosexuality, and who therefore supported, as happened in
most Western countries, changes in the law which meant that
certain forms of homosexual behaviour ceased to be unlawful.
Homosexuality itself was still to be publicly regarded by society,
let alone by the churches, as a great moral evil, but men who
engaged in it, within strictly defined limits, would no longer be
sent to prison. We believed this change to be the maximum
homosexuals deserved or could reasonably expect. We were
proved totally mistaken. Decriminalisation made it possible for
homosexuals to organise openly into a powerful lobby, and it
thus became a mere platform from which further demands were
launched. Next followed demands for equality, in which homo-

sexuality was officially placed on the same moral level as standard forms of sexuality, and dismissal of identified homosexuals from sensitive positions, for instance in schools, children's homes etc., became progressively more difficult. This was followed in turn by demands not merely for equality but privilege: the appointment, for instance, of homosexual quotas in local government, the excision from school textbooks and curricula, and university courses, passages or books or authors they found objectionable, special rights to proselytise, and not least the privilege of special programmes to put forward their views – including the elimination of the remaining legal restraints – on radio and television. Thus we began by attempting to right what was felt an ancient injustice and we ended with a monster in our midst, powerful and clamouring, flexing its muscles, threatening, vengeful and vindictive towards anyone who challenges its outrageous claims, and bent on making fundamental – and to most of us horrifying – changes to civilised patterns of sexual behaviour.

Here indeed we have sexual politics in action. And, as with other alternatives to God, the result is not human happiness, but human misery. The homosexual community, as they now styled themselves, by their reckless promiscuity during the 1970s and 1980s, helped to spread among their members the fearful scourge of AIDS, a killer disease of a peculiarly horrible nature, for which there is no cure, and no immediate likelihood of a cure. Nor are homosexuals the only persons to suffer from sexual politics. Venereal diseases of all kinds, some unresponsive to even the latest antibiotics, are spreading rapidly. So is divorce. The percentage of one-parent families, with all the misery that entails, rises remorselessly. The number of illegitimate births, another prime source of human unhappiness, is now over 50 per cent in some great cities; in parts of Washington, the capital of the Western world, it is now as high as 90 per cent. The object of sexual politics is supposedly hedonistic. What bitter irony is there! I often think of my old friend and college contemporary Ken Tynan, another figure I describe in my book *Intellectuals*. Marvellously gifted, world-famous early in life, he became a leading evangelist of sexual liberation. It was his religion, and sex was his god. He distinguished himself, if that is the word, by being the first person to use a four-letter word on British television, and later by devising the first pornographic stage-show, *O Calcutta!* But the god he worshipped proved false and vengeful: his career, his private life, his health, all collapsed, and his end, at a tragically early age, was sad, lonely and hopeless.

Race politics, like sexual politics, constitute an alternative religion for some, and in many ways are open to the same objections. They begin with a legitimate demand, and then proceed rapidly to request, indeed insist on, unwarranted privilege. Positive discrimination is a moral evil, almost as great as its negative form, for by giving one person more than justice it must, by definition, give another less. It does not work, nor is it ever likely to achieve its objects, but instead, like all forms of extremism, it arouses hatred and disgust, and countervailing forces. What is essentially wrong with race politics is that they are fuelled not by love and reason, but by fury and bitterness. How much more valid, and helpful, and likely in the long run to raise the condition of hitherto underprivileged races, is the Christian teaching that all men and women are equal in the sight of God. It is the true multiracialism, just as it is the true sexuality, and – dare I say it? – the true socialism.

It is possible to detect the same incipient signs of extremism in other items on the new radical agenda. Environmentalism, for instance, starts from the sound premise that the earth is our heritage and our responsibility, and that we must conserve it for our progeny. That, indeed, has always been orthodox Christian doctrine, which teaches that people have no absolute rights of possession and that all is on leasehold from their maker. But environmental politics can degenerate into a new form of pantheism, indeed of paganism, in which notions like Mother Earth assume spiritual and mystic significance, and we are in danger – rather like the Nazis, themselves notable Greens in their origins – of reverting to primitive patterns and, like our distant ancestors, worshipping woods and rocks and rivers and animals. I see somewhat similar dangers in the developing movement of health politics, a new name for what used to be called eugenics. The quest for health at almost any cost characterised the inter-war period and was particularly marked in totalitarian societies. Stalin treated his opponents as insane, and locked them up in psychiatric hospitals. Hitler murdered the insane, to improve the stock of his race, and when this practice was abandoned in response to Christian pressure – the only success the churches ever had in deflecting him from a policy – he used the death laboratories thus prepared as a pilot project for the 'final solution' of the 'Jewish problem'. We do not yet murder the insane – perhaps we never will – but we slaughter unborn babies throughout the world literally in their millions. There are already countries – the Netherlands, for example – where euthanasia is on the verge of legality and is indeed already widely practised. In some ways health politics are already the most threatening item of all on the secular agenda which constitutes the contemporary alternative to God.

But the practice of abortion and euthanasia reminds us of one important point. It lies at the very heart of humanity's failure to find the alternative spiritual comfort and moral leadership which only belief in God can provide. These alternative secular systems can kill. They can do that only too easily: whether the six million Jews slaughtered by Hitler, or the twenty million Russians done to death by Stalin, or Pol Pot's massacre of a third of the population of Kampuchea, or Mao's prodigious mass-slaughters on a scale we do not yet exactly know – or the millions of infants we do not permit to be born at all, let alone live. All these systems can end life, but they cannot prolong it. The greatest of all human problems – the problem of death – they cannot solve. The secular mighty of the world – the tyrants, the kings, the arrogant intellectuals, the gifted men and women who think they know all the answers, the clever dons, the brilliant writers – all alike are sentenced to death from the moment of their birth, and sooner or later, that sentence is carried out.

The point was made with sombre brilliance by that great adventurer and writer Sir Walter Ralegh, on the last page of his *History of the World*. It was written in the Tower of London, while under sentence of death from his implacable enemy, King James I. The passage is plainly directed at this conceited king, once called 'the wisest fool in Christendom', but it applies to all who set themselves above law and morality:

O eloquent, just and mightie Death! Whom none could advise, thou hast persuaded. What non hath dared, thou hast done. And whom all the world hath flattered, thou only hath cast out of the world and despised. Thou has drawn together all the far-stretched greatness, all the pride, cruelty and ambition of man, and covered it all over with these two narrow words – *Hic jacet* – here lies.

It is because sensible men the world over, at all times, have recognised and accepted the inevitability of mighty death, that they have turned to God to explain its significance. Without God, death is horrific. With God, death is still fearsome, but it can be seen to have a meaning and purpose and a hope. The great strength of Christianity has always been that it brings men and women to terms with death in a way which offers them comfort and an explanation. Of course, the explanation is not complete. How could it be? As St Paul writes, in his first Epistle to the Corinthians, 'For now we see through a glass, darkly; but then, face to face'. God cannot be replaced, because only belief in him offers a 'then'. There is a famous passage in the first volume of history, and it is a great one, written by a member of the English-speaking race, St Bede, after whom I am proud to be named. In his *Ecclesiastical History of the English People,* he tells the story of how Paulinus first preached the new doctrine of Christianity at the pagan court of King Edwin of Northumbria, and in particular of how he gave the Christian explanation of death and what followed it. The explanation has always been clear and unequivocal; it was then, as it is now. And so it struck these simple pagans. There was a moment of silence, and then a wise old earl spoke. Life, he said, was short. It was like a sparrow, in winter, flying through the king's hall. 'It goes from darkness into the light, then into the darkness again – that is life.' 'This life of man,' he added, 'appears for a short space, but of what went before, and what is to follow, we know nothing. If, then, this new teaching gives us certitudes, we should follow it.'

There is no substitute for God: this our own dreadful century has abundantly proved. But I do not myself think that belief in God can be demonstrated like some mathematical theorem. It cannot be proved, in the sense we humans understand the word. It is something we intuit, and accept, and something too we reach, or reinforce, by prayer. Those who try to find substitutes for God not only fail, and often bring down misery on themselves, they throw away something marvellous. Some lines from the Catholic

poet Francis Thompson make the point with enviable eloquence. Thompson was an unfortunate man, whose own life became and remained a mess; but on the central issue of the purpose of life he was strong and sure. We do not, he wrote, need to look for an explanation of our existence in the distant universe. Our quest for an alternative is wholly unnecessary, for the real thing is before our eyes, if only we will open them:

> Not where the wheeling systems darken,
> And our benumbed conceiving soars! –
> The drift of pinions, would we hearken,
> Beats at our own clay-shuttered doors.
>
> The Angels keep their ancient places; –
> Turn but a stone, and start a wing!
> 'Tis ye, 'tis your estranged faces,
> That miss the many-splendoured thing.

There is, then, no alternative to God, so far as I can see – so far as our twentieth-century experience teaches us. But that is only the first step on our quest. If our need for God is such that no alternative which human ingenuity can devise will satisfy us, what is the nature of this enormously important and essential being? Can we in fact know God, describe him, define him?

CHAPTER 4

What is God, then?

Most of us believe in some kind of God, at any rate part of the time, but what do we mean by this? What is the nature of this God we half-believe in, occasionally? Is he truly omnipotent, ubiquitous, ever-present, watching our every move, privy to our most intimate thought? Or is he remote, distant, one who has set the universe in motion but thereafter holds his hand until he decides that time must have a stop? Or is he something in between these two extremes, or something quite different from any of these possibilities, something so remote from our imaginations that no writer on the subject – and there have been countless thousands – has even begun to conjure him up in words or images?

Some people today take the view that everyone is entitled to construct his or her own personal image of God, and worship accordingly. Throughout most of history those set in authority over us have denied this individual freedom. They have insisted on having an official state religion, or recognising an official church, and commanded all those subject to them to abide by its teachings – not least about the nature of the divinity. Rome had its state gods and official forms of worship, and then at the beginning of the fourth century AD it abruptly switched to Christianity, which soon became the official religion in its turn. Until quite recently, most states had an official church. One or two predominantly Christian countries still do, and nearly all Islamic ones – indeed some of the latter are theocracies, in which church and state are indistinguishable, and church law is secular law. In such regimes, the characteristics of the deity worshipped are closely defined by legal codes. That does not mean, of course, that all citizens accept such definitions in their hearts.

Today, most Western countries remain, as it were, agnostic on the issue of God. All the same, most of them – perhaps all of them – prefer their citizens to be God-fearing. Precisely what God is feared is secondary, so long as he is feared: then, it is felt, citizens are more likely to keep the peace and obey the secular laws. In 1954, the phrase 'under God', as used by Lincoln in his Gettysburg Address, was added by Congress to the United States Pledge of Allegiance. Two years later, the device from the US coinage, 'In God We Trust', became the nation's official motto. Which God? God as defined by whom? In the United States, church and state are constitutionally separated and Congress is not empowered – indeed it is specifically forbidden – to lay down forms of religion. So the God in whom Americans trust is left undefined, constitutionally vague and mysterious. Indeed, at the time of these changes, the head of the American state went out of his way to insist that the precise nature of the belief was a matter of indifference to authority. President Eisenhower told the country: 'Our government makes no sense unless it is founded on a deeply-felt religious faith – and I don't care what it is.'

That frank statement raised some eyebrows at the time, and even a few titters among intellectuals, who had a low opinion of Eisenhower anyway. How, they asked, could a man seriously lay down that he did not care what people believed so long as they believed it strongly enough? No doubt the sentiment could have been more tactfully phrased, but it is obvious what Eisenhower meant, and what he meant made good sense from his point of view. He was concerned with public behaviour, not with private truth. As First Magistrate he was anxious to keep crime low and obedience to the law high, as Commander-in-Chief he had a responsibility to ensure that the armed forces were obedient and loyal, as the only public official elected by all Americans he must do his best to see that all citizens perform their duties and pay their taxes. They were more likely to do this if they believed in an external power, higher and more permanent than the state, who was aware of all their shortcomings and would punish them in the next world even if they escaped retribution in this. That is what he meant by faith, and the precise form it took was a matter of individual choice, not state policy. All that Eisenhower was doing, in fact, was expressing his belief in religion as an effective form of social control.

Governments, then, prefer us to be God-fearing, but they do not, as a rule, go any further into the kind of God we are to fear. They leave that to us. But how do we set about inquiring into the nature of God? That is a question no one, not even the most acute theologian – or all the theologians put together – has ever been able to answer. It has often struck me that the two most important questions about existence – is there a God and what happens after our death? – are not only unanswered but probably unanswerable. Ever since they came into existence and acquired self-consciousness, human beings have known they are sure to die. Thus they have been speculating about what happens after death for about 250,000 years, and they are no closer to an answer today than they were a quarter of a million years ago. In that respect, human knowledge has not advanced one iota. It is the same with God – whether he exists and, if so, what kind of being he is. The savage from the Early Stone Age, or even earlier, is as well informed on this point as we are. His intuition, his guess, is as good as ours, perhaps better. We can spend a lifetime in a library, studying theology, but at the end of it all we have is knowledge of what men and women have thought about God. This undoubtedly has a certain value, possibly great value, but it is not empirical knowledge about the subject itself.

Recently, an American scholar, Jack Miles, produced a book which he called *God: a Biography*. This fascinating study involved a careful reading of the Bible using the techniques and the spirit of a literary exegetist studying, say, a play by Shakespeare – *Hamlet*, for instance. Such an approach can dig an astonishing amount out of the text, as the writings of A. C. Bradley on Shakespeare's tragedies show. Miles notices a lot of things about the God of the Bible, notably the way in which he changes as the Old Testament proceeds. For instance, when the Bible opens, in the Book of Genesis, God is talkative: so talkative that he talks to himself because there is no one else to talk to – he has not created them yet. He remains talkative for a long time, conversing with various of his creatures, laying down his commandments and other instructions in considerable detail and communing with his prophets at length. Then a change comes with the Book of Job. During it, at a certain point, he ceases to speak, though he continues, of course, to do things. After the Book of Job, he scarcely speaks ever again, though sometimes his earlier commands are reiterated. He becomes a Silent God. In the New Testament he speaks once, to say, 'This is my beloved son, in whom I am well pleased.' Thereafter, Jesus Christ talks, a great deal, as though the Father, feeling his age, had decided to hand over the firm, or the government, or whatever the concern is, to his son and heir, who would henceforth speak for him.

Miles notices that God appears to age in the course of the Bible. Equally significant, he becomes more mysterious and remote. In the early books he is active, often visible, doing things as well as talking, showing himself, brisk and proud of his works. At one point, in the Book of Deuteronomy, he even insists, almost irritably, that all his commands are perfectly plain and that there is no excuse for any Israelite who does not understand and follow them. But slowly he begins to veil himself. Not only does he age, and his beard grow – he changes from the powerfully athletic God of Michelangelo to the Ancient of Days portrayed by William Blake – but he retreats into the mist and half-light, and ascends into the distant empyrean. He himself, as it were, undergoes an apotheosis from a God-of-this-world into an infinitely distant being, about whom we suddenly seem to know nothing.

All this is interesting, but the only real information it conveys is about the imaginations of ancient Israelite historians, poets and theologians. It tells us that, as they became more sophisticated, they ceased to anthropomorphise God, equipping him with all kinds of human characteristics, such as pride, boastfulness, irritation and anger, vengefulness and forgiveness. Instead, they confessed their inability to visualise God with any conviction and pushed him further and further up and indeed off the stage, so that he is merely a remote presence in the wings, and is eventually written out of the script almost entirely.

Then, suddenly, God's son makes his appearance. He is not just anthropomorphised but is actually man, a real man, 'begotten not made', as the Nicene Creed says, born of woman, who grew up in a specific place, Palestine, preached, suffered and died. With the New Testament, human interest switches from God the Father, now wrapped in impenetrable mystery, and concentrates on his son, who is completely humanised, while remaining divine. At this point we come to the great parting of the ways between the

Jewish religion, which remains strictly monotheistic, concentrating exclusively on the remote and mysterious original God,
and the followers of the New Testament, who call themselves
Christians, quite rightly, because their focus is on the human and
tangible and visual form of Jesus Christ, the Son. As Christ is a
historical figure, as well as possessing a human nature, it is possible
to discover a lot about him, knowledge of an empirical nature,
and to imagine a great deal more, so that Christ becomes a very
real person in the minds of men and women. He is indeed 'made
flesh and dwells among us', and this helps to explain why Christianity spread so rapidly across the world and is still a living thing
for a billion human beings, while Judaism remained the religion
of an austere élite, who can get by without anthropomorphic
props. However, on the question of the Father, Christians are in
exactly the same position as the Jews – God is indefinable, invisible, unknowable, and in the last resort almost unimaginable.

Almost unimaginable – but not quite. Whether we like it or not,
we do exercise our imaginations about God and produce pictures
in our minds. Bertrand Russell, albeit an atheist, told me he had
an image of God in his head, a relic of childhood which he could
not quite drive away – a rather frightening image. A. J. Ayer, again,
tried to conjure up notions of God, if only to dismiss them: he
told me this was routine procedure for a professional philosopher,
but it may be that he could not help it. I dare say the redoubtable
atheist leader Professor Dawkins also has his personal image of
God, just as we envisage what Dagon looked like or Thor or Jupiter.
Indeed, it is hard not to do so: artists have created so many images
of this kind for us that it is beyond our power, even if we wished,
to sweep our minds clear of them. In one sense, then, we are stuck
with God. My personal image of God has not changed much since
I was a child, and I suspect this is true of most people.

The process of reasoning comes in, however, when we speculate
not on God's appearance or being, but upon his doing – his
power, his activity, his function. Here there are huge areas of
disagreement. A. P. Herbert, the English MP and writer, used to
tell a story about H. G. Wells, who was a lifelong atheist, and the
novelist Arnold Bennett, a wise old bird who reserved judgment
on such matters. Herbert had a house alongside the Thames, from
which the Oxford and Cambridge boat-race could be splendidly

seen, and every year he gave a party so that friends could watch it from his garden. On one such occasion Wells, surveying the immense throng of people, turned to Bennett and said, 'Look at those numbers – how can you say there is a God?' Bennett replied, 'Oh, he is not dismissed so easily as that.' Wells thought that the infinity of human beings who have come into existence since the world began, and who may be infinitely exceeded by those still to come, was quite beyond the power of any supreme being to cope with, especially if he inquires closely into the behaviour of each and every one of them, to decide whether they are to be saved. Bennett, on the other hand, thought that, if we endow God with supernatural powers, it is not for us to set a limit to them or to deny his ability to manage mere numbers, however great.

It seems to me that Bennett had logic on his side, and that Wells was thinking in terms of gods in the Greek sense, or demi-gods, rather than the Almighty God who created the universe out of nothing. A God with vast but still restricted powers makes no sense at all to me. If there are things God cannot do, then he is not God. Of course, there may be plenty of things he does not choose to do. Many people, perhaps taking their cue from the later books of the Bible, where God is increasingly remote and mysterious – not exactly supine but, on the whole, a God who lets events take their course – believe God is reluctant to interfere with his creation, though not unmindful of it, and watchful, and reserving his right to intervene if it is his pleasure. Such a one was George Washington. He was, so far as I can see, a characteristic late eighteenth-century deist, who felt – as Newton and Locke had taught – that God designed the world and set it in motion but did not normally fiddle with the operating machinery of events. As president, too, presiding over a constitution which separated church and state, Washington was most reluctant to invoke the deity. But in his Farewell Address to Congress, perhaps the most considered and sincere statement of his general views, he did indicate his belief that the new country was in the special care of divine providence and that, provided its citizens behaved themselves honourably, God would not allow the nation to founder.

This is a view many share: a God who is watchful, all-seeing, but who seldom interferes. Abraham Lincoln's concept of God was similar. After his death, his widow said he never felt he belonged to any church, and he clearly had difficulty in believing in a personal God of any kind. On the other hand, his love of righteousness, which went to the very foundation of his being, would not allow him to envisage a universe in which there was no ultimate power of good, and in which frail human beings were abandoned to moral anarchy and blind events. His letters and papers before and during the Civil War are fascinating not least because he was struggling within himself to know to what extent he could rely upon or be guided by a divine providence. Distinguishing between Hellenic and Hebrew philosophy, St Paul says: 'The Greeks ask for a reason, the Jews look for a sign.' In this sense Lincoln was with the Hebrews: he was always looking for a sign, especially in the anxious times leading up to the public Emancipation of the Slaves. He would not allow himself to think that God awarded victories or inflicted defeats. He specifically said, 'God is not on our side – but I hope we are on his side.' But he hankered for the sign of righteousness and he evidently felt that God – or whatever he was – did sometimes speak clearly to his creatures, albeit rarely.

President McKinley went further. He thought the president actually had a right, perhaps even a duty, before taking a momentous decision, to implore the Almighty for guidance, and that if the president so prayed, in all sincerity, that guidance would be provided. Shortly after the United States annexed the Philippines, he told a delegation to the White House how he reached that decision:

> I am not ashamed to tell you, Gentlemen, that I went down on my knees and prayed Almighty God for light and guidance that one night. And one night late it came to me this way ... There was nothing left for us to do but to take them all and to educate the Filipinos and uplift and civilize and Christianize them, and by God's grace do the very best we could with them, as our fellow men for whom Christ also died.

I suspect that most presidents have, in practice, behaved from time to time as McKinley did. Any man or woman who exercises huge powers, and whose decisions may send young men to their deaths, or whose failure to take the right decisions will imperil the entire country of which they have charge, will most probably turn to God for guidance on momentous occasions, even if their belief in a deity, in normal times, is a little shaky or vague. Harold Macmillan told me he prayed in this way, when he was prime minister; and so too did Margaret Thatcher. Probably democratic leaders, who feel their responsibilities acutely, come into the same category as soldiers before an action and sailors in bad weather – they have a *déformation professionelle* in favour of belief. Most people, I imagine, would want it that way. I always found it oddly reassuring when Nikita Khrushchev, who as ruler of the Soviet Union was an atheist by definition, brought God into his utterances, as he often did. And the great majority of us would prefer our rulers to pray for guidance before taking an important decision, rather than rely simply on secular considerations. It is always better to have God in the equation than left out of it. That is a natural feeling: we are more comfortable with God than without him. When Dr Johnson finished the last piece of much-retarded copy for his infinitely delayed *Dictionary,* he said to the boy who had delivered it to the printer, 'Well, boy, and what did he say to you?' 'He said, Sir, "Thank God I have done with him." ' On which Dr Johnson commented, 'I am glad that he thanks God for anything.' It is not only reassuring that we ourselves feel God is there; it is doubly reassuring that others, too, feel he is there.

On the other hand, there are many who feel that God, while indispensable in great matters, is too mighty to trouble himself about small ones, and that it is quite wrong to expect him to do so. We are reassured to hear that the president prays for guidance over Bosnia. But if we heard that he prayed for guidance on whom to invite to a White House dinner, our reactions would be mixed. We might think we had a religious fanatic in charge: worse, a man suffering from religious mania. There is an old legal saying '*De minimis non curat lex*' – the law does not concern itself with trivial matters. Many assume this applies equally, or even *a fortiori,* to God. My wife Marigold takes this view. When I explain to her that I am worried about what God may think about an article I am writing – the subject being important to me but not, perhaps, to many other people – she exclaims in exasperation, 'God has better things to do than worry about *that!*'

There is a common variant on this approach which sees God as absent-minded, or at any rate as an authority who does not necessarily take note of everything his creatures are doing or not doing. This is particularly favoured by the timid and humble. A friend of mine quotes her aunt, a self-effacing lady with a difficult and sometimes neglectful husband, who said on one occasion, 'Things are going so well. Alfred is so attentive and he hasn't got anyone else at present. The farm is paying its way. None of the children is giving trouble. Honestly, I'd get down on my knees and thank God, but I'm afraid of drawing attention to myself.'

We have here, of course, more anthropomorphising. If God is indeed Almighty then he is certainly all-seeing too, and his eye had been on the self-effacing aunt throughout. It is less likely that he should be inattentive than that he should be impatiently awaiting her thanks. And equally, an all-powerful God is not bound by stuff about *de minimis*. Nor is his time limited. God is not a busy Chief Executive Officer of the Universe, who cannot be bothered with this or that. He has, quite literally, all the time in the world. It is not for us to say what he considers trivial. Probably he does not think anything is trivial, any more than he makes distinctions between the moral behaviour of an emperor and a shoe-black. It is far more likely that everything is important to God than that he is guided by what *we* think important.

We have to anthropomorphise God to some extent because there is no other way, in practice, that we can imagine him. But beyond a certain point seeing him as man, or rather a superman, is misleading and dangerous, because he is not a man, and his powers are not those of a man multiplied an infinite number of times. We are particularly misled when we try to set limits to God's concern. There are no restraints whatsoever on God's ability to take cognisance of phenomena, human or any other kind. When it comes to quantitative aspects of God, we are probably safer to follow the analogy of a computer than the analogy of a man. It is already possible for us to imagine a computer of such size or power or complexity that it is capable of performing, almost simultaneously, more operations than the entire human race could manage, even if it took many years. But we are only at the beginning of computer technology. Plenty of people still alive were around when the first mainframe computer was built just before the Second World War and can remember when such things did not exist, other than the stately machines, made by Charles

Babbage in the 1830s, which are kept in London's Science Museum. What, we must ask, will be the power of computers made in a thousand years' time? Or in a million years' time? We cannot even begin to comprehend their capacity – the number of operations they can simultaneously undertake, the amount of information they can absorb and act upon. Yet God's power, in these respects as in others, is infinitely greater than that of the most advanced computer our descendants will design billions of years hence. So God will have no difficulty in concerning himself with the minutest details of all his creatures, until the end of time.

Personally, I have always taken the view, and do so now more than ever, that Almighty God, far from setting the universe in motion and then letting the drama enact itself – as many think – is an ever-present, ubiquitous arbiter in all affairs. I may sometimes doubt the existence of God altogether, or rather push the fact of his existence to the back of my consciousness, but when I am thinking about God at all, I do not doubt for one second that he is privy to all my thoughts, let alone conscious of my actions, and that everything about me is important to him. If I speak to him, he listens; if I pray to him, he considers; if I thank him, he is gratified; if I disobey him, he knows and notes; if I defy him, he is saddened; if I love him, he responds. Or rather, I should correct that last statement: I do not even need to perform an act of love to evoke that response, since his concern is uninterrupted and perpetual. That concern extends to every human being who has ever lived, and it does not cease with death and judgment. That God is conscious of those who have joined him in Heaven, or who are preparing to do so while still in Purgatory, is obvious. What is less obvious, but equally certain in my view, is that God continues his concern for those who have rejected him finally and so are in Hell – if indeed there be such creatures, as I fear there may be. There is no finality with God, and his concern for the damned remains, one guarantee that they will not be damned for ever. Again, it is not difficult for us to imagine God caring for a great and intelligent creature like an elephant, which has so many human characteristics, including a tenacious memory, and which has some kind of consciousness of the cycle of life and death, since it seems to venerate its dead peers or wish to lay its own bones alongside theirs. What is also less obvious, but which

I nonetheless believe, is that God is aware, and cares for, every single member of a swarm of locusts – that he follows the existence of each of these ephemeral creatures, however many billions of them there may be, and notes what happens to them all. They may not be conscious of themselves, but God is conscious of them. He is conscious of each flower, and each leaf and each blade of grass – every living and growing thing capable of separate identity. It is true to say, I think, that there cannot be any molecular event, any event at all, however minute or transient, in the entire universe, which is not known to God. He takes an interest in all things, because he is the cause of all things.

Now this view I hold of God's ubiquity and all-consciousness and concern – which is also the view, I should add, of most orthodox Christian theologians through the ages, and of most Jewish theologians too – must in no way be confused with pantheism. God is conscious of all, and is in a sense everywhere; but he is not everything. He is outside his creation, and must have been outside it to create it in the first place. I regard pantheism, the belief that God is everything or in everything, and that everything is God, as a most mistaken and dangerous belief. In a sense, it is the negation of belief, an escape, a cop-out from all the difficulties of theology. Spinoza, I think, became a pantheist because he was not prepared – as he would have been today – to admit, even to himself, that he was an atheist. He chose pantheism in the seventeenth century, just as similar sceptics chose Unitarianism in the eighteenth century – it was, in effect, a form of disbelief and a convenient half-way to open admission of disbelief. Pantheism, it seems to me, is a mere tautology; it equates God with matter and really tells us nothing about either. It is also liable to promote various forms of paganism – gods as streams and rivers, woods and mountains. It betrays a feebleness of mind, an unwillingness to work out for ourselves what exactly God is and what he wants us to do.

Of course the God I have tried to describe, who is all-present, all-knowing and all-involved in the minutest detail of our lives, is not an easy God to live with. In a sense he is an impossible God to live with, because it is beyond our capacity, in practice, to conduct our lives in communion with God at every second of our existence. Some of the saints, the mystics in particular, have come close to it, at any rate for part of their time. But for the great majority of us, God enters our lives only occasionally, period-ically – spasmodically, one might say – when we remind ourselves that he is there, watching, listening. We pray to him in the morning and in the evening. We may say grace before or after meals. We may give him a word of thanks at moments of pleasure or success or satisfaction, and we may call on him when we are frightened or longing or desperate. The rest of the time – by which I mean nearly all the time – there is silence or inattention or even indifference on our part, though God is always there. His line to us is perpetually open, even when we do not respond for long periods. For many, contacts with God are suspended for years at a time, sometimes for half a lifetime. That is sad, it can be tragic, but it is not irreparable. When we will it, when we remember that God is always there, contact can be resumed instantaneously: there is no waiting, no probationary period, no 'technical diffi-culties'. We can be back on the same footing in an instant.

Now you may ask: why should it be that Almighty God, who is infinitely powerful, should always be in the role of suppliant, as it were, while we mortals, who are infinitely weak, should ignore God for years at a time, then be welcomed back, like a prodigal son, the second we feel the urge to call on him again? The answer is that we are not talking about justice, we are talking about love. So far I have left out this key word. Nevertheless it *is* the key. The universe without God is, to me at any rate – and I think to most of us – unimaginable. God without the universe is indeed conceivable, for God, being all-powerful, must be all-sufficient too. The universe did not need to exist at all. The only reason God created it was love. It is the nature of God to create from nothing, and in his imaginative genius he conceived of a universe which he could love, and peopled it with creatures who would have the power of choosing whether they loved in return. Without love, the universe makes no sense at all. Love is its creative principle, its sustaining principle and its energising principle. God's love, being perfect, does not need or even expect reciprocation, while delighting in it, so there is no symmetry between his love and ours. But clearly, the more we do reciprocate, the better the universe – or at any rate that part of the universe we inhabit – functions. This is a very important point, I think, and I will try to elaborate it.

But first we must try to get a little closer to God, and his nature, and in particular we must attempt to discover what exactly the love of God is, and why he feels he must express it.

CHAPTER 5

He, she or it: divinity, gender and sex

God's motive in creating the universe was to express his love, to search for reciprocation of love, and to this end he created free-willed creatures who are at liberty to give or withhold their love for him. This poignant and elegant scheme teaches us that God is a being but not exactly a person as we understand it, still less a person with gender. We are accustomed to refer to God as 'he' and I will continue to do so throughout this book, but it is purely a matter of convenience and it does not signify that I regard God as masculine.

Our distant ancestors lived in a world where brute strength was important, and where the greater physical power of men, their skill and courage in hunting, and their superior daring and risk-taking, gave them an unassailable predominance. They were the masters. They had to be. There was no alternative way of organising society. We live in a world where physical strength is of rapidly dwindling importance and where intellect is all. Women are, on average, marginally more intelligent than men, albeit they seem less inclined to take risks and therefore less innovative. It appears to me probable that, during the third millennium, they will gradually attain a mastery over men in most respects, and then it will be necessary to organise society in a different way. But in the days when the human race was first exploring the possibility of divinity, and was assembling pagan pantheons, then moving to monotheism, society had a patriarchal structure. It was only natural to assume that the heavens were a mirror-image of earth, and had a patriarchal structure too. Of course there were female gods – often very powerful ones – but the head-god was almost invariably a male and his superiority was underlined by his marriage to the senior female goddess. Thus divine families reproduced earthly ones and the patriarchal principle was maintained. When first the Ancient Egyptians, then the Ancient Hebrews, started to worship a single god, it did not occur to them that this god could be anything but masculine. When gods became God, they acquired an umbrella masculinity in this single *persona*, who absorbed the female attributes of the old goddesses.

But of course all this anthropomorphism merely reflected the limitations of the human imagination. The ancient peoples found it very difficult to think in terms of abstractions – most of us still do – and it was beyond their capacity to visualise God except as some superhuman creature. So God was presented as male, seen as male, made to speak as a male and to some extent even think as a male. But that does not in any way mean that he is male or even that the more sophisticated ancient theologians themselves thought of him as male. It is significant that, even within the Old Testament, as it develops, God tends to lose his gender. In the process of becoming silent, and more mysterious, he forfeits his masculinity and becomes increasingly non-specific. Jewish theologians have always tried to avoid referring to God as He or attributing any human, let alone masculine, characteristics to him. Gender is no more than a linguistic device, for want of a better. Christian theologians have been less rigorously mono-theistic in this respect, as in others, because the theology of the Trinity means God is presented as the Father, and there is no getting away from the fact that the Trinity is a patriarchal concept. Women do not come into it. The Virgin Mary is needed to enable Jesus Christ to be conceived and born as man, but Mary is emphati-cally not divine, albeit she is miraculously born without sin, thus giving her a unique singularity as a human. (She is also assumed into Heaven, rather than dying, so both her beginning and her end are miraculous and non-human.)

However, none of this means that Christians think of God as masculine, as opposed to feminine. Christian monotheism may be compromised, as some think – certainly Jews think – by the Trinity, but Christians still see God as a totally different being to humankind, with no human characteristics at all. In this sense, their theology is exactly the same as Jewish theology. Indeed, God the Holy Ghost, the third person of the Trinity, is precisely the disembodied, non-gender-specific, totally immaterial God of strict

Jewish theology. God the Holy Ghost represents the love between the Father and the Son – is pure love, in fact – and it may be that this is the way we ought to look at the Trinity as a whole, at God as a whole. But most human beings are frail and limited creatures, not given the powerful conceptual intellects of philosophers, and it is hard or impossible for them to think of God in this abstract way. They prefer the Father and so, I must confess, do I.

There is no reason, therefore, why women should not refer to God as She, if they find it more helpful, and think of God as womanly. Female visual images of God are possible, even easy. I suspect that great female saints like St Monica or St Catherine have always thought of God as predominantly female, and that such an attitude has been common among nuns of many orders. But this is a matter of private choice and convenience, not a theological point. St Teresa knew perfectly well that God was neither masculine nor feminine. Women, and possibly some men too, are perfectly entitled to think of God as a woman if that aids them in their devotions, just as most Christians use images and holy pictures. They do not really believe God has male or female characteristics any more than they believe statues are divine.

At the same time, it is wrong for feminists to press for changes in the liturgy to make references to God non-gender specific, and still more wrong for the ecclesiastical authorities to give way to them. Such changes upset most people, including most women, and are quite unnecessary. I am all for tolerance in religion, except when intolerance is absolutely essential. Here, surely, is a case of latitude, and for everyone to tolerate the susceptibilities of others. The theologians have made it perfectly clear – clearer today than ever before – that God is without gender, and we must see him as such if that is the way we choose to love him. But if it is helpful, it is perfectly permissible to see him as a Father, or a Mother, or both. Meanwhile, let the liturgy, which has acquired the creative patina of age, so important in our devotions, stay as it is.

Now let us turn to what I believe to be a far more interesting and instructive question: why did God, being himself without gender, create gender in the first place? This question is not often asked because we are taught by science that the masculine/feminine principle is essential to all generation, in the vegetable world let alone the animal and human world, and that there was no alternative but for life to evolve in this way. I do not accept this. God is all-powerful and he did not need to plant the gender-principle in organic life at all. The material universe itself was created, and propagates itself, without gender. Stars do not marry or breed planets by fusing masculine and feminine elements. They expand or explode or separate themselves on quite different physical principles, which do not involve gender-dualism at all. That was God's conscious decision, in setting the laws of astrophysics. But equally, in setting the laws of organic life, he chose to introduce gender, and it is interesting to speculate on what was in his mind.

My belief is that there was a fundamental purpose in this decision. If, as I have argued, God's motive in creating the universe was love, if love is the ultimate organising and sustaining principle of the universe, if God himself, in so far as he has characteristics beyond his own self-sufficiency, is the very embodiment of love, then it is clear that, in his mind, one of the principal objects of the universe was the exploration of love to its ultimate possibilities. God himself is one, unique, alone – he has to be, in order to be all-powerful. But his very omnipotence imposes limitations: the option of sharing power is not open to him. One purpose, then, of the universe was and is to explore such options by introducing the principle of power-sharing. This principle is most universally expressed in gender, for by definition neither party to a male/female duality is potent without the other. Neither can love fully without the other, and certainly neither can create, can make their love flesh, without the other. Now God can create alone; his love can express itself in creating from nothing. But that is his unique power and he cannot share it with anyone else. In order, therefore, to examine love in all its possibilities, he had to create this alternative form of love which only becomes possible, and fulfils itself, when the two unequal parts merge.

You may say, indeed, that God created gender out of curiosity, as well as love (curiosity, of course, is a form of love). Singular love, like his own, has only one expression. Blindingly perfect though it may be, it lacks variety. Mutual love, on the other hand, as generated by the gender principle, has an infinity of expressions. Not only does it make possible evolution through natural selection but, in its higher expressions, it produces perpetual dramas – histories, comedies, tragedies. It combines endless physical possibilities with endless emotional possibilities. We accept gender, take it for granted, because we have never known anything else. But without it the world could not function. God, as I say, might have chosen to operate it on a different principle. But a world without gender, even if it functioned, would be stale, flat and unprofitable. It would be a form of living death. So gender supplies both dynamism and interest. It is an amazing thing. Next to the Big Bang itself, it is the most remarkable and ingenious of all God's acts of creation. It is the most fascinating too. Its operations and permutations, creating life, are more interesting to observe than the expansion of the universe itself. They have the further merit that, the higher the forms in which they exist, the more interesting they become, and will become. We are only beginning to explore the potentialities of gender, which are inexhaustible, in so far as anything is.

Now what follows from this analysis of God's use of gender? Two things. First, we must have a special respect for gender: it is evidently very dear to the heart of our maker. It is fundamental, not accidental. It is essential to his purposes, not a mere means to an end, a purely practical device. 'Man and Woman created He them.' The Book of Genesis got it right with this direct statement of inescapable fact. God did not create human beings who, for reproductive purposes, had certain differences. I have often seen it stated – it is a point made for the purposes of feminist propaganda – that the differences between male and female bodies are minute compared to their similarities. That may well be so. But if it had been God's plan to minimise the difference between men and women, he would surely have created hermaphroditic humans who would have bred by parthenogenesis. But he did no such thing; he created male and female and he had good reason for making them entirely separate entities with quite different purposes and functions.

Now I am not making an anti-feminist point. It may be well to say here that I am, in my own way, a feminist. I believe in the fullest possible participation of women in the governance of our world, which is coming anyway whether people like it or not, and I have always striven, in so far as it has been in my small power, to promote and accelerate it. But I am not an ideologue. I want to have real women in actual jobs of importance, not to impose rules and quotas and positive discrimination in their favour. Still less do I want to introduce equality, except the only form of equality which is possible and desirable – equality before the law. Men and women are not equal. They are different. Their differences are their strengths, so that men and women together are more than the sum of their parts. And their differences are their glory too. The fact that they are different is essential to their creativity. Hence if anything I want to accentuate their differences, emphasise them, cultivate and nourish them. I believe that this is the natural wish of most men and that, as women secure equality of opportunity – which they are rapidly doing in Western societies at least – this will become the overt, as it is instinctively the natural, wish of women too. For there are, in fact, huge differences between the male and female sex, and it is plainly God's purpose that they should exist and fructify. So let us dismiss from our minds any merging between men and women. They are separate – and unequal – and will always be so.

You will notice that, for the first time, I have replaced the word 'gender' with 'sex', and this is quite deliberate. In speaking of the universe as a whole, it is well to refer to gender as its most interesting generative principle. But when we come to human beings, sex is a more appropriate word because gender differences cannot be usefully discussed without reference to human sexuality. Now we come to the second conclusion which flows from God's invention of gender. God is particularly interested in, and anxious to stress, sexuality, particularly human sexuality. It may be objected: how can this be so? Is not God himself sexless, at least in so far as we understand it? It is remarkable that, in the Old Testament, as opposed to virtually all other religious systems of the Ancient Near East, the cosmogony is sexless. God does not produce the universe from his semen, nor does he generate man: he makes both. It may be said that, in the Christian New Testament at least, God produces the Son by some kind of generative process involving the Virgin Mary, But sexuality, on God's side at least, does not seem to come into it: the Holy Ghost, an entirely non-personified spirit, is produced for the purpose, and all that Mary is told, by the further mediation of the Angel Gabriel, is that she is already pregnant. Furthermore, it may be objected, God's son,

Jesus, is in all the circumstances a remarkably non-sexual creature. Since he lived until the age of thirty-three without marrying, he could be accurately described, in terms of the society in which he lived, as a confirmed bachelor, quite a rarity then. Despite all the efforts of blasphemous movie-makers, there is no indication whatever that Jesus had a sexual liaison of any kind. He has a taste for the company of women, even when matters of importance are discussed, he obviously attracts them, and he sympathises with and understands them – his rapport with women is one of the central themes of the New Testament – but that is as far as it goes. Jesus does not perform sexual acts of any kind. The Jewish God, and even the Christian God, is set apart from sexual activity.

All this being so, why do I say that God seems anxious to stress human sexuality? The answer is that, as with his deliberate decision to create gender, his stress on sexuality is part of his divine plan to explore love to its ultimate possibilities. Human sexuality is a physical and emotional, even a psychic instrument, of enormous power. It can drive men and women to acts of madness and despair and enormous cruelty. It is no accident that the national myth-epic-history of the Greeks, the war against Troy, is set in motion by an elopement. The pull of sex underlies the whole of Dante's epic, *The Divine Comedy*, the most sublime work of art of the Middle Ages. Shakespeare, in one of his most powerful plays, *Othello* – later to be the theme of the masterpiece of Italy's greatest operatic composer, Verdi – shows two noble lives destroyed by sexual jealousy. Sexual desire is the energising mechanism of the most pervasive and often-elaborated European myth, the story of Faust, in one of its incarnations the most justly celebrated dramatic poem in the German language. Why did God make sexuality so powerful? Its forceful effect on both men and women seems disproportionate to its primary purpose, reproduction. In the animal world, let alone in the vegetable world, the operations of the gender-principle require no such enormous incentive. The vegetable world reproduces itself compulsively without the aid of sexual desire, and the animal world desires sex only to propagate. Among human beings sexuality has a life of its own quite apart from reproduction – often a death of its own too. It is a huge force unanchored in the urge to perpetuate the species, or rather a force which can break free of this anchorage and roam the world raging, inspiring and destroying. Or, to vary the metaphor, it can become a loose cannon on the deck of human life.

God created this force, and freed it from the exclusive demands of reproduction because, in his human experiment, he wanted to see the interaction of varieties of love. It is part of God's creative genius that the love with which he desires to fill the universe has infinite gradations. In its purest form, as it radiates from God itself, it is utterly selfless. It seeks no more than to express itself and will do so, perpetually, unanswered, even though it delights in reciprocation. In its least pure form, it is utterly selfish and treats the subject on which it is lavished, even if another human being, as a mere object. By giving his human creatures free will, God offered them all kinds of choice. The most important one is whether to reciprocate his love, and how intensely to reciprocate it. The choice would not be genuine, and thus interesting, if the kind of selfless love provided by God was the only one on offer. By creating sexual love of great power and complexity, and by endowing humans with it, God sets up not just another form of love, which can attain sublime expression and which is akin to and supplementary to the selfless love which he desires to be reciprocated. He also sets up a rival to this kind of love – a rival to himself – and bids his human subject choose. He tells them how they should choose, but he leaves them free to choose differently. He thus intensifies the human drama which the universe came into being to make possible.

We are not at this stage discussing the problem of good and evil – that will be discussed in the next chapter – but it is clear that once love, and especially sexual love, can find selfish expression, as well as the selfless expression of which God sets the supreme example, then we are confronted with love which has infinite gradations between good and evil. All these forms of love are natural, in the sense that God willed they be possible. But some conform to his purpose and some do not. Once we grasp this principle, many of the most difficult problems of moral theology, and the way in which the churches have tried to deal with them, become much clearer. In the first place, the Christian churches, and especially the Catholic Church, are said to be obsessed by sex and to devote a disproportionate amount of time and spiritual energy to dealing with it. In the light of what I have argued, I think it is right to do so. For sex among human beings is a huge force and can have a disproportionate effect on the extent to which we conform to God's wishes. It is a rival to God, often a successful rival. The church is sensible to take it with the utmost seriousness.

Then there is the question of celibacy. On this point I think I will part company with many of my readers, especially my Jewish readers and Protestant readers. No matter; I must follow my line of argument to see how convincing it is. The universe is about love, and there are different varieties of love, and intensities of love within it. The most powerful and intense variety is God's love for us, which is entirely pure and unselfish, and is given whether or not it is reciprocated. Clearly, our human love reaches its highest expression when it comes closest to approximating to God's love. We can do this in more ways than one. When men and women love each other, they can do so selfishly or unselfishly, with many gradations in between. The less selfish their love is, the purer it is, and the closer to God's love for us.

The love of men and women for each other, then, does not preclude their love for God – far from it. In fact the more they love each other selflessly, the more likely it is that they will love God too. Sexual love can be a rival to the love of God, but it need not be. In theory, indeed, a man may have a perfect, selfless love for his wife and a perfect, selfless love for God, both existing simultaneously, in fact reinforcing each other. But, since human beings are imperfect, fallen, unsatisfactory creatures, such a dual perfect love is inherently improbable, or at least very rare. Moral theology deals with the generality of mankind, not the exceptions; and God himself is interested in the generality of mankind – though he takes great interest in the exceptions too, of course. Most men and women find it difficult to balance the rivalries of love. Men and women may learn to love God by loving each other – some undoubtedly do. But it is far more likely that they will love God with some of the intensity with which he loves us if God is without a competitor in their hearts and they can concentrate wholly on him. That is the case for celibacy, and especially the celibacy of the priesthood, of those who have taken special vows to devote themselves to God's service and who have made a lifelong profession of it.

It is objected that a celibate priest, who has not known human love, is not a fit person to administer to souls: he may be all right in a monastery, praying, but he is unsuited for pastoral work. It is particularly objected against the present Pope John Paul II that, being celibate, he ought not to pronounce, *urbi et orbi*, on such important questions as family planning, divorce and sexual sin. I must say, I find this a very feeble argument – one which, incidentally, applies equally to Jesus Christ himself, indeed to Almighty God too. If experience is the chief qualification for preaching God's will on sexual matters, then the most debauched will make the best pastors, a manifest absurdity. There is more than one way of acquiring sexual knowledge and experience. The average husband and wife, who remain faithful within marriage, may be – probably are – happy sexually, but they cannot be described as particularly experienced. The average celibate priest, by contrast, acquires through the confessional an insight into the varieties and power and problems of sexuality denied to most married couples, indeed to many psychiatrists. One old priest, who has been hearing confessions for half a century, said to me, 'The burden of sexual knowledge I carry is sometimes very onerous.' Pope John Paul II, when he was Archbishop of Cracow, was so conscious of the problems of sexuality that he set up a marital institute, serving the entire vast archdiocese, whose function was to work on the problems of sex, including unfaithfulness, divorce, incest, illegitimacy, venereal disease, prostitution, wife-beating and marital violence, and impotence. He put in charge of it a remarkable and saintly woman who had survived the horrors of Ravensbruck, the Nazi concentration camp reserved for women, in which some of their more bestial medical–sexual experiments had taken place. This women herself had been subjected to them. The work of the institute has proved very valuable, and has been widely circulated and imitated; it serves to draw attention to the seriousness with which celibate clergy, and John Paul II in particular, can and often do approach their pastoral work.

Priests have often told me that the very absence of direct experience in sex, which can be confusing and lead to prejudices, can make their approach to dealing with the sexual problems of parishioners more objective and successful. But a point far more important than any of these is that the particular concentration on devotion to God made possible by celibacy also makes it far more likely that a priest can reciprocate God's love with its own intensity, and so inevitably receive more in return. And the love which God gives us is the source of all grace and wisdom. The more we are capable of receiving, the more likely it is that we will take right courses and lead others along them. So what the celibate priest loses in direct experience of sexual love – and that loss, as I say, may not be great – he more than makes up in the wisdom and patience and understanding God imparts to him.

It is worth adding, at this point, that what applies to a masculine celibate priest applies just as much to a woman priest. I believe that the all-male priesthood of the Roman Catholic Church (and, for that matter, the even fiercer opposition to woman priests in the Orthodox churches) is a lost cause, and rightly so. God had all kinds of reasons for introducing the principle of gender into the universe, but a desire to differentiate between the spiritual capacities of men and women was not one of them. Quite the contrary: the whole history of Judaism and Christianity shows that women as well as men are capable of the utmost expressions of spirituality of all kinds. There are those who argue that both Judaism and Christianity have suppressed the natural abilities of women and degraded their role in spiritual society. That is not my reading of the scriptures, either the Old Testament or the New. Quite the reverse. One of the most remarkable facts about the Bible – in some ways *the* most remarkable fact – is that it is history with the women left in. It appeals as strongly to women as to men for that reason, among others. In this respect it is without rival among the religious texts of the Ancient Near East, or among the secular texts too. From the very beginning, women are part of the Bible story, acting, reacting, talking, scheming, suffering and comforting, as well as merely breeding.

Indeed, it is a curious and most significant fact that God, as presented in the Bible narrative, uses women to introduce into the world one of the uniquely human propensities – the ability to laugh. *Homo sapiens* is a laughing animal perhaps even more than he is a tool-making animal. Indeed, next to self-con-sciousness, the ability to laugh, which is of course a consequence of self-consciousness, is perhaps the most important human characteristic. The earliest written mention of laughter in the whole of world literature occurs in Chapter 18 of the Book of Genesis, when God appears to Abraham as he sits at his tent door in the Plains of Mamre, and tells him that his old wife Sarah is to have a son. Sarah was 'well stricken in age; and it had ceased to be with Sarah after the manner of women'. Sarah too was listening at the tent door to what God said, though unobserved, and when she heard she was to become pregnant she 'laughed within herself, saying, After I am waxed old shall I have pleasure, my lord being old also?' There are many striking things about this passage, notably the fact that Sarah associated sex with pleasure as well as with the honourable duty of a wife to bear sons. Notable also is the fact that she laughed to herself, indicating that humour, especially ironic humour, was already a woman's defence in a man's world. Indeed, both God and Abraham are annoyed to hear her laugh, God particularly because he interprets it as a reflection on his power to do the impossible – 'Is anything too hard for the Lord?' God insists. As laughing is a form of womanly defence against overbearing masculinity, Sarah is abashed at being over-heard to laugh by God, and there is an altercation between the woman and the Deity: 'Then Sarah denied, saying, I laughed not; for she was afraid. And he said, Nay; but thou didst laugh.'

The fact that God used the gender-principle, which he had invented, to bring into the world the laughter-principle, which he had also invented, and that his agent in this was a woman, is an instance of the way in which God exploits the creative possibilities of gender. It also illustrates the importance he attaches to women, and the stress he places on the ways in which they differ from men. Men learned to laugh too, but women laughed first, just as women, in the person of Eve, were the first to allow their curiosity to overcome their sense of obedience – something which God angrily deplored and punished, but with which, being curious himself, he also sympathised. God did not make men and women equal. He made them different, and each has gifts and qualities the other lacks, or possesses in a lesser degree. In terms of total value, it is impossible to choose between them. For all these reasons it is not acceptable that God should have intended only men to serve as his priests indefinitely. Of course it was natural that Jesus Christ, conducting his ministry in the Palestine of the first century AD, when women were discriminated against in countless ways and denied freedom of movement and speech, should have selected his Apostles – whose principal duty was evangelism – solely from men. But in every other respect he treated women with the utmost seriousness and it is evident that he believed them capable of understanding his message as well as any man could. He deliberately commended Mary, the woman who quested for truth and knowledge, as opposed to Martha, who put domesticity first – Mary, he said, 'hath the better part'. It is inconceivable to me, in the light of the New Testament record, that Jesus Christ would have denied today the right of women to serve him in any capacity whatever, as priest or bishop or indeed as pope. I believe I shall live to see woman priests in the Catholic Church, and my grandchildren may well live to see the first woman pope.

God's doctrine of love, gender and sex, then, is inclusive. He does not prefer men to women, though he makes them very different. He does not prefer non-sexual to sexual love, though he sees, as we can see for ourselves, that non-sexual love which is entirely selfless is likely to be purer than the most self-effacing form of sexual love. But the criterion of purity of love, and therefore the acceptability of human love to God, is the absence of self. In the moral economy of God's universe of love, the conquest of self is the most valuable of all attainments – to God, and ultimately to ourselves. It is the key to all other forms of moral progress. And it is particularly the key to love. God made sexuality very powerful so that it would generate intense dramas among the human beings in whom his curiosity is infinite, so that it would be a powerful force for good, and so that it would be a worthy and honourable rival to the non-sexual love he offers to mankind as the exemplar of all love. He also made it powerful so that it offers the greatest possible challenge to the selflessness of spirit he wants to encourage. Overcoming self in sexual love is supremely difficult. But it is the only way in which sexual love can become as pure, or nearly as pure, as the non-sexual love which God radiates. The rules of sexual conduct, as laid down by the churches in God's name, are strict, and necessarily so, because God has made the sexual forces within us so strong. But the conquest of self is more important

than adherence to these rules because they are means to an end
and the end is the expression of a love akin to God's own. It is
possible to imagine situations in which an adulterous love, or a
homosexual love, or even perhaps an incestuous love – a love
which violates the traditional rules – is more acceptable to God
than a licit love, precisely because it involves a more complete
conquest of self. That is a hard doctrine, but it follows logically
from the love-economy of God's universe.

Equally, it is hard to imagine a more complete moral anarchy
than the one which reigns at present in the Western world in
sexual matters, where selfishness in the pursuit of satisfaction is
the imperative norm, where sexuality is completely separated
from duty, responsibility, social need and communal harmony –
as well as from reproduction – where, indeed, sexuality is separated
from all forms of love itself, except self-love, so that it becomes
the absolute negation of the love God extends to the universe.
We seem to have set up in the West at the end of the twentieth
century a sort of sexual antithesis to the universe of love God
planned for us, in which the immense power of sex is directed
almost exclusively to selfish and so to evil ends, Here is our little
pandaemonium, when men and women behave like devils and evil
reigns. And that, inevitably, brings us to the problems of evil in
the world, and why God permits it.

CHAPTER 6

Why evil exists – and why we can distinguish it from good

In this chapter I will try to deal with the problem of evil, and I shall tackle it in two sections. First I will examine God's toleration or co-existence with evil, then I will go on to inquire why it is that human beings instinctively recognise evil as such, and have no real difficulty in distinguishing between evil and good. These two questions are interconnected, but neither is easy to unravel, and I shall not be at all surprised if I fail to carry many readers with me: I myself am fumbling my way.

God's evident willingness to permit evil to exist has been a stumbling-block to many throughout history. If God is infinitely good, and infinitely powerful too, why should evil exist at all, when it is within his capacity to eliminate it once and for all? Or, since he is the author of all creation, why did he bring evil into existence in the first place? This has always worried people, ever since they learned to think clearly for themselves about great issues. The Brahmins pondered it, and the early Buddhists, and the Manichees – the last saw the world as a dualism, a mighty struggle between good and evil forces. Most of the Asian religions explain evil by introducing an element of pantheism. Plato and the Stoics produced other solutions. But none of these systems of thought will allow, as Jews and Christians do, that God is absolutely all-powerful, and therein lies the real difficulty.

I suspect that the problem of evil drives more thoughtful people away from religion than any other difficulty. I know a case of a brilliant Catholic priest, who lost his faith and resigned from the priesthood, and then married and pursued a secular career, entirely because he could not reconcile the existence of God with the existence of nuclear weapons. I cannot follow his line of reasoning at all, though I respect it. More common are those sensitive and imaginative souls who know of a case where an innocent small child – perhaps their own – has died in agony from an incurable disease. They cannot reconcile this guiltless, pointless suffering with God's goodness. So they cease to believe in God at all.

This is an old argument and it was presented brilliantly by the sceptic Pierre Bayle in his *Historical and Critical Dictionary*, published in the 1690s, which became a kind of bible for eighteenth-century anti-Christians, deists and agnostics. Bayle thought that the ubiquity of evil, often triumphant, made the existence of an omnipotent, benevolent God incredible, though he maintained that, religion and morality being independent of one another, it was perfectly possible for men to practise the private and public virtues, and so fight evil, even if they did not believe in God, or even if God did not exist at all. Bayle's arguments led the philosopher G. W. Leibniz to attempt a refutation by coining a new science which he called theodicy, literally the justification of God. In 1710 he published *Essais de theodicée sur la bonté de Dieu*, arguing that evil was not just inevitable but actually necessary because it threw into relief and brilliance the virtues of goodness, just as shade and obscurity revealed the highlights of a painting. Just as a great master, like Caravaggio, cannot reproduce three dimensions on a two-dimensional canvas without the use of shadows and darkness, so God cannot bring home to us the splendour of goodness, including his own, without the contrast of evil.

This is an elegant proof, rather than a convincing one, and I am not sure that Leibniz and his many imitators and successors have succeeded in their object. The Book of Job, which for many people is the greatest work of art in the Old Testament, also tackles the problem of evil, by examining the appalling sufferings inflicted on this innocent and righteous man by a testing Deity. It certainly succeeds as art and it probably fascinates more people today than any other part of the Bible – an American friend of mine has recently written a whole book about it – but I am not sure that it succeeds as theology. The ending, in particular, in which Job suddenly and inexplicably becomes rich and happy again, strikes one as weak and has led some critics to suppose it was added by a later hand, and that the original text of Job, being true to itself, ended in tragedy.

One Judeo-Christian explanation of evil, which is suggested by the scriptures themselves, runs as follows. Evil was created by the sins of the rebel angels, especially by the sin of pride committed by Satan or Lucifer, their leader. Once Hell came into existence to house them, evil was always an infection which could spread. When God created man, as it were to take the place of the missing angels, and made him without knowledge of good and evil, and set him in the Garden of Eden, where evil certainly did not exist, Satan was able to tempt Eve to eat the fatal apple, by which such knowledge was conveyed, and she gave it to Adam too. So God expelled them from the Garden into the vale of tears which we call earth, where evil in all its forms co-exists with goodness, and sinful man is left to choose between the two.

This rather tortuous explanation is not of a kind to satisfy most people nowadays, and it has a crucial weakness. If God is truly omnipotent, why did he allow the rebel angels to rebel in the first place, and why did they – Satan being next to God in intelligence, as we are told – knowing God was all-powerful, think they could get away with it? A more plausible case is suggested by Origen, to my mind the cleverest of all the early theologians, who argues that evil necessarily springs from God's bounty in giving free will to his human creatures. It is an act of God's nobility to allow them to choose evil as well as good, and evil must exist to make the choice meaningful. This is a line followed by St Thomas Aquinas and others. Clearly evil and free will are somehow connected. But this does not explain the many evils in the world which have nothing to do with human choice, good or bad. The death of a child in a Nazi camp can fairly be attributed to the freedom of will enjoyed by Hitler and the members of the SS, and thus a sacrifice on the altar of human choice. But an innocent child dying in agony of meningitis or buried alive in an earthquake has nothing to do with human volition. Evil in man is easily explicable, in my view, and may well be justified by the overriding demands of the freedom of will, which is what makes humankind so noble and extraordinary and – to God – so endlessly interesting. But evil in nature is harder to grasp. I suppose it might be said that God, having created the universe, and subjected it to general laws, feels it right to allow those laws to operate, and human beings, placed in the universe so that they can exercise choice, have to take their chance with nature also, and some inevitably become victims of nature before they are rational and can exercise choices.

I am not easy in my mind about this reasoning, however, and I must confess that my own answer to the problem of evil – my own theodicy – is much more simple, some would say simplistic. I honestly do not know why God permits evil in all its forms. I take Leibniz's argument up to a point and can understand that the existence of evil, both in nature and in man, makes the universe a much more interesting, if dangerous, place than a morally one-dimensional Garden of Eden. God is infinitely curious, just as he is infinitely everything else which is desirable, and curiosity is clearly one reason why he brought the universe into existence in the first place. God's curiosity in observing humanity is more likely to be stimulated and satisfied if human-kind has to struggle both against the consequences of choosing evil instead of good, and against the objective facts of evil in nature – often overcoming or mitigating those evils by his or her ingenuity. But I do not pretend this is a complete answer. My instinct, rather, is to trust God. Our understanding, compared to God's infinite knowledge and wisdom, is so puny that it seems to me hazardous to set ourselves up in judgment over God's righteousness. God always has a purpose, and that purpose is always for the good and for our welfare. I am content to believe that no one who innocently suffers here on earth will be without full and ample recompense in Heaven. The tiniest child, crushed out of existence by blind nature or human wickedness in this world, will live to enjoy God's bounty and praise his justice and munificence in the next. No evil will go unpunished, no injustice unrighted, no suffering unrelieved in the end.

Some people will object that this answer is too easy, indeed complacent. And they have a case. Our attitudes to the problem of evil are influenced by our own experiences, and by the number and cruelty of the blows of fate we have had to suffer. I have to admit that my own life has been amazingly fortunate. I was the youngest child of a happy family and got more than my fair share of love. The only really devastating blow I suffered in the whole of my life was the sudden death of my father when I was thirteen. This occurred without warning while I was away at school, and it was particularly hard to bear because in the previous vacation I had first got to know him well and was rejoicing in his decision to treat me as someone worth being with, sharing ideas with and consulting. Of course, there have been other blows too, but far less serious or sudden ones. There has certainly been nothing comparable to shake my faith in the justice of God. I have always been healthy and so has my wife, my children and, so far, my grandchildren. I have had a modest success in life and have lived throughout in a country favoured by fortune. I have my faith in God, more important to me than anything else.

So I have good reason to thank my maker and I do, daily and most earnestly. I also have a fear, real if irrational, rather like the pious aunt in the story I told, that God may suddenly become aware of my good fortune, largely undeserved as it is, and decide to give me what I call a biff. This theory of a Divine Biff, for those who have been having it too good, finds no place in any volume of theology that I know of, but it has a morbid grip on my imagination. Indeed, I find it is shared by many other people, with whom I have discussed it. They too, when things are going undeservedly well, fear a corrective biff from the Deity.

But this is a digression, and the point I am really making is that I may not be the ideal person to advance justifications for God's tolerance of evil, having had to suffer so little of it. Better to turn to the countless people who have led lives, objectively viewed, of unrelieved misery and misfortune, through no fault of their own or, like Job, have been lifted on high and then inexplicably dashed to the ground. Those who have undergone huge and continual sufferings, and have emerged without bitterness or have contrived to overcome their resentment, are the ones to justify God's ways to man, rather than someone like myself, who has little reason to grumble. But, having thus disqualified myself, I am still convinced that God sees infinitely further than the rest of us, that he has reasons for all things, and that in his good time there will be explanations forthcoming for all he does, or does not do, or permits to happen. Here, patience and forbearance are the great virtues – difficult virtues too and ones I in particular do not find it congenial to practise.

Whatever the justification, however, it is a fact that God permits evil to exist. Therefore men and women have to cope with evil, and this brings me to the second part of the problem. I said at the outset of this book that one reason why men and women tend to believe in God is that they are aware they have a conscience, and therefore assume God put it there. It is a remarkable fact that awareness of good and evil, and an instinctual feeling that good is morally preferable, even if our baser instincts do not permit us to prefer it, seem to be implanted in us by nature. This is what is called Natural Law: that is, the law fixed in nature by God the Creator which human creatures can discern by the light of natural reason. As such it is contrasted, by theologians, with the Revealed Law, such as the Ten Commandments presented directly to Moses by God and written in tablets of stone. Theologians argue that those commandments – except the one about the Sabbath Day – are to be found in Natural Law too, and are common to most societies, and that Revealed Law merely gave them added emphasis and specific terminology.

Until comparatively recently, the doctrine of Natural Law was accepted by most theologians almost as axiomatic. St Paul refers to it in his Epistle to the Romans (2:14ff.) when he says that the Gentiles, even though they have not been taught the Torah, or Mosaic Law, 'show that what the law requires is written in their hearts'. The Stoic philosophers of Athens in the fourth and third centuries BC believed in Natural Law, expressed in the law of conscience or duty. Stoics argued that God is the immanent, all-pervading energy which sustains the natural world, and the reason or Logos which is reflected in the world's order and beauty. So the good and wise man conforms to nature: that is, he lives according to the law of the universe embodied in the divine reason. There is an old tradition that St Paul was in correspondence with Seneca, the leading Stoic of his time, and it is evident from the very opening of the gospel of St John, with its memorable passage about the Logos, that it was pervaded by Stoic philosophy. Natural Law has thus been part of Christianity since its inception and that is as it should be, because Natural Law is a form of moral absolutism and therefore akin to Christian teaching, which I believe is true for all times and peoples.

In more recent times, however, there has been less stress on Natural Law, and I notice, for instance, that there is no entry for it in the index of the new *Catholic Catechism*, comprehensive and admirable though that volume is in most respects. This decline of belief in Natural Law has been accompanied by the growth of moral relativism, the teaching that axioms of right or wrong vary according to time and place and custom: there are no absolutes, merely the norms of particular societies. In short, what is done, is what ought to be done.

Now I have learned from the experience of our own times what reason and instinct teaches me also – that moral relativism is a great evil, one of the greatest of all evils because it makes possible so many other evils. I am surprised to hear intellectuals defend it, as they frequently do on radio and television, because it is my conviction that no one really practises in moral relativism. Or, to put it paradoxically, there is no such thing as absolute belief in relative morality. All who profess to accept relativism in morals in fact make exceptions – to steal, to murder, to lie, for instance, they admit is always wrong. Even the most insistent moral relativist finds, if he examines his conscience closely, that he accepts a core of morally absolute beliefs. I use the word 'conscience' advisedly, for the existence of a conscience is incompatible with moral relativism – a conscience rises above relative values and insists on absolute ones.

Moral relativism has been the cardinal sin of the twentieth century, the reason why it has been such a desperately unhappy and destructive epoch in human history. Both the great evil philosophies of the century, Nazism and Communism, were morally relativistic; they argued that the 'Revolutionary Conscience' or the 'higher law of the Party' were superior to the ancient prescriptive moral wisdom of humanity, expressed in the Decalogue – Natural Law and divine law. The arrogant insistence of these two totalitarian systems, that they made up their own laws and imposed and changed them at will, was too much even for a morally easy-going world, which is always only too ready to forget absolutes and sink into moral sloppiness. So the world rose up and eventually overcame the Nazis, and uncovered the bestiality of the death-camps, those ultimate symbols of moral relativism with their repudiation of the absolute doctrine 'Thou shalt not kill'. And the world also repudiated and isolated Communism, which eventually collapsed of its own hopeless implausibilities and inefficiencies. But that does not mean that moral relativism has been banished from the world – far from it. The relativistic notion that what is done in any particular society is right, constitutes a slippery slope which is inviting and easily followed and eventually ends in complete moral anarchy. The decline of organised religion is an encouragement to moral relativism. The growth of mass-communications – especially television – is a compelling visual aid to moral relativism. The churches themselves, or rather the weaker of them, are inclined to indulge in moral relativism in the forlorn belief it will boost their declining numbers. So in the United States and Britain we have the pathetic spectacle of some churches trying to justify perverted sex – because there *are* such people as practising homosexuals – or divorce – because so many people *do* get divorced – or pre-marital sex – because couples who live together without benefit of marriage are *so* numerous nowadays. On the other hand, Pope John Paul II makes himself unpopular with many people, especially those in the media, where moral relativism is particularly common, simply because he insists on moral absolutism and will not bend the law of God and nature for a sinful generation.

This is an old battle and will go on to the end of time. And of course, just as there is no such person as an absolute moral relativist, so there is no such doctrine as absolute moral absolutism. Even the most absolute rules are a little ragged at their far edges, as particular societies, while absolutist at the core, yield to custom or particular problems in some matters of detail. There are unresolved contradictions, too, in some of the most important absolute rules. 'Thou shalt not kill', good for all times and places, is qualified by the undoubted right of society to take human life in certain circumstances – in the cause of justice in civil society, for instance, and in the course of a Just War. The present pope is opposed to capital punishment and believes it is hardly ever necessary to inflict it – and that it should be avoided at almost any cost. He is closer, therefore, to being an absolute moral absolutist than I am, for I believe capital punishment is necessary in some cases – many cases, as a rule. But such disagreements in detail do not undermine the general conviction that absolute morals are the norm and that society must abide by them. That is undoubtedly the lesson of history, apart from anything else.

It is also, I would argue, the lesson of genetics. I do not think the existence of the conscience in human beings, and their deep, basic convictions that certain things are always wrong, has come about by accident, or that these beliefs are just metaphysically or miraculously implanted in us by Almighty God, from outside as it were. I think they are part of his divine scheme, and always have been, and that they are written into the laws of the universe as surely as the laws of thermodynamics or any other of the unalterable axioms of physics. Since it has been right to call us humans or rational creatures, or even perhaps before that, it has been written into our genetic codes that we should make distinctions between good and evil, and that we should have a moral preference for good. That indeed is why we tend to adhere to Natural Law, and have a conscience and will ourselves to follow it – even if that will often proves too weak to combat other instincts in our genes. Our genetic coding and the necessity of absolute morality are closely connected and both form part of the divine scheme. I am not arguing that positive moral coding is confined to humans – it would be surprising if it were. Anyone who has been used to keeping horses or dogs, for instance, is aware of moral tendencies in these noble creatures – animals saints and sinners as it were – which reflect genetic codings and sometimes malign genes, albeit at a cruder level. But just as *homo sapiens* is the rational creature *par excellence,* so he is the morally coded creature *par excellence,* and that is undoubtedly part of God's scheme for the universe. Ours is not a chaotic universe but a universe of laws, and they include moral laws. We ignore them individually at the risk of our immortal souls, and mankind ignores them collectively at the risk of its social health and even its existence.

CHAPTER 7

The God of beauty

When I was a child, I always associated the notion of God with beauty. There were several reasons for this. The first was that, in our house, the only things which seemed to matter, which were treated as important, were religion, education and art. My father was headmaster of an art school, and a practising painter. He produced watercolours mainly, but also etchings, drypoints, lithographs and other kinds of prints, and at his schools the pupils were instructed in sculpture and pottery as well. In our house was an art room (it was always called that, not a studio, regarded as an un-English expression), where my father worked. Art and education were intermingled and both were sacrosanct. My father's very limited resources were primarily devoted to the education of his children, and great significance was attached to our schooling, and our performance at school. But even more important was religion: that is, attending church, prayers, holy pictures and statues, fasting and abstinence, keeping the commandments and pious practices. I became aware of this order of priorities at a very early age.

The second reason I associated God with beauty was our local church. Shortly before I was born, our parish priest, an ambitious and energetic man, decided to build a new church and bought a virgin site, not far from our house. He consulted my father at every stage of this undertaking, from the original design, throughout the construction, and during the completion and decoration of the building. The church was conceived on the largest possible scale. No architect was employed, but our priest, sometimes accompanied by my father, travelled in Europe to look for models, and eventually hit on a compromise between two which had taken his fancy. So the church had a large Gothic tower joined to a series of Romanesque domes, and three-and-one-half in number, the half-dome covering the high altar, and the other three the nave. The edifice was built of stone and in order to carry its immense weight, in a part of Staffordshire riddled with old mine-workings and liable to subsidence, a thick raft of concrete was placed under the foundations.

Most local Catholics did not believe in the ability of the parish to carry through and finance this immense undertaking – and non-Catholics were scandalised by our audacity and pride. Even my father was worried by the responsibility of it all, and by many other aspects of the design and construction. But our priest was a man possessed by a vision and he was determined to carry it through, no matter what. And he did carry it through, at remarkable speed. The main construction period coincided with the Great Depression, when there were thousands out of work in the neighbourhood and the evidence of dire poverty was everywhere. This made it more difficult to borrow money or to raise funds to finance what was known as 'the Debt'. On the other hand, it may be that it was easier and cheaper to get labour at this time, and to spur it to exceptional efforts, and this explains why the church was so soon completed.

At all events, by the time I came to consciousness the church was nearly finished, and the internal decoration was proceeding. My father was much involved in this, and so was I as a small, wondering and rapt spectator. It was as though, in a modest way, I was a witness to the topping-out and the embellishment of the great basilica of St Peter's in Rome. As the church was so near, I was in and out of it many times a week. It was not so much that I was fond of it as completely dominated and overawed by it. It was, physically and in every other way, a huge presence in my life. My father often drew and painted it and so, in due course, did I. It did not occur to me, in my childhood, that God and art had separate existences, since both were so intimately united in the church itself. Only later did I perceive there was such a thing as secular art, and even then it seemed to be more a tributary of religious art rather than an autonomous entity. God presided over everything, it appeared, but he had a particularly close connection with any artistic endeavour – architecture, of course, painting, sculpture, but also brass- and ironwork for the church fittings, stained glass for the windows, needlework for the vestments and altarcloths, and various kinds of precious metalwork for the holy vessels. God was also somehow involved in the casting of the massive bronze bells, and the elaborate process whereby they were hoisted to the top of the great tower, so that they could ring out over the surrounding countryside, proclaiming triumphantly that the magnificent church had, indeed, been finished.

The association between God on the one hand, and art and beauty on the other, was thus impressed upon me from the earliest age, so that I took it quite for granted. Hence, when I studied theology at school, what attracted me most among St Thomas Aquinas's various proofs of God was the fourth one, from beauty. St Thomas argued, as I recall, that we were aware, through our senses, not just of beauty but of degrees of beauty. It follows from this that there is an absolute beauty, and that thing or being is God himself. We love God, in this life, as the very epitome of goodness, which we perceive from his works and from the love for us which radiates from him. But we cannot – yet – see God and we thus have no conception of the absolute beauty which is him. That, I imagine, will be among the chief delights of Paradise, the contemplation of an effulgent and myriad-natured beauty, which is perpetually changing and modulating, yet permanent in its serenity and power. I suppose we shall all – if we get there! – be beautiful then, and one of the characteristics of salvation will be the acquisition of power to enjoy beauty in ways we cannot now even imagine. Heaven will be a celestial academy and gallery of living art, whose beauties will penetrate and envelop our very souls. We will walk among and converse with those Raphael madonnas and Botticelli angels and Michelangelo and Donatello Davids. But it is the beauty of God himself which will most entrance us.

God, it is clear, gives us a foretaste of his beauty in the universe he has created. Its beauty, like its energising forces, radiates from him. Indeed, the fact that God rejoices in beauty is one reason why he created the universe in the first place. The universe, like God himself, is living beauty, constantly changing its form with fresh delights. It creates beauty by its motions. The starry heavens were the first intimations of beauty which penetrated the minds of primitive men and women, who had no possessions and had not yet taught themselves to make things, but already possessed the power of ecstasy. During those long nights of distant antiquity, they lay on the ground and contemplated with wonder and satisfaction the movements of the stars. It was almost certainly then that they grasped what beauty is about – an intimation of God. The stars taught them that God was there, and that he was even greater than the stars because he had made and arranged them and set them in motion. So beauty did indeed lead men to God, as St Thomas later argued.

The universe, from its inception – from that first Big Bang – has had an awesome beauty but, as it expands and develops, its beauties multiply and intensify. We can see this ourselves, as the number and variety of flowers increases, and we and nature together produce finer specimens. Human beings, always beautiful, become more so as new and healthier generations succeed each other. The girls are prettier than ever before, and there are more of them to catch the eye. The young men are taller, stronger, more handsome. The universe is so full of beauty that it is difficult for one limited human being to take it all in. We travel more than ever, and have far easier access to the splendours of the world than any of our forebears, but it is beyond our power, even in a lifetime, to absorb more than a fraction of what God has provided for our delectation. God is, if anything, too generous, as Martin Luther is recorded as observing in his *Table Talk*: 'Dr Luther, holding a rose in his hand, said: "Tis a magnificent work of God: could a man make but one such rose as this, he would be thought worthy of all honour, but the gifts of God lose their value in our eyes from their very infinity."'

God provides us, then, with countless models of beauty, and it seems to me manifestly part of his purpose for us that we should learn to reciprocate, by producing beauty ourselves. It is one important way in which we return God's love for us. We cannot give him power or possessions, for he has everything of that kind already, but we can give him beauty of our invention, and he rejoices in it, however inferior it may be to his own inventions, just as fond parents enjoy the drawings of their tiny children. Artists of all kinds are dear to God. He endows them with their skills and, in rare cases, their genius, and delights in the way they make use of them. Woe betide an idle artist, neglecting God's gifts! – a point Milton makes in one of his greatest sonnets when he writes of 'talent which is death to hide'.

Some visitors to Rome, seeing the marvellous works of art created there under papal patronage, especially from the fifteenth to the seventeenth centuries, deplore the expenditure of so much time and money and energy on mere artifice. They see the glories of papal Rome as materialism triumphant, sanctified secularity, paganism enthroned. That is an arguable point of view and throughout the millenniums of belief austere souls have sought to praise God without any aids of beauty. But to my mind, and I think to most people's, to create beauty is one way in which we respond to God and praise him. To erect buildings and to adorn them with art specifically so that God may be worshipped in them is a worthy occupation for a pope and his cardinals. And it is no bad thing, incidentally, for an ecclesiastical ruler to have the physical means to overawe his secular rivals. Not long ago I was in Rome with Margaret Thatcher on a private visit, and Pope John Paul II kindly arranged for her and one or two of her friends to be shown the Sistine Chapel, reopened after the most extensive restoration in its history. It was a rare privilege to see Michelangelo's frescos without the perpetually milling crowd which fills the chapel throughout its official opening hours. It was a still rarer experience to see Margaret Thatcher, this Queen of Politics, this outstanding exponent of the art of ruling, quite overcome – rendered speechless, in fact – by the splendour of beauty brought into being by a genius under ecclesiastical patronage. She saw that the church can command, as well as the state!

No pope or archbishop should be deterred from erecting monuments to Almighty God by mere difficulty or expense. We have to think of future generations, as well as our own. And we have to think what God himself wishes. The catholic ruler of a West African state has been much abused for building in his capital a huge cathedral only slightly smaller in size than St Peter's itself. He should, it is argued, have spent the money on the poor, with whom his country is plentifully provided. But it may be that the poor in West Africa rejoice in this immense creation. In my observation and reading of history, the poor love cathedrals and always have done and will continue to do so. A cathedral is something a poor man or woman can visit and share with God.

It was Wordsworth who pointed out that a poor man is just as capable of enjoying beauty, and putting it high in his scale of values, as a rich man. The poor of West Africa, who have little but their native pride, may well be happy to observe that their small country is capable of creating a cathedral on the scale of Europe's largest, and that the black African can pay his or her tribute to Almighty God just as munificently as the white Westerner.

The 8,000 medieval parish churches which we still possess in England – the greatest single item in our national dowry of art – were built and paid for by a society most of whose members had few material possessions. They now constitute a monument to their generosity and magnanimity, which we will continue to use and enjoy so long as we have the sense to preserve them. They give us as much satisfaction as they give to God, for whose glory they were erected. And do not the souls of those medieval men and women, now in Heaven, rejoice that their churches, created with so much sacrifice, still sound forth God's praises?

Early in the century, both the Protestant and the Catholic communities of Liverpool, a city then famous for its religious fervour, decided to build new cathedrals. Paradoxically, the Protestants chose a gifted young Catholic architect, Giles Gilbert Scott, and he produced for them the design of a masterpiece in Edwardian Gothic. With prodigies of effort, the work was financed and built, and finally completed in the 1980s, long after sponsors and architect were in their graves – as usually happens in the case of cathedrals. But this marvellous building, the finest erected in Europe this century, survives to do them honour, and to honour too the resolution and faith of the Anglican Church in Liverpool. The Catholics of the Edwardian age also chose a fine architect: the great Sir Edwin Lutyens, an Anglican by conviction but a Catholic by artistic sentiment. He designed a glorious church, on the scale of St Peter's, in the most sumptuous Baroque, to be built of marble. This was an even greater labour and expense than the Anglican cathedral, but the immense crypt was in due course completed. Then came the war, which halted construction. Some time after the war, Archbishop Heenan – later cardinal – estimating that the cost of completing the project was more than the Catholics of Liverpool could bear, decided not to complete it. Instead he commissioned and built a much cheaper thing, by a meretricious

Modern Movement architect, with a peculiar tent-like roof, which has led the jeering Protestants of the city to christen it 'Paddy's Wigwam'. The Catholics, who were barely consulted by Heenan in making his decision, now hang their heads in shame that they must worship in such a hovel, already showing signs of decay. They are indeed poor, but they would have found the money for Lutyens' magnificent basilica. I reproached Heenan at the time, as being a man of little faith. I told him about the church which our parish priest had insisted on building, against much advice, when I was a child, and how the money had been found to complete it. He expressed contrition, and maybe it is still not too late to resurrect Lutyens' ambitious scheme, for the glory of God in the dawning twenty-first century. We shall see.

In the meantime, there can be little doubt that among the most privileged of human beings are those who have the honour to erect a great church to God. They must be considered the most fortunate of artists, and dearest to their maker. Most, as I say, do not live to see their work finished, Michelangelo and Brunelleschi being among their number. But there are exceptions. Sir Christopher Wren designed the new St Paul's, supervised its main construction, and lived to see it completed. This immense work brought him little material reward, caused him endless heartache and anxiety, brought him opprobrium and eventually dismissal, and received surprisingly little recognition in his lifetime. But at least he saw it finished, and thereafter he came once a year, to sit under its dome, to pray, to meditate and to rejoice. Those must have been cherished moments – both to him and to God.

However, no good purpose is served by designating a hierarchy of God's favour for creative geniuses. All artists endear themselves to him by depicting his creations to the best of their ability. Painters are often genuinely pious men and women, despite their wild notions about the Deity. It is common among them to kneel down and pray in dedication before beginning a canvas, and kneel down in gratitude when they have completed it. Sometimes they have misgivings about their failure to use their talents exclusively to praise and explain God's works – thus Botticelli, one of the purest and most gifted of them all, came bitterly to regret his secular works, with their voluptuousness and riot. He is even said to have destroyed some. But that was foolish – as foolish as the iconoclasts who, in most faiths, Orthodox, Catholic, Protestant, Islamic, have gone around destroying works of art in churches, as vain, idolatrous and blasphemous. It is not for any one or any group of us to decide that people have been wrong to worship God in their chosen fashion.

Far more likely it is that God takes particular pleasure in seeing our attempts to use our skills to replicate the beauty he has created. God is the greatest of all connoisseurs. All my life I have been a landscape painter, after a fashion, as my father was before me. I now regret not having painted more, but I chose to earn my living by writing and the demands of that trade are exigent and for many years I painted little. During the last decade I have tried to make up for lost opportunities by painting what I see wherever I go in the world, even if I only have a few snatched minutes for a quick sketch. The results have been rewarding far in excess of my expectations. Not only have I accumulated a large stock of sketches and finished paintings, from all continents, but the quality of the rendering has improved. I feel, increasingly, that I am painting for God, as much as for myself and my friends. God gave me this certain, limited talent, and I am serving him by seeking to improve it while making a record of what he has created in the world. To me at any rate, painting is prayerful. It is also one of the most innocent of enjoyments. And it instructs. There is no doubt that painting forces us to look very closely at what God has done and so to grasp the design of nature, just as painting a building gives us a marvellous insight into the intentions of the architect. Hills and mountains, rivers and waterfalls and lakes do not just come into existence haphazardly. They are formed over long periods by powerful natural forces, and studying them closely while painting enables one to understand these processes and so paint better. No one who spends long hours and days painting landscapes can be without considerable knowledge of the way God has made the world, and of the relationships between beauty and purpose in natural forms. For a long time I was singularly inept in drawing, and still more painting, trees, so that I almost despaired of them. But they are among the finest of God's creations – noble things, so full of majesty and honour, and so varied. So I persevered and made a special, painstaking study of their structure, and at long last I began to understand how God designed them, and how it was their functional efficiency which made them works of natural art. So I improved and now take enormous pleasure in painting trees, albeit with occasional failures still.

What I have undoubtedly neglected is the human form. I like to put figures in my landscapes, as my father taught me, just to indicate scale, and I am often ashamed at how poor they are. So I often tell myself that I must go back to life-class and really master the human form by drawing it patiently and industriously. So far this has not happened, and the months and years go by, and I realise yet again the importance of resolution and persistence and will-power in all schemes of human improvement. I say to myself now: 'I will find time to carry out this resolve, as soon as I have finished this book.' For who can deny that the human form is in many ways the finest of God's works of art? The scriptures tell us that God created man in his own image. We do not know exactly what this means, and it certainly cannot mean that God looks like a man in an ordinary visual sense. We are left with a mystery, but perhaps we can begin to solve it by studying and painting the human form with the diligence its radiant beauties merit. There is, indeed, a certain holiness about the body, in both its male and its female varieties, and it is with some reverence that we should approach it – there is a connection with the divine. That was the spirit in which William Etty RA, an artist I much admire, approached the nude. He worked on it all his life and, though he attained remarkable proficiency in both drawing and painting human flesh – no English artist ever did it better – he was never content. He continued to attend life-classes at the Royal Academy right to the end of his life, sitting among the students and not too proud to receive their critical comments on his work, or to listen to the presiding master. I possess some of the results of his dedicated industry and value them as evidence not just of his skill, but of his determination to improve it. There is no better way to serve God.

Studying the works of God and trying to reproduce them visually brings us close to our creator. It is one way to know him. But it may be that the musician gets even closer. The universe is an exercise in harmony as much as in shape and colour and texture, and none can doubt that there are celestial sounds as well as visions. Then again, all creation is a series of abstractions as much as a series of material realities, and these abstractions can be expressed musically as well as mathematically and algebraically. Composing, reproducing and hearing sounds of exquisite beauty and profundity can give us extraordinary insights not just into beauty, but into goodness itself. After hearing a great symphony, telling us, but entirely in abstract terms, of truth and justice and heroism, we arise better men and women. The musicians in the orchestra feel it, the conductor feels it, the listeners feel it. The mood may not last, but it is much to have felt it at all. It is akin to the lifting of the heart and spirit we experience at a religious ceremony when we have concentrated our thoughts well and meditated deeply. So music works on our minds, and God listens too. It must be a fine thing to have composed the music which has so held players and audience and so raised their minds to God. That is why, I think, Jean Sibelius told me, in the summer of 1949, 'to compose is often an agony but it is the quintessence of privilege too'. Many composers have been deeply religious people, humbly rejoicing in this privilege – none more so than Joseph Haydn, whose long, industrious and painstaking life, so modestly conducted amid so many difficulties and setbacks, is a model of artistic integrity in God's service. Or there is the case of Anton Bruckner, childlike and wholly innocent in his devotion to God, who spent so many hours seated at the organ, alone with his music and his maker, and then poured forth his prayers in vast symphonies, few of which he ever heard performed. His ninth, last and greatest he dedicated, quite simply: 'To Almighty God'.

In contrast to architects, painters and composers, writers have a mixed record in God's service. They are so numerous and varied that it is risky to generalise in any way, but it is remarkable how many writers, in all civilisations, have tended to take a critical view of established order and sought to subvert it. It is probably the single most striking characteristic of the mind which wishes to express itself through the written word. Now, of course, in subverting order they may be carrying out God's purpose, and there are plenty of instances in the Old Testament where that is exactly what its more passionate writers are doing. But I have spent my entire working life among writers and I know very well that the cast of mind which they habitually possess, and which

harbours huge resentments of the world as it exists, is not necessarily motivated by selfless altruism. To praise God is not usually
the writer's intention in picking up a pen or sitting down in front
of a word-processor. More likely it is to express a grievance or work
off a resentment or articulate a personal longing or simply to
rage – in addition to making money, of course. Writers are sinful
and fallen and unsatisfactory man writ large. It will be, for me at
least, one of the great points of interest of the next world to see
how God, in his justice, sorts out all the giants and pygmies of
the pen. How will Voltaire fare? Some Christian polemicists write
as if he were already in Hell, but I am not so sure. A man's writings
have to be judged in their effects, if any, over many generations,
and these may be contradictory and, in aggregate, difficult to
assess. We may be sure God will do them justice, however, and
this may often in the end surprise us. Where will he place Tolstoy,
that astonishing combination of humility and arrogance, wisdom
and madness, piety and destruction? He will have difficulty with
Milton, too, who sought – so he said – to justify the ways of God
to men and ended by writing a masterpiece whose hero was Satan.
I do not know how Shelley will fare, he who professed atheism
and practised a kind of exalted pantheism, who preached socialism
and was a monster of personal selfishness. The fact is, nevertheless,
that men and women have been uplifted and inspired by Shelley's
poetry and become better people in consequence.

How will God reward or punish, sanctify or damn the immense
mass of gifted men and women who have given contradictory
messages to the modern world? All will come up for judgment –
the Baudelaires and the Hugos, the Hemingways and the Joyces,
a mad genius like Ezra Pound and a calculating operator like Zola,
the reckless like Rimbaud and the thoughtful like Emerson, the
sinners like Byron and the saints like Chesterton. I cannot imagine
how God will arrange Sartre and Bertrand Russell, Wittgenstein
and Rilke, Yeats and Lorca in any order of sanctification or devilry
which makes sense. But it will undoubtedly be carried out: therein
lie the fascinating things to come. What evil have their writings
done – then and since? What good – in their lifetimes and thereafter? The heavenly computers will whirr and deliver and the
notices of judgment will be posted, and the writers, dishevelled,
apprehensive, ashamed or defiant, struggling or abject, will be

brought out to be given their laurels or punished, in front of all the watching world.

But there are also those writers who have not sought to tell the world what to do, to create Utopias out of their own unaided intellects and incited people into trying to bring them about, but instead have simply set themselves to portray God's universe and his people in loving words. They will have a smooth passage through the storms of that tremendous judgment day. There are writers who, by their modest genius, or even merely by their carefully husbanded and honed talents, have sought chiefly to enable their readers to see God's creation with fresh eyes – have taught us to look, again and again, at the world around us and the way humans behave. To teach us about the universe, to encourage us to explore and value and treat tenderly all its manifestations and inhabitants, is a salient work of art in itself and an act of worship. Such writers are dear to God, and they are valuable to us too: for the understanding and reverence we bring to the world around us is a salient part of our duty, as we are beginning to discover. Let us now turn to that aspect of our religious faith and practice.

CHAPTER 8

God's world – or ours?

Human beings are ingenious and resourceful creatures and, being such, do great things, become self-congratulatory and suffer from *hubris*. Man must be perpetually on watch against the sin of pride, the real killer, of souls as well as bodies. The scriptures say that God not only made man in his own image, but gave him dominion over the earth and all that is on it. But the scriptures were written by men (and sometimes by women). Yes: I know we are taught they are divinely inspired: 'So have I heard and do in part believe', as Horatio says in *Hamlet*. It may be that God indicated what was to be put down, and the writer placed his own construction on it. The dominion over the earth and its creatures, given by God to man, was heavily qualified, more so perhaps than the Bible makes out. To begin with, it is not a freehold but a leasehold, and I suspect that it is one of the pernickety kinds issued by such conservationist bodies as the National Trust. We must do this and we may not do that. It is a fully repairing lease and periodically monitored to secure compliance. God is a jealous God – there, the Bible was exact – and watches over his freehold with an eagle's eye and a tiger's rage and an elephantine memory. He knows from long experience that mankind is a bad tenant. Man is exceptionally wasteful and, until recently at least, rarely troubled himself with disposing of his waste sensibly. It is sometimes tempting to characterise *homo sapiens* as a rubbish-making animal. Accumulations of noxious and disgusting rubbish appear very early in his discoverable history and·are much older than cities. When cities do appear they are often built on earlier layers of rubbish, sometimes dozens, scores or even hundreds of feet deep. I am not saying that man is alone in making rubbish. In the Scottish highlands, for instance, I know of a large eagle's nest, in part of the surviving aboriginal Caledonian forest, which is many hundreds of years old and whose foundations, high in the tree, are made up of the rubbish of many earlier nests, just like cities in antiquity. Many birds live on their own rubbish dumps. But man wastes things out of all proportion to his needs or consumption, and accumulates rubbish with terrifying speed and scatters it about him in the most careless manner. It is amazing how soon he produces and distributes rubbish, even in the most unpropitious circumstances. The South Pole and large parts of Antarctica are already littered with rubbish. So are the slopes of Everest. So, increasingly, are prominent areas of space.

What is Almighty God to make of this rubbish-excreting and scattering creature he has put in a position of trust over the world? There is now virtually no part of the planet so inhospitable that man cannot penetrate it and, if he chooses, lay waste to it. He already has a foothold in space and will soon be clambering about it freely, in search of raw materials and precious metals and stones, energy and power – all the valuables whose production entails rubbish in colossal quantities. Stout Cortés of the twenty-first century will soon be on his way in space, brave, greedy and messy.

Now it is obvious that, while making purposeful use of the world and the universe is not only lawful for man but actually enjoined on him by God – that is one reason he created it in the first place – wastefully to despoil it or to consume it selfishly is sinful. The Judeo-Christian tradition teaches, and I think has always taught, that the Seventh Commandment, 'Thou shalt not steal', protects the world around us, as well as our neighbour's possessions. As we are leaseholders, we must not diminish God's freehold needlessly and without warrant. The new *Catholic Catechism*, which seems to me – on balance – an unrivalled compendium of clear-sighted moral theology and, for that matter, good sense, tells us: 'Man's dominion over inanimate and other living beings granted by the creator is not absolute; it is limited by concern for the quality of life of his neighbour, including generations to come; it requires a religious respect for the integrity of creation.' I like that use of the word 'integrity': for the universe is indeed a whole and we must try to see it and treat it and preserve it as a whole. We are now rapidly acquiring the knowledge to work out what this commandment means in practice, and to observe it accordingly. So our responsibilities increase with our understanding, exactly as a growing child's do. We are beginning to move about the universe as adults, and we must behave as adults.

No sensible person will disagree with this, and it only remains to work out what it means in practice. But it is at this point that the trouble begins, on account of what I do not hesitate to classify as a new form of paganism – environmentalism: an ugly name for an ugly thing. Paganism is a periodically besetting sin of the human race and it can take a variety of forms. In our times it has re-emerged with enormous force as a movement, especially among the young and educated (perhaps one should say half-educated) to sanctify nature in all its forms – oceans, rivers, rain-forests, wetlands, uplands, bats and herons, elephants, whales and white rhinos, and many other objects and species, common or rare. It has taken advantage of the fact that we live in the Age of the Lobby to make itself immensely strong. But it is much more than a lobby or a series of lobbies – Greenpeace, Friends of the Earth, the Club of Rome, etc. It is, undoubtedly, a form of religion. Its adherents, who are mostly young or youngish, but not without the odd bronzed and scrawny guru or fakir among them, betray all the signs of religious enthusiasm: absolute conviction, lack of interest in any arguments except their own, contempt for evidence except the canonical 'facts' they present as such, extreme activism, and a tendency to take part in processions, demos, marches, martyrdoms and miraculous happenings. Most of these people, in another day and age, would have been religious persons: in the Middle Ages, Franciscans; in the sixteenth century, Jesuits and Carmelites, Calvinists and Baptists; in the nineteenth century, revivalists at Camp Meetings, fanatical Emancipationists and John Brownists, missionary nuns, Salvationist blowers of bugles and strummers of tambourines. They are now too 'modern' and rationalist, too up-to-the-moment and of their age to believe in the God of the Judeo-Christian tradition. So they take up this new form of pantheism instead. It fills the vacuum in their hearts and souls left by the waning of formal religion. They see themselves as strictly reasonable and scientific, in their presentation of apocalyptic visions of the earth ruined by the greenhouse effect, acid rain and global warming. They are replete with charts and graphs and statistics and infra-red aerial photographs, and they can rustle up professors and experts galore to endorse their objectives. But in reality they are no more level-headed than the ancient Israelites who, while Moses was up in the mountain communing with the real God, made a gold calf and danced around it.

One piece of environmental dishonesty which left a profound impression on me was their initial differentiation between capitalist destruction on the one hand, and socialist conservation on the other. At a time when the Soviet Empire, in Europe and Asia, was doing everything in its power to stamp out organised religion and traditional morality, the environmentalists were holding it up as an example of responsible behaviour. All their critical venom was concentrated on the capitalist West, whose very system was presented as an organised orgy of waste and artificially created needs, which by its nature consumed but did not conserve or replenish, which destroyed but did not restore. The capitalist system, they argued, was intrinsically and by its very nature anti-environmentalist, incorrigibly so, and the underlying assumption of all their propaganda, throughout the 1970s and much of the 1980s, was that to get a saner, purer, ecologically sound world we would have to replace capitalism altogether, presumably by some form of socialism.

In fact this presentation of the case has proved wrong in every particular. One of the virtues of capitalism is that it is self-corrective. It responds remarkably quickly to popular demand, and if the demand is for a cleaner environment and a less wasteful use of resources, then that demand will be quickly met. The point made by the more sensible kind of environmentalist, that careful and intelligent use of resources, and respect for nature, actually produces greater efficiency, is one that capitalism is peculiarly well suited to grasp. And it has grasped the point. Over the past three decades, with increasing speed and even enthusiasm, Western commercial institutions, great and small, have often been ahead of the state, with its slow and clumsy systems of statutes and regulations, in addressing environmental problems. But all this is perfectly well known to those who take the trouble to study objectively what is being done.

What was less well known until the collapse of the Soviet Empire in 1989, which thereafter laid bare the evidence for all to inspect, was the degree of devastation which the command economy, or socialism, or Communism, or whatever you care to call the Marxist-Leninist way of running things, has inflicted on the environment in Eastern Europe and West and Central Asia. We are only now beginning to understand the magnitude of the damage which has been done, some of it irreparable. The physical injuries inflicted on the surface of the earth – plainly visible if you fly over Siberia, which is now possible – are exceeded only by the wasteful use of natural resources. The Soviet Union ruined the entire Aral Sea and some of the largest river systems in the world. It destroyed whole oilfields, for ever, by incompetent and even criminal exploitation. That story, too, is now becoming well known. What is notable, however, is that the environmentalist lobbies, once so noisy in contrasting capitalist shame with socialist pride, have made no apology at all for thus misleading the world. They have simply passed on to fresh battles, usually against Western governments and international companies.

But, before we follow them, there is an important point to be made in this contrast between the performance of capitalist West and socialist East. It is not exactly surprising that an atheist system, based upon what Marx called dialectical materialism, which denied the existence of God formally, and sought to explode the spiritual element of life completely – as a 'bourgeois super-structure' – should have treated the earth with such contempt and harshness. Even in the heyday of the early capitalist system, in late eighteenth-century Britain, when it was at its most wasteful and destructive, there were powerful spiritual voices raised against it, in God's name. William Blake animated the ghost of Milton, to pronounce the *réquisitoire* against unbridled capitalism. In his great poem of that name he included the magical verse turned into the hymn 'Jerusalem', whose radical sentiments, by one of those ironies beloved of the British, have not prevented it becoming a favourite of traditionalists, so that it is reverently sung at annual Conservative Party Conferences, as a right-wing alternative to 'The Red Flag'. Blake's voice was not alone, however. Edmund Burke and William Wordsworth, Samuel Taylor Coleridge and John Henry Newman were among many others who, with a variety of arguments springing from Christian religious principle, called for restraints on the new industrial capitalism. The Judeo-Christian moral tradition has always provided a critique of commercialism which has been used by legislators to introduce statutory restraints – not just humanitarian ones, like those limiting working hours and the employment of children, but others directly designed to protect the environment, like city and country planning regulations, anti-pollution laws, wildlife protection acts, the creation of national parks and reservations, as well as measures to provide pure air and water, and healthy food. Some of these go back to the early nineteenth century, and in the whole effort to place industrialisation within a legal framework, the key figure was the Christian fundamentalist the Earl of Shaftesbury, father of factory legislation.

The early history of the environmentalist movement, in fact, shows that it sprang up among men and women grounded in this religious tradition, who always brought God into the argument. God, they argued, had a right to be there (it is hard to think of an argument where he has no right to be) because he made the universe and man is his mere tenant. But in putting this point of view, and insisting that God's freehold rights be respected, they never fell into the trap of pantheism or paganism, or invested inanimate nature itself with rights which properly belong to God alone. Nor did they ignore the rights of man, complementary to God's, as tenant-in-chief and, under God's law, ruler of creation in this world. The early environmentalists, being mostly enthusiastic Christians, were never anti-human. But the movement has always had a tendency to slip into extremism and to attract fanatics, and in the last generation it has been not only de-Christianised and paganised, but rendered irrational and destructive of the legitimate interests of the human race.

Indeed the force and fury of environmentalist lobbying is doing an increasing amount of damage, often to the cause itself, as weak and confused governments bend to its will. I was dismayed, as many other reasonable people were, in the early summer of 1995, when a plan to sink in deep ocean waters a Shell oil-platform, which had reached the end of its working life – a plan arrived at as the least-damaging solution to the problem, after many studies and much deliberation and consultation – was abruptly dropped after environmental extremists started a noisy boycott of Shell products. Here was an unpleasant demonstration of the irrational power of the new paganism. Shortly afterwards I found myself in a moral dilemma over the open clash between Greenpeace, which had led the campaign against the Shell plan, and the French government, over the issue of French nuclear testing in the Pacific. I greatly dislike French governments, notorious for their arrogance and selfish intransigence, and I greatly dislike Greenpeace for its pagan fanaticism. Which, then, to support? When the French refused to bow to the clamour and actually seized the Greenpeace propaganda ship, I found myself reluctantly forced to take sides, and raised a feeble *Vive la France!* And I think my instinct was right. The French did not leave God out of the argument. They rested their case for building nuclear weapons, which involves testing them, on the right of self-defence, enshrined in Natural Law and endorsed by the law of God. They may have given it a wrong interpretation in this particular instance – that is a genuine matter of argument – but they were not acting outside a moral and legal context. Greenpeace was simply invading national sovereignty in pursuit of an irrational point of view which holds all nuclear energy to be inherently evil. But nuclear energy is not inherently evil: it is a gift of God, like other inventions, to be used subject to the appropriate restraints which qualify all God's gifts. To deny people the right to use it, on a pagan principle that the earth and oceans are sacrosanct, seems to me sinful.

A similar drift to dangerous and morally flawed extremism can be observed in the animal rights movement, whose lobbies are often closely connected to the environmentalist ones, and even overlap. The way in which we treat animals, and all living things below the level of humanity, has already become an important issue in advanced Western societies, and will become still more important in the twenty-first century. Here again, we will get the argument all wrong – certainly confused – if we leave God out of it. I must tread carefully here. As a veteran journalist, I discovered long ago that nothing is more calculated to inflame the reader – especially British and American readers – than an ill-considered reference to animals. Animals are much loved in our world, and their interests jealously protected, sometimes over-protected. That God created all forms of animal life, of set purpose, and that he loves them accordingly – as he loves all his creation – is certain. He has their interests at heart and perceives them better than anyone else. All that remains for us is to interpret his teaching. Therein, however, lies the difficulty. Animal lovers and the Judeo-Christian tradition have had an uneasy relationship. The Old Testament is not exactly the animal-lover's bible. Therein animals are treated as wild enemies of the human race – the psalms see the Devil as a 'roaring lion, seeking whom he may devour' – or as cherished objects of human property, to be protected and legislated about accordingly, but essentially to be used by humans without regard for the interests of the animals themselves. Abraham's abortive sacrifice of his son Jacob, which is held up to illustrate the mercy and humanitarianism in God, actually ends in a young ram getting its throat cut. It is a curious fact that, in the whole length of the Old Testament, there is only one reference to an animal being kept as a pet. The New Testament is no different. Jesus Christ has no particular concern for animals. He is born in a manger and the beasts of the field keep him warm, therein producing a mass of sentimental Christian iconography, but as an adult he uses a great draught of fishes to perform a commercially attractive miracle and he causes the Gadarene swine to go to their maddened deaths without compunction. His most intimate contact with the animal world occurs when he chooses on Palm Sunday to enter Jerusalem on an ass, and this was ingeniously seized upon by Chesterton to compose a triumphalist pro-animal poem. But Christ's choice of animal was made to emphasise his modesty not to suggest he was fond of asses. No, there is not much in the New Testament, any more than in the Old, for animal-lovers.

All the same, the teachings of the religious tradition on how we should treat animals are perfectly reasonable. I am not going to get involved in the intricacies of Jewish dietary laws, and I am aware that some people object strongly to the slaughtering procedures involved in the production of kosher meat. They may have a case. But in general, Jewish theology lays down that the animals are part of God's creation and entrusted to the stewardship of those whom he created in his own image. People may thus use animals for their legitimate purposes, but we must respect their integrity and we owe them decency and kindness. Christian teaching continues this tradition and elaborates it. God has a providential care for his animals and they, for their part, by their mere existence bless him and give him glory. Not only is habitual ill-treatment and needless cruelty to animals gravely sinful, but the love of animals – within proper limits – is meritorious. We have a positive duty to prevent animals from dying needlessly, and there is strong approval for organisations which look after animal welfare in a sensible manner. But the new *Catholic Catechism* specifically permits medical and scientific experimentation on animals 'within reasonable limits' where it 'contributes to caring for or saving human lives'; it condemns as 'unworthy' spending money on animals 'that should as a priority go to the relief of human misery'; and it concludes: 'One can love animals; one should not direct to them the affection due only to persons.'

So far so good. But the church does not, I note, talk about animal rights. That is wise. It is not clear to me that anyone has rights, apart from God himself. And certainly it is hard to see how a creature can possess rights without also possessing complementary responsibilities. Men may have rights and they certainly have duties. Animals, so far as we can judge, have dutiful instincts to their kind, and they can be taught to perform duties to us, but so far as we can see they have no autonomous sense of responsibility such as all humans possess. Rights and duties are and must be reciprocal. I conclude from this that to talk of animal rights is wrong and misleading and will simply lead us into moral confusions – as it is already leading the animal rights enthusiasts. The right approach is to begin with the duties of human beings to animals, which are numerous and imperative. It is by ignoring these duties, rather than by failing to respect imaginary rights, that we have fallen short in the past. If we work out and list these duties correctly, and then perform them, we will be doing God's will.

All the same, I feel that a great change is coming in our relationship with the animal world. Great saints like St Francis, St Cuthbert and St Philip Neri, who were particularly close to animals, and specially sensitive to the way in which they manifested God's will and love, saw this change coming and were ahead of their times. The understanding of animals they individually and intuitively acquired is gradually becoming more general as we use all the resources of modern science to get closer to them. We are indeed beginning to understand how animals think and why they do

nderstanding makes us appreciate them far more
ɔre intelligently. The more we understand about
e more we value the lives of all creatures. Veg-
etarianism is spreading, inexorably I believe. God allowed us to
live off the beasts of the fields and the forest because there was no
other way, then, for humankind to survive and prosper. But our
technology is now such that we can produce endless varieties of
nourishing and delicious foods without resorting to animal flesh.
Gradually this realisation will take hold of us. The rise of factory
farming, whereby food-producers cannot remain competitive
except by subjecting animals to life-cycles of unspeakable deprivation, has hastened this process. The human spirit revolts at
what we have been doing.

A Danish friend of mine, who has a large farm which, following
the Danish tradition, dealt largely in pigs, has ended his share in
the trade. He told me: 'I came to know my pigs well. They are
highly intelligent and sensitive creatures. They are quite unlike
cows, let alone chickens. It is quite wrong – obviously and unques-
tionably wrong – that we should breed them in the ways that
have become universal under modern trading conditions.' So he
has stopped raising pigs, and he is turning the buildings which
once housed them, and the land where they browsed, into an
opera house. These feelings of revulsion will spread and intensify,
and gradually take hold of the West, and eventually the East and
South too. I believe we shall gradually come to regard eating the
flesh of animals as no more acceptable than cannibalism – and no
more necessary, either.

I detect a change in myself too. Perhaps it is because I am
growing old, and coming closer to the day when I must say
farewell to my own life and body, that I am becoming increasingly
respectful of life in any form. It is hard to think of any mani-
festation of God's creative spirit – any living thing he produces,
however frail or primitive – which is less than wonderful. An
ordinary house-fly, closely inspected, is a miracle of contrivance.
It now seems to me that to swat such a remarkable being, except
under the clearest necessity, is an outrage against nature. I am
now very careful in the way I deal with annoying insects, let alone
larger vermin. The idea of killing game is now to me abhorrent. I
now very much regret that, nearly half a century ago, I shot and

killed a bear in Scandinavia. There appeared, at the time, some justification for slaughtering the beast, but that now seems to me special pleading.

The last time I took part in a punitive expedition was a lesson to me. I went with my host, a large Highland landowner, on a search-and-destroy mission against herons which were devastating the river-salmon. Herons are beautiful and amazing birds, and heavily protected by law, but they have amazing appetites and are capable of eating their entire bodyweight – and more – every day. Their slaughter of salmon in the pools is horrific. We have duties to salmon as well as to herons, and my host had duties to the estate, much indebted to its salmon fishery, and to the many estate-workers who depended for their livelihood on its survival. That, at any rate, was our rationale for this expedition. We detected two herons very quickly, and my host shot them. He reckoned two were enough: the rest would take the hint and go elsewhere, as indeed they did. But when I examined the bodies of these large and once-splendid birds, I was abashed. They had changed in the instant of death from confident and graceful aerial monarchs of the river into mere huddled bundles of lifeless feathers, utterly insignificant and pathetic. One felt that a crime had been committed. So my uncertain and reluctant career as a hunter finally ended.

In the twenty-first century, then, we are likely to see our relationship with the animal world – and the other world of living creation – change fundamentally, as we sort out our moral ideas and adjust our economic habits accordingly. All that will be in accordance with God's will, as we come to understand it more fully. What is less clear, however, is whether our greater knowledge of the animal world, which we are acquiring through more sophisticated instrumentation and systematic observation, will help to revise our ideas about the place animals have in the providential scheme. Have they something akin to our souls? Will they, like us, have a place in the afterlife? The churches usually answer no to the first question and are silent or unforthcoming on the second. St Francis would have said yes to both. But he, and his views, were *sui generis*. The church as an institution, like Judaism as an institution, insists on the uniqueness of humanity – the animal world is no more than an appendage. The right answer, surely, is that we do not know enough to say. Despite our science, we have no more knowledge of what goes on inside the head of a dog than our Stone Age forebears who first domesticated him. In fact they may well have known more than we do, intuitively, because they depended more on the creature for their survival.

I had my fine dog Parker for the entire eighteen years of his life. I loved that dog and he loved me. We each studied the other, noted intentions, moods, likes and dislikes, pleasures and pursuits, prejudices. He studied me more intently and intelligently than I studied him, and he responded to my wishes with a hairtrigger speed and exactness which did immense credit to his heart and head. I could not conceivably have asked more from a dog. But did he have a soul? At the end of those eighteen years, when I parted from him with much sorrow, I was none the wiser. I looked and looked into those bright, far-sighted eyes, so anxious to respond and to please, and could detect nothing spiritual whatever. At the end of it all, the only sensible maxim is to be kind to animals and to love them with all appropriate love. Lockhart, in his marvellous life of Scott, which shows he was everything a good man should be, remarks: 'He was a gentleman even to his dogs.' That is indeed a tribute. Anyone who has owned dogs knows that it is not easy to treat them in a gentlemanly fashion. They are too subservient, too anxious to please, too forbearing of bad temper and selfishness, too forgiving of ill- or inconsiderate treatment, to bring out the gentleman in you. Nonetheless, Scott somehow contrived to be a gentleman to his, and that is the heroic example we should follow towards all animals.

CHAPTER 9

The problematical uniqueness
of mankind

On a clear night, when countless stars are visible and many of
them shine with intensity, we humans are filled with awe. But we
draw different conclusions from the experience. Blaise Pascal, in
his *Pensées*, wrote: 'La silence éternelle de ces éspaces m'éffraye.'
He was frightened not just by the immensity of God's power, but
by the sheer size of the setting in which man's insignificance is so
marked – and the unwillingness or inability of that immensity to
say anything about itself. Thomas Hardy, who found it difficult
to believe in a God whose actions, in his view, displayed blind
malignity rather than benevolent providence, made much the
same point. He uses the experience of night-time observation of
the heavens, from the plateau of Egdon Heath in *The Return of the
Native*, to show how, watching the stars, we actually become
conscious of the rolling of the earth, and can perceive that it is
not flat but round, and hurtling through space. Thus we are made
painfully conscious of how small we are, and how endless the
universe, and if – as Hardy concluded – there is no Almighty God
for us to look to, how much we have to fear! Far better, then, for
mankind to behave like an animal, and burrow deeper into the
familiar, comforting earth, burying our heads and hiding like the
ostrich from the nameless terrors in space.

For some people the sheer size of the universe is the most
obvious disproof of the existence of God. That, as we have seen,
was H. G. Wells's view. It is very common among scientific materi-
alists. In my arguments with Richard Dawkins, recently promoted
Professor of Public Understanding at Oxford University, I discovered that this was the point he found most conclusive in
demonstrating the impossibility of a supreme being: there was
just too much for him to be supreme over. Try as I may, I cannot

see the logic of this. It seems to me that quantitative argument works more cogently against atheism or humanism than against deism. The more our radio-telescopes enlarge our notions of how big space is, the less likely it seems that physically fragile creatures like ourselves, living in time and space, can ever achieve mastery of the universe – or think and behave as if we could – and the more likely it is that something metaphysical, like God, whose powers are not limited by any system of measurement, must exist, to keep it all in order.

If we cast our minds back to the age of primitive man, we can see him spending many of the night-time hours, after hunting was done but sleep had not yet claimed him, lying on his back and gazing up at the heavens. He saw those same stars as we do, and wondered about them. He had an acute sense of visual distance – much better than ours, for he needed it for hunting – and he must have realised how far away they were and therefore how enormous the heavens must be. I suspect it was precisely this night-gazing which implanted in his mind the idea that there must be a God, not just the familiar, local gods of nearby streams and woods, but something – someone – much bigger and mightier. The power of local gods radiated over limited distances only, and other gods and charms had to be carried around to remain effective. But the god of the heavens was a mighty god of gods precisely because space was so enormous. It is significant that all the earliest pantheons contained supergods like this, as though primitive man's study of cosmology, crude though it was, already pushed him in the direction of monotheism. I think his instinct is surer and sounder than the half-knowledge of a clever twentieth-century scientist, dazzled by statistics and calculations about billions of light-years.

However, in one respect our greater knowledge of the immensity of the universe has changed our perception of man's place in it – and God's – and the relationship between the two. Until recently, primitive man shared one belief with all his descendants: a conviction that man, as a species, was unique and therefore his relation to God singular. Whatever else we might think, there was only one human race, only one lot of beings 'made in God's image', and we were therefore the principal object of God's attention. All the drama of creation, the Fall, Original Sin and human redemption, the Incarnation, Death and Resurrection of God's Son, Death and Judgment, Hell and Heaven and Eternity – all was entirely for our benefit. Neither the Old Testament nor the New hints at any other possibility. Plato and Aristotle both assumed the human race to be unique in its potentiality. So did Maimonides on behalf of Jewish thinkers, Avicenna and Averoës for Islam, St Thomas Aquinas for the Christians. Our entire framework of thinking about religion is conditioned by this polarity: Man – and God. But what if there are other parties?

It is surprising how little thought theologians have given to the possibility of stars or planets being inhabited by creatures more or less like ourselves. Or rather it might be surprising if the scientists themselves had not also largely ignored this field of speculation. But they do, probably because they do not want to be laughed at or forfeit the esteem of colleagues. Ever since some early man or woman spotted the Man in the Moon – and that happened thousands of years ago – the idea of creatures in space has been associated with comedy rather than mystery: little green men with eyes on stalks or ant-like things in flying saucers. As a result the only kind of people who have taken them seriously have been fiction-writers and cranks, the latter not above a bit of faking to impress fellow-fanatics. The serious scientists have kept well clear and theologians have considered the entire subject beneath their notice.

Leaving divine agency aside for the moment, the evolution of human life on our planet seems to have been the consequence of an amazing series of happenstances or coincidences or accidents of nature. The chances of this combination of circumstances occurring at all are slim, and seen from this viewpoint our very existence, as *homo sapiens*, is an amazing piece of good fortune. The chances, therefore, of a similar combination, producing a comparable end-result, must seem inconceivable – rather like the standard impossibility of monkeys, sat down at typewriters and bashing away at random, producing the entire works of Shakespeare. But we know that it is theoretically possible for precisely this to happen. Equally, a type of being similar to ourselves emerging somewhere in space is also theoretically possible if space is big enough. But we now know that space is so big that such a happening can theoretically have taken place not once but many times – perhaps hundreds, thousands, even millions of times. And if it *can* have taken place so often, then surely it *must* have taken place in reality, at least once.

This opens up alarming possibilities. I am not concerned here with the possibilities of such creatures existing and making contact with us, or of us making contact with them – or of their invading us, as in Wells's *The War of the Worlds*. I leave that to the writers of science fiction. More practical and serious-minded scientists are also at work on the possibility of other worlds and their inhabitants. We are not merely sending large-scale probes into the space which immediately surrounds us; we are also radiating signals to much more distant space, in the hope that somebody or something will pick them up, and reply. American, British and French defence experts are also working on these possibilities, as it is their duty to do.

My concern is quite different. If there is another world somewhat like ours, and on it there are creatures with intelligences and sensibilities comparable to ours, then two questions immediately arise. First, did God put them there, in the same way as he 'put' us on earth: that is, made possible the physical circumstances in which we could evolve? Second, have they become aware of God's existence, and intentions, in the way that we have done? These are very disturbing questions indeed. They need to be considered separately, to begin with, though they are in fact closely connected. The answer to the first question need not necessarily upset us too much. God may well have put thinking and sentient beings rather like us on another star or planet, just as he 'put' the native peoples in North and South America. For many thousands of years the existence of the American Indians was unknown to the peoples of the Eurasian land-mass, among whom the biblical story was situated. Abraham arose and became the father of the Israelite people, and in due course Moses led this people from Egypt to the Promised Land, and was given the Law by God on Mount Sinai, and transmuted the Law into the Pentateuch or the *Torah* or the Old Testament or whatever we may wish to call it, and the dominant form of human monotheism – amended by the New Testament into Christianity and by the Koran into Islam – came into existence. It was a Eurasian creation, originally the work of a small collection of tribes inhabiting a very limited portion of Eurasia.

But the Jews were a people of the diaspora from very early times, and even by the age of Christ their scattered communities were all over the Mediterranean and constituted about 10 per cent of the population of the Roman Empire. Under the aegis of Christianity, and later of Islam, the form of monotheism described in the Bible spread to large areas of Eurasia and even of Africa. Then in the fifteenth century it crossed the Atlantic, 'discovered' the American Indians, and introduced them to the Christian form of monotheism. By analogy, then, it may be the task of us monotheistic earthlings to carry the truth to the 'natives' of space, and 'convert' them to our way of religious thinking, just as the Spaniards and Portuguese originally evangelised and baptised the American Indians. There may be problems of acculturation, and a need to incorporate or translate or transmute the religious customs or practices of the space 'natives' into Christian norms, but that problem already exists, particularly in Africa, and we are used to dealing with it, albeit we have not always handled it successfully.

This comforting scenario, however, presupposes that the space 'natives' have reached only a comparatively early stage of progress – earlier than ours, anyway – and have yet to evolve towards monotheism. It also presupposes that we 'discover' them, and evangelise and baptise them. And it may well be that one or more of the inhabited other worlds are of precisely this kind, and that it is God's purpose that we should eventually get to them and bring their peoples into the faith, just as Europe sent out missionaries to the world. But there is an alternative possibility, and if there be many inhabited worlds, a strong possibility – almost a certainty – that some of these 'natives' are actually a good deal more advanced than we are, and have already developed their own forms of monotheism, which are better than or at any rate quite different to ours, and that far from us discovering and colonising and evangelising them, they discover and colonise and evangelise us.

Where does this leave the uniqueness of human beings, and the singularity of their relationship with Almighty God? At first glance it leaves both in ruins. We then have to imagine ourselves as far less important than we had supposed. We may still be lord of all we survey here, for a time at least. But we may turn out to be a rather puny and insignificant species in terms of the universe: not very numerous and not very powerful and rather under-developed – in fact exactly like the native American Indians, when first Columbus, then Cortés and Pizarro stepped from their boats and waded ashore. Man's imagination has already been exercised by the prospect of being visited and colonised and conquered from outer space – though the stories we tell ourselves usually have a happy ending, as in Wells's prototype – but we have given little or no thought to the prospect of being evangelised from outer space, though it is only too likely. If outer-space invaders come here and bring their superior technology and weapons, they are virtually certain to bring their religious beliefs too, and these will very likely seem superior also.

This intriguing possibility brings us inevitably to the second question: have these distant creatures like us become aware of God's existence and intentions, as we have done? This is really the key question: is he the same God for them, as he is for us? Now if we believe that God is indeed omnipotent and ubiquitous, and that his power extends to the whole of creation – and we really have no alternative but to believe this, if we believe in God at all – then we must suppose that their God and our God is the same. How could it be otherwise? At a certain stage of their evolution, God must have manifested himself to them, as he did to us, communicated with them, as he did with us, and given them his instructions – his commandments – as he did with us.

However, what we must find it difficult to believe, and I for one find it impossible to believe, is that religious development among these other peoples followed exactly the same trajectory as ours, or even a similar one. There cannot have been a similar Eden in outer space, and a comparable Fall, and a Flood, and an exile in Egypt, and an outer-space Moses and another planetary Ten Commandments. Whatever God planned for these other, distant creatures of his, it must have been somewhat different even at the beginning of their story, and have followed a radically different line as things developed. I reject absolutely that these other crea-tures are, in each case, clones of mankind, and that the entire biblical epic has been re-enacted elsewhere in space, perhaps many times. The story of the relations of these space creatures with God must have been quite different, and if there are many such races of creatures, we are faced with the existence of a whole series of different stories, a multiplicity of religious epics, each unique in itself and contrasting – perhaps clashing – with the rest.

For Christians a particular problem immediately raises itself. Jesus Christ was sent by God to earth to sacrifice himself and thus to redeem mankind. St John's Gospel says that 'God so loved the world that he sent his only son' to achieve this. When the first Christian priests went in Columbus's ships, this raised no difficulty for them. The native Americans were clearly part of mankind and God's son had died for them too. They were just as eligible to receive the Christian message as the Gentiles to whom St Paul had originally preached it. But what of those creatures in outer space? Again, if they are comparatively primitive creatures, and we get to them before they get to us, then the problem is soluble. They are to be treated as mankind or as an appendage to it, and we can assume Jesus died for them too. But what if they are superior creatures, and they get here first? What if they have their own salvation story, and worship Jesus in another name? Obviously, there are going to be problems of concordance, and they will be less and less easily soluble the more the rival salvation story – or stories – varies from our own.

Now let me posit another alternative. Suppose these creatures arrive here with the story of their God, who resembles ours in omnipotence and so on, but they have no story of a Fall and Redemption. What becomes of concordance then? Are we to suppose that God created two quite separate kinds of sapient creature, one which was tempted and fell but the other of which did not, but lived in accordance with God's word *ab initio* an idyllic, Eden-like existence? Or is there a possibility that this other order of God's creatures was subjected to a quite different providential plan, the nature of which we cannot even begin to guess at? How do these two sets of creatures fit in with each other? Does God appear in one guise to us and in another, quite different, guise to them? Do they come higher than us in the order of creation? Are we, perhaps, to be their creatures, intended by God to be so, just as God made us masters of the world and all *its* creatures?

Now it may be said: this is mere mischievous speculation. By discussing such possibilities – and they are no more than possibilities, highly unlikely ones at that – you tend to put needless doubts into the minds of men and women and undermine settled faith for no good purpose. But I have a reply to this criticism. Has not the time come to be less globocentric? Until the twentieth century was well advanced, Christians tended to see the church with almost exclusively European eyes – America being judged an appendix of Europe – and this necessarily narrowed our vision and range of sensibilities. We have since learned to be less Euro-centric and to bring all the varied peoples of the earth into our religious considerations. That has proved an advantage. In the Catholic Church, for instance, when there is a papal conclave, we see cardinals of all races and colours coming to Rome, and when there is a General Council the bishops come in their thousands from all parts of the globe, speaking all tongues and embodying a vast range of customs and attitudes – thus the universality of the church is visibly proclaimed.

Similarly, I think it is right and profitable to imagine a wider church still, a truly universal church, in which emissaries speed from one solar system to the next, from one galaxy to another on the other side of space, just as, many centuries ago, the patriarchs and bishops of the primitive church sailed about the eastern Mediterranean to attend councils. It is not too difficult for us to imagine this happening among an interterrestrial community which is an extension of our global one. But we ought equally to consider the possibility that a truly universal church may be very different indeed to anything we have so far experienced here on earth. We may be a junior and insignificant part of it, with a lot to learn and little if anything to teach.

It is good for our incipient *hubris* to think of these possibilities, and right to become accustomed to the possibility that our vision of faith may be subjected to a rude and alarming shock one of these days. When rumours reached the outside world in the late 1940s that a huge depository of ancient religious texts had been discovered somewhere near the Dead Sea, there was widespread anxiety among senior religious men, not least in the Vatican, that these texts might contain revelations about the Old Testament or the New – or the actual life of Christ – which would prove mighty awkward. There was a good deal of position-taking in advance, and a certain amount of skulduggery in getting possession of the texts and supervising their transcription and exegesis. In the event, no one need have worried: the Dead Sea Scrolls, immensely interesting though they proved, upset no fundamental tenet of anyone's faith and did not even introduce a stupendously new historical fact affecting our knowledge of the Old Testament or the New. I confess, I was myself disappointed. More important, as it happened, was a tiny papyrus fragment which enabled scholars to confirm the early dating of the Synoptic Gospels in 1994, and which had been lying in Magdalen College Library, in Oxford, all the time. I mention the Dead Sea Scrolls simply to indicate that the Christian faith, like the Jewish faith from which it springs, is a historical set of beliefs, which attests to actual events in the real world, and therefore can be fundamentally modified by the production of new evidence. As we begin to explore space, and – more important, perhaps – as people in space begin to explore us, we have to be prepared to be able to accommodate, within our traditional system of belief, stunning new knowledge which will challenge the singularity of our own relationship with God and may be exceedingly difficult to reconcile with our own religious understanding of what has happened in history. In short, God may have some surprises for us, which may well seem like nasty surprises to begin with.

In all this speculation, however, there is one comforting fact. Whatever mysteries and surprises space may hold for us, none of them need have any disturbing effect on our individual relation-ship with God. God, as I believe, created each one of us; God speaks directly to us, personally, intimately, confidentially; and we in turn speak one-to-one with God in our prayers. That is the absolute certain fact about God and each of us, and nothing to come in space and time can change it. Whether the human race be singular or not, whether we are unique as a God-worshipping species, or must share him with other or even many sets of creatures throughout the universe – some of whom may be rad-ically different to ourselves – nothing can prevent God entering our hearts and dwelling there, if we invite him.

Therein, of course, lies the wonder of faith, as I understand it. It is gigantic enough to stretch across the universe, however vast it may be, but it is also small and special and particular enough to be a single soul reaching out to God. There is a sense in which time and space and magnitude are quite irrelevant. God created the universe out of love, and love is its energising and sustaining principle. The principle expresses itself as intensely and perfectly in the communion of one individual with God as it does with the collective worship of countless billions, living in worlds an infinity of light-years apart. God and his universe are equally macrocosm and microcosm because in the end love is not to be measured by time and space. With God, quantitative considerations do not apply, because he transcends them. As William Blake puts it (*Auguries of Innocence*):

> To see the World in a Grain of sand,
> And a Heaven in a Wild Flower,
> Hold infinity in the palm of your hand,
> And Eternity in an hour.

This important point, that for each of us our personal relationship with God is the key to faith, needs qualification, however. Each of us has this individual relationship with our creator and nothing can take it away from us. Each of us can lose our soul, and each of us can save it. It is an undoubted and possibly a tragic fact, as Pascal remarks, 'On mourra seul' – we shall die alone. We come to individual judgment. But that is not the end of the story. We are part of a vast collectivity of souls. We belong, as Catholic theology puts it, to the mystical body of Christ, which is the church. This membership is or ought to be a source of strength to us. There is a point in the sacrifice of the Mass when the priest, on behalf of the congregation, asks God: 'Look not upon our sins, but on the faith of thy church.' Our individual failings can be, and often are, counterbalanced by the collective goodness of the church as a whole, 'the communion of saints', as the liturgy puts it. This belief is not confined to the Roman Catholic Church. It is to be found, in one form or another, in all the branches of Christianity, in Judaism and in other serious religions. We are born individually and we die alone – there is no escaping these facts. But we also have a collective status by virtue of the faith and worship we share with countless others, and this gives us access to privileges which no one individual, it may be, is worthy to receive.

A church, then, is a source of strength. As it is devoted to the worship of God, it is, almost by definition, a divine institution.

But it is also, necessarily, a human one. That raises problems, serious and almost intractable problems, of organisation, leadership, discipline and authority. That is the subject of the next chapter.

CHAPTER 10

The church, dogma, authority, order and liturgy

The idea that worshipping God is a matter of individual choice, and that men and women can decide for themselves the manner in which they do so – or whether they do it at all – is a comparatively recent idea. It has been an axiom of the United States constitution right from the start, but it is only in the twentieth century that most countries have followed her example. In the past, state churches were the rule. They still exist in some countries. Nominally, Britain still has a state church, and her head of state must be an Anglican. Most Muslim countries give state recognition and special status to Islam, and some are actually theocracies: that is, there is no real distinction between secular and priestly rule, and Islamic law is the law of the land.

These theocracies are, in fact, a modern survival or revival of what was the norm. In antiquity, the state was identified with the god its people worshipped and infidelity was treason. Israel was like all the rest in this respect – the great Jewish philosopher Philo called Israel a 'democratic theocracy', using the word 'democratic' to signify that all its people, irrespective of rank, were equal under God's law. That was unusual in the Ancient Near East, for in most states the ruler was also an emanation of the god, or high priest, or both. It was the Persians, under Cyrus, who found it convenient, as imperialists, to accord religious toleration in their empire. Their liberalism made it possible, for instance, for the Jews to return from Babylon to Jerusalem and resume worship in the Temple there. The Greek successors to the Persian Empire maintained, on the whole, this policy of toleration, and when the Romans succeeded the Greeks they, too, permitted a variety of religious worship provided it did not challenge the state. Hence Jesus's prudent words: 'Render, therefore, to Caesar the things which are

Caesar's, and to God the things which are God's.'

It was Christianity which began the tradition of religious independence because it emerged in an empire where it was usually tolerated but had no connection with the state. Imperial governments sometimes turned on it furiously, precisely because it was so successful and attractive, and Christians were transformed into living torches or thrown to the lions or crucified. But as a rule the church was allowed to exist, provided it made itself inconspicuous. Thus for over 300 years it developed its organisation and internal law all by itself, without the help or hindrance of the state, and this was a novelty. Hence, when Christianity eventually became the religion of the Roman Empire, in the fourth century AD, the church was already formed and characterised by its own independent history, and its institutions were autonomous and capable of defending themselves. When, in post-Roman times, Europe was progressively Christianised, the church acquired a monopoly of all religious worship and was closely identified with the secular power, but it nevertheless preserved its own identity – it was never Erastian. In the eleventh century, under Hildebrand, Pope Gregory VII, during what was called the Investiture Contest (the right of the church versus the right of the king to choose bishops), the church showed that it was willing to challenge and fight the state to preserve its autonomy and to assert its rights over ecclesiastical matters.

Hence, though the Christian Church, especially in its Roman Catholic branch, is often seen as an instrument of oppression – and sometimes was an instrument of oppression – it was in fact the first institution in history to stand up systematically to the claims of the state. This became of enormous importance in Europe and was one reason why, unlike the rest of the world, freedom began to be established there. Hildebrand undoubtedly saw himself not only as a servant of God, but as a campaigner for justice and liberty under the law, and one who in consequence had to endure great and bitter sufferings. Hence his dying words: 'I have loved justice and hated iniquity, therefore I die in exile.'

My reading of the history of Christianity is one reason why I, unlike many people in Britain and the United States, refuse to see the Roman Catholic Church, to which I belong, as an authoritarian institution. It is that of course, at any rate in theory, but it is much more than that. What I am doing in this chapter is to examine why it is I value and love my church and to try to convey a sense of this value and love to others who do not share my faith. Now in one sense, and a very real sense, this affection is based on familiarity. Catholicism – the Holy Roman Catholic Church – Rome – the Scarlet Woman – the Whore of Babylon – has no terrors for me because I am as used to it as a much-loved old teddy bear or a favourite armchair or a smelly old favourite dog. I was born a Catholic and my family has always been Catholic. I come from the north of Lancashire, which for complicated reasons that I need not particularise – they are set out in my book *Elizabeth I: a Study in Power and Intellect* – was never Protestantised in the sixteenth century. There is also an Irish strain in my family, from the Catholic South. So I think I can honestly say there is not one drop of Protestant blood in my body. Occasionally I boast of this fact, which my wife Marigold judges to be childish. I have, as it were, been married to the church all my life and am used to her ways, whether they be slatternly or tiresome, noble, loving, admirable, foolish or insupportable. Quite apart from anything else, I have a fondness for old institutions which have high pretensions but are also timeworn and manipulable, theoretically rigid but in practice accommodating, which demand everything but will settle in practice for less, often much less. I found exactly the same with the army, in which I spent two happy years as a National Serviceman. Here was a totalitarian institution living under martial law and committed to efficiency at any human cost, but which in practice – once you became familiar with her habits – was quite a comfortable set-up. You had to know your way around the army, but once you acquired this knowledge and the knack of utilising it – and not all acquired the knack, by any means – the institution held no real terrors. It could, of course, deal you a painful and unexpected blow once in a while (so can the Catholic Church), but in general it is a dear old thing.

Now the Catholic Church certainly does not see itself as a dear old thing, so perhaps the next thing I should do is to describe how it sees itself. In the first place it does not see itself, as others often do, as a formidable cluster of buildings round an enormous Baroque church: the Vatican. Nor does it see itself as a collection of black-suited or gorgeously vestmented ecclesiastics: the clergy.

It sees itself, rather, as something ghostly, mysterious and poetic, and this self-vision is not entirely fanciful either. In certain moods it is absolutely sincere. Strictly speaking, 'church' from the Latin *ecclesia*, the Greek *ek-kalein* ('to call out of') signifies a convocation or an assembly. The Jews figure in the Greek Old Testament as the Chosen People before God, especially when they assembled before Mount Sinai to receive the Law. The early Christians, by calling themselves an *ecclesia*, saw themselves as the heirs to that elect people. In the church God 'calls together' his people from all over the world. The Greek term for this, *Kyriakon*, whence we get the word *church*, or in German *Kirche*, means 'what belongs to the Lord'.

But from the very beginning these etymological realities have been smothered in metaphor and imagery by writers who have served the church with overwhelming passion and devotion – sometimes losing their lives in the process. The church is the mystical body of Christ; it is a sheepfold where the sheep are safe, but also the flock – the flock of God. It is a cultivated field, a vineyard, a forest of olive trees. It is also a building. Jesus Christ compared himself to the stone the buildings rejected but which was made into the corner-stone. The church is also a rock on which the building is erected. It is a family, a house, a dwelling place, a holy temple. The people of the church are the living stones from which the temple is built. It is also the bride of God, the 'spotless spouse of the spotless lamb', she whom Christ 'loved and for whom he delivered himself up that he might sanctify her'. St Augustine, in a striking passage, says that, just as Eve was formed from Adam's side, so the Church was 'born from the pierced heart of Christ hanging on the cross'.

It is important to remember, all the time while we are looking at this fanciful imagery, that what is meant by the church is not the Vatican or those ecclesiastics, but the living church of countless souls seen collectively. Otherwise one dissolves in laughter. But if the church is seen as this mystic unity of souls, longing for goodness and to be united to God and sharing his love, the metaphors make sense. In a way, the church is an enormous abstraction. That is how Clement of Alexandria sees it: 'Just as God's will is Creation and is called "the World", so his intention is the salvation of men, and is called "the Church".' Building on this thought, the great statement of faith, *Lumen Gentium*, which the Second Vatican Council adopted as one of its Apostolic Constitutions, puts it as follows:

> The Eternal Father, in accordance with the utterly free and mysterious design of his wisdom and goodness, created the whole universe, and chose to raise up men to share in his own divine life ... [He] determined to call together in a holy church those who should believe in Christ. This family of God is gradually formed and takes shape during the stages of human history ... [It was] already present in figure at the beginning of the world [and] prepared in marvellous fashion in the history of the people of Israel and the old alliance ... it will be brought to glorious completion at the end of time.

The church, then, is more than a convocation, a gathering, it is the actual process, also, whereby men and women are saved and share God's divinity. Yet it is also a human institution as well as a divine one. It is visible as well as mystical, and it does manifest itself in powerful buildings and gorgeously attired clergymen – and rulers and bureaucrats and red-tape and belligerence and sheer idiocy at times. There is in fact a striking passage written by St Bernard of Clairvaux. He was a great servant of Almighty God who founded the magnificent Cistercian Order, and preached a Crusade, and was the friend and ally of popes – and their critic and opponent – who made his considerable weight felt throughout the Christendom of the twelfth century. St Bernard was bitterly aware that the church was worldly as well as divine and said so:

> O humility! O sublimity! Both tabernacle of cedar and sanctuary of God; earthly dwelling and celestial palace; house of clay and royal hall; body of death and temple of light; and at last both object of scorn to the proud and bride of Christ! She is black but beautiful, O daughters of Jerusalem, and even if the labour and pain of her long exile may have discoloured her, yet heaven's beauty has adorned her too.

This is how I have come to see the church, as a fallible human institution which has been capable of great enormities, which is still liable to misjudgments and even folly, but nonetheless in some ways radiates the divine. I love it – and I watch it with a wary and critical eye. I do not believe that there is no salvation outside the church. This doctrine makes no sense at all and I find it hard to accept that it was ever seriously taught by anyone who understands what the church, and salvation, is about. There is some misunderstanding here – a host of misunderstandings, I suspect. There is a significant passage in the Acts of the Apostles, Chapter 10:

> Then Peter opened his mouth and said, Of a truth. I perceive that God is no respecter of persons: But in every nation he that feareth him, and worketh righteousness, is accepted with him.

That puts the matter plainly enough. God gave all of us a conscience, whatever church we belong to, or whether we belong to none. That conscience is the instrument of absolute morality, of Natural Law, and if we follow it, we cannot go wrong. But the conscience in its natural state I imagine to be rough-hewn. It needs to be sculpted and refined and polished, needs to be made into what we call the informed conscience. That is the process of moral education, and it is best conducted within a church and a family which belongs to the church. Which church? What the Catholic Church says is this, and I quote from the Decree on Ecumenism enacted by the Second Vatican Council:

> For it is through Christ's Catholic Church alone, which is the universal help towards salvation, that the fullness of the means of salvation can be obtained. It was to the apostolic college alone, of which Peter is the head, that we believe that Our Lord entrusted all the blessings of the New Covenant, in order to establish on earth the one Body of Christ into which all those who should be fully incorporated who belong in any way to the People of God.

This apparently exclusive claim is then qualified in a number of ways. First, 'All who have been justified by faith in Baptism are incorporated into Christ; they therefore have a right to be called Christians, and with good reason are accepted as brothers in the Lord by the children of the Catholic Church.' Furthermore, 'many elements of sanctification and of truth are found outside the visible confines of the Catholic Church ... Christ's spirit uses these churches and ecclesiastical communities as means of salvation.'

The official Catholic line, therefore, is that the Catholic Church constitutes the direct and obvious and surest line to salvation, but that one can get there perfectly well through the route of other

Christian churches. It then adds – and few will disagree – that unity is nevertheless most desirable and we should all work towards and pray for it. I am going to deal with the relationship between the church and the Jews (and indeed other non-Christians) in the next chapter. Here it is simply necessary to say that the Catholic Church no longer claims, if it ever did, that good men and women cannot get to Heaven except through Christianity in general and Roman Catholicism in particular.

The position I have reached, after a lot of thought and some experience, is as follows. There are all kinds of ways to God. In Chapter 16 of St John's Gospel, Jesus says: 'In my father's house are many mansions.' This is an unfortunate mistranslation, but it is a striking phrase nonetheless, and what Jesus means is obvious. There is room for everyone in Heaven and not just room for all, but for all types. God, in his infinite wisdom, and in his insatiable curiosity and love of variety, made men and women very different. He poured the genes, as it were, into a gigantic celestial melting pot, and they come out within a united framework but in infinitely varied combinations. Therein is the delight and genius of mankind. God does not want a uniform spiritual personality. He wants the mystics and the activists, the crusaders and the praying monks and nuns, those whose mission is in the world and those whose work is contemplation. Everyone who recognises God and wishes to serve him will have strong instinctual ideas of how this service can best be performed and in what institutional context, or none. And these ideas can be further shaped by prayer for God's guidance. In the end, the individual has to take the responsibility and make a choice as to what is best for her or him. That is exactly what the conscience is for.

After what is already a fairly longish lifetime in the Catholic Church, my view is that it is an institution which provides unrivalled opportunities for most people to get to know and understand and serve God. In one way or another it can accommodate a remarkably wide variety of souls, and does in fact house over a billion – it has 'many mansions' of its own. But it cannot serve all temperaments equally well. Not only do I believe there is salvation outside my church; I also think that, for some people, salvation is more likely outside my church – in other churches or in no church.

Having said that, however, I must add that my experience, and my knowledge of history, shows me that the riches of Catholicism are enormous – much greater than anyone outside the church can possibly imagine – and the more people who enjoy them, the better. I want everyone I love to be part of the church because I am acutely conscious of the comfort and security, the stability and certitude, the happiness and the wisdom – yes, and the freedom – which being a Catholic has brought to me. I want to share these gifts. But I proceed cautiously. I never proselytise, as such. I know people who do, like my old friend the Earl of Longford, himself a convert of half a century or more, who is anxious to bring everyone whatever into the church and makes his feelings plain. I prefer to let the Holy Spirit work in people's hearts slowly and silently. Hence, when someone comes to me and asks for advice about becoming a Catholic, I give it as truthfully as I know how. If I perceive that they are ready, and keen, I arrange for them to have professional instruction. If a dear friend comes to me for advice, I sometimes give preliminary instruction myself. I always respond positively when the question of the church comes up in conversation among my friends. I want to help – I do help when asked or when it is clear my help is needed and will be useful. But I also confess my own woeful ignorance and shortcomings and uncertainties. I never pretend that conversion to Catholicism is easy or simple or the solution to all ills of the spirit. Indeed, it may be the beginning of new ones. But it is, for me, the source of immense happiness, and I want to share it if possible – if it is, in fact, God's will.

One reason I find great comfort in the Catholic Church is its sense of authority. I am in some ways a chaotic person, a wild person, and I need discipline. A lot of that discipline I can impose upon myself. For a quarter of a century I have been a self-employed freelance writer, and during that time I have produced a number of very long and complicated books: that requires self-discipline and I am capable of providing it in full measure in my professional life. But there are other areas in which I require discipline from outside. I recognise the fact and I look to the church to provide it. Many people feel like me. They want some external discipline of the spirit, they need the help of some informed and insistent and confident guide to push them in the right direction and keep them moving. They think the Catholic Church does this better than any other institution of its kind, and they are right.

They want certitude as well as discipline. Here again, the Catholic Church provides it. It does not say: it is likely that God wants this or that, or that he may require us to believe this doctrine and to perform that duty. The Catholic Church speaks the language of 'must' and 'will' and 'is' and 'therefore', not of 'might' and 'maybe' and 'on the other hand'. A very large number of people require this certitude. They find life complicated and difficult to understand. They are not skilful at working out what it means to them and what they ought to do in all circumstances. They have views and opinions, of course, and likes and dislikes; but there are large areas where they need firm truths to cling on to and firm instructions as to their path ahead. They like a church which lays down the spiritual law and insists on it and, insofar as it lies in its power, enforces it. The Catholic Church is such a body. Especially under the present pope, John Paul II, it has made its teaching absolutely clear on a large number of points of conduct, not least those which are particularly contentious and difficult and where public opinion is not on the side of strictness – such as birth control and abortion and divorce. John Paul's many and detailed encyclicals have clarified Catholic teaching on virtually the whole range of faith and morals, and they have been accompanied by the publication of the largest and most comprehensive catechism ever issued by the church, which outlines, explains and justifies the faith, citing scriptural and patristic authority, with admirable lucidity and force. The Catholic Church, under this formidable pope, has reinforced its reputation for being unyielding and changeless in essentials of faith, and for insisting on teaching what it sees as the truth, without the smallest concession to current fashion or popular clamour or temporary expediency. That is certainly what I want, it is plainly what an enormous number of Catholics by birth want, and it seems to be also what a great many from other Christian churches, or no churches, want too. In the two societies I know best, the United States and Britain, large numbers of people are turning from the moral chaos they find in the contemporary world, and the uncertain teachings of the churches into which they were born, to the sureness and steadfastness of Catholicism.

Whence does this church derive the authority it insists on displaying? The argument runs as follows. Jesus Christ always spoke with a note of authority. He was gentle and compassionate, the very reverse of aggressive. On the contrary, he was wonderfully persuasive and beguiling. But he did not mince words on the salient points, he never prevaricated or dodged issues or left his hearers in doubt. He spoke with all the authority vested in him by his Father and he spoke to be obeyed. At times he displayed righteous anger, against those who knew the truth but did not teach it or wantonly neglected it or obscured it, and against those who openly flouted God's wishes to the scandal of the innocent. On these occasions he did, indeed, display the Wrath of God. I do not know whether it is correct to characterise him as authoritarian, because he had no power except that which radiated from his own personality or was conveyed by his miraculous gifts of healing. But he was an authority figure: a leader, a teacher and a charismatic head of mission.

Christ's appointment of the Apostles, 'the Twelve', prepared the way for his own departure and ensured the continuity of his mission. They were an elect, a chosen group who understood his teaching and were commanded by him to propagate it. He specifically gave them the authority and the charismatic ability to do so, and they began their historic mission on the feast of Pentecost, when the Holy Spirit breathed into them and gave them skills of communication which, we are told, were miraculous. Their direct successors, by apostolic appointment, were the bishops, and it is a source of great pride in the Catholic Church – and a certain scepticism among historians of antiquity – that from the very beginning of the church the apostolic succession has been uninterruptedly maintained.

The bishop is primarily a teacher, in Latin *magister*. He alone possesses the complete panoply of teaching authority and the administrative and disciplinary powers which necessarily accompany it. He sits in the teacher's chair, in Greek *kathedra*, and so his church, where the chair is next to the high altar, is called a cathedral. The collective teaching power of the church, expressed through the college of bishops, with the pope at its head, is therefore known as the *magisterium*. All this is plain enough. We now come to the difficult bit, for many the stumbling-block. The

Second Vatican Council and canon law lay down plainly that the pope's presiding presence is essential for the college of bishops to exercise their authority, and he must confirm or recognise what it decides for that to be valid. In addition, because the pope is the successor to St Peter, who was invested with special authority by Jesus himself, and is therefore the Vicar of Christ on earth, he can exercise 'unhindered' full, supreme and universal power over the whole church. In short, the bishops are powerless without the pope, but the pope has full power even without the bishops. When it comes down to it, the Roman Catholic Church is indeed an autocracy and the pope is an autocrat. He runs the church in more or less the same way Jesus Christ ran his mission. I am not sure that an authoritative church or a mission to the world can be run in any other way, and the fact that the church is an autocracy may well be one reason it has survived for 2,000 years and is still flourishing. The pope's powers are administrative and disciplinary and pastoral. But he also, and above all, has teaching power, and there his authority is at its highest. But it is also restricted. The pope cannot teach error when he is speaking *ex cathedra*, from his chair, on matters of faith or morals, and addressing the church, *urbi et orbi*.

Note that important limitation. Modern popes have a habit of making announcements or giving a little homily from the window of their private apartments, overlooking St Peter's Square, at noon on Sunday, popping out like a cuckoo clock dead on time. These discourses are sometimes of no consequence and sometimes significant, but they are not infallible. Nor are the papal encyclicals, which are guides to and interpretations of the faith rather than *ex cathedra* pronouncements. They usually have great authority and often reiterate teachings of the church which are indeed essential parts of the *magisterium*, but an encyclical is not an infallible document as such. Needless to say, if the pope goes in for weather forecasting or political pronouncements, what he says is his opinion, no more. The present pope evidently has a horror of capital punishment, but the church does not teach that it is wrong. I feel at liberty to dissent from the pope on a number of issues. He has a hostility towards the free enterprise system which springs from his peculiar background in Poland and which leads him to put it on the same moral level as collectivist economic systems. I find this nonsensical and annoying. But then I find the philosophy of Husserl, to which the pope is greatly attached, nonsensical too, and the philosophy of Heidegger, who took over many of Husserl's ideas, deeply annoying. So what? We disagree, and that is all.

But I also listen to the pope with respect, because he is wise and experienced and the Holy Spirit is with him when he speaks on faith and morals, and no doubt at other times too. And when the pope does speak *ex cathedra*, on the central points of faith and morals, I follow him. To be frank, I do not always feel tested on this issue. The last great dogma proclaimed by the church was the Assumption of Our Lady. The Mother of God did not die naturally, she was assumed into Heaven. I find no difficulty in accepting this teaching. It is not something which particularly interests me or which seems of much importance, though it is obviously important to many theologians. The pope and the collegiate church wills it, so I accept. It might be a different matter if the church suddenly produced, as it often rumoured it might, a dogma insisting that Mary is the Co-redemptress. This would smack to me of Mariolatry and my gorge might rise. On the other hand, it might not. I will face that problem when I come to it, if ever. My conscience will be my guide. I recall a testy remark by Hilaire Belloc, made when someone drew his attention to some Vatican nonsense: 'What can you expect from an institution run by a pack of Italian clergymen?' The nonsense was not a dogmatic pronouncement, needless to say, but you see the drift of Belloc's thought. I return to my comparison of the church with the British army. The army commands, and I obey. When so ordered, I go over the top and take part in the attack. But I do not necessarily believe that the Commander-in-Chief is a military genius.

There is a further role to be played by a church which is sure of its teaching and not afraid to speak its mind – the battle for life. I often reflect on the disasters of the twentieth century and wonder what fresh horrors the twenty-first will bring. We have learned some lessons from the twentieth. In particular we have learned to fear the state and see it as it is: useful, even friendly when small and chained, a mortal enemy when it breaks its constitutional bonds. So that, I hope, will not be the problem during the twenty-first century – we have got the totalitarian virus out of our system, though it is well to remember that China, with over a billion people, is still infected. But I think it is already evident what we will have to fear in the new century. In our own, we allowed vicious men to play with the state and paid the penalty with scores of millions done to death by state violence. The risk in the twenty-first century is that we will allow men – and women too – to play with human life itself. And by play I mean to use and abuse and change the life-forces as though there were no laws except those we ourselves determine.

I was much struck by an exchange which occurred in September 1994 at an Oxford conference on medical ethics which my wife organised at St Anne's College. One of the speakers, the British journalist Melanie Phillips, used the phrase 'the sanctity of human life'. Another, a dauntingly clever philosopher, interjected: 'Now wait a moment – let's look at that expression, "the sanctity of life". You may be right. Perhaps human life *is* sacred to us. But I don't know it as a fact. Prove it to me. *Why* should human life be sacred?'

I found this a chilling moment, and many of those to whom I have described the incident found it chilling too. I had always thought that the sanctity of life was one of those 'truths' which sensible men and women 'hold to be self-evident'. It did not need to be proved. It just was. Proving it is not easy. I doubt if I could prove it. But then I do not need to prove it because I know it to be true just as surely as I know that I am a human being. I think most of us feel that way. There are a number of beliefs to do with behaviour and morality and civilisation which are so self-evident that the request to prove them creates uneasiness.

Yet that, I fear, is precisely the kind of uneasiness we are going to experience in the twenty-first century. All kinds of axiomatic certitudes about human life will come under challenge from the innovators who plan to use new technologies to 'improve' the human condition, just as the Nazis and the Communists planned to use the state to improve it. There are, of course, continuities between the two forms of social engineering and human engineering. The Nazi plan was to 'cleanse' the human race by an extreme form of eugenics which involved eliminating Jews, gypsies, Slavs and other types of *Untermenschen*. Communist eugenics involved eliminating the exploitative bourgeoisie and introducing a new, cleansed kind of human being, without acquisitive instincts. Looking back it is hard, now, to decide which was the more dangerous kind of nonsense. Both involved mega-murder and both rested on the assumption that those in authority have the right to make up the moral rules as they go along. The innovators who will endeavour to exercise power in the twenty-first century have, likewise, a contempt for absolute morality and a belief that morals and laws should be relative, and changed from time to time to suit the convenience of men and women.

Are they not having their will already? In 1994 in Britain alone, 168,000 unborn children were lawfully destroyed. The number of legal abortions which have been legally conducted in the world exceeds the numbers of human beings killed by both the Nazi and the Communist tyrannies. At the other end of the life-span, euthanasia is already lawful in the Netherlands, or at any rate unpunished. Efforts are being made to introduce this approach in various other Western countries, including the United States and Britain. Abortion and euthanasia are merely the plinth on which the innovators – those who need to have it 'proved' to them that life is sacred – intend during the twenty-first century to erect a system in which they will be allowed to do virtually anything with human life which technology makes possible.

So, with only a few years to go before the twenty-first century begins, John Paul II, a tenacious freedom-fighter for life, a positive crusader for life, published his 1995 spring encyclical, *The Gospel of Life*. It firmly restated the sanctity of human life as an absolute. It defended human life in all its manifestations in a manner robustly grounded in natural and divine law – truths presented as unassailable, unalterable and eternal – and it identified all acts terminating innocent human life, however speciously defended by courts and parliaments, by philosophers and even churchmen, as forms of murder. Thus the Catholic Church's teaching on human life, as expounded by Pope John Paul, is internally coher-ent and consistent, massively brave and unfashionable, a hard doctrine to follow – as all good teaching is – and is being and will be resisted, ridiculed and cursed by all the evil forces of the modern world. But it has been sent out to all men, with all the eloquence of an old pope who has personally lived through the Nazi and Communist tyrannies and knows a threat to life when he sees one, and with all the resources of a large, ancient and well-organised church which is used to clinging to what it sees as the truth in the face of fashionable opinion. It is at such moments that I thank God that my church is an authoritarian one, and so is habituated to speaking out with a clear and authoritative voice, just as its founder Jesus Christ did two millenniums ago.

There is another aspect of the church's existence which is important to me and which I will try to explain to myself, and to others. Belief in God is only the beginning of religious life. The substance of that life is learning to love God with the fullness and intensity he deserves, and to express that love by our behaviour in everyday life. A few rare souls among us can do this unaided. Their spiritual imagination is so strong, their disciplined nature so reliable, and their ability to engage in solitary worship – and to take themselves through a lifetime in the world without external supports – so complete that they can be, as the Greek Orthodox Church has it, *idiosyncratic* – they can devise their own practices of religion and observe them. Thus the hermits and mystics and coenobites. But that is certainly not for me or for the over-whelming majority of people. We need a framework of prayer and worship and sacramental celebration. The communion, presence and solidarity of our fellow believers are essential to us. We lean on each other and hear each other's voices raised in prayer. Our faith is mutually reinforcing. Our good works act as exemplars to each other. A church full of people who have come together to worship God of their own free will is a peculiarly blessed and happy assembly, and to be part of it, regularly, is a reinvigoration of belief and of our determination to lead useful and decent lives.

The principal way in which the church provides this system of support is through the liturgy. The liturgy of the Catholic Church is very old and retains elements of the ancient Israelite liturgy – readings from the Old Testament and the psalms, recalling the tremendous events of the providential story, the Fall of Man, the Flood, the escape from Egypt, the giving of the Ten Commandments and the coming to the Promised Land, the Exile and Return, the prophecies and the adumbrations of the Messiah. Embedded in the Catholic liturgy, in fact, are surviving Hebrew and Aramaic words, as well as the Greek *kyrie eleison*, which recalls the time when the Early Church was largely Greek-speaking. The

liturgy of the Dark Age Church was in Latin, added to and modified
in the Middle Ages, completely recast and updated during the
sixteenth-century Counter-Reformation and finally rendered into
the vernacular as a result of the decrees of the Second Vatican
Council during the restless 1960s. But the essence of the liturgy
has been constant for nearly 2,000 years. Theologians have a
rather elevated and flowery way of presenting the liturgy. They
describe it as the work of the Holy Spirit, quoting the saying of
Jesus in St John's Gospel (14:26): 'the Comforter, which is the
Holy Ghost, whom the Father will send in my name, he shall
teach you all things, and bring all things to your remembrance,
whatsoever I have said unto you'. Hence, the Spirit and the church
are said to co-operate to manifest Christ and his work of salvation
in the liturgy. Through the Eucharist and the other sacraments,
the liturgy is the memorial of the mystery of salvation, and the
Holy Spirit is the church's living memory.

All that is undoubtedly true but, as I say, it is a little flowery and
for me the liturgy is something much more down-to-earth. It is
the routine of religion. We are told that Tibetan Buddhists put
little paper wheels with prayers written on them into streams, and
let the water spin the wheels and say the prayers, as it were. This
was often cited to me, as a child, by pious nuns as an example of
pagan superstition and silliness. But I do not think it silly. I am
comforted by the idea of all those paper wheels spinning endlessly
even when their fat and lazy monk-owners are asleep. A prayer-
wheel keeps the machinery of devotion going, after a fashion. So,
too, I am comforted by the thought of the whole vast machinery
of Christian worship continuing, all round the clock, in a world
where the sun never sets, in countless grand cathedrals and
humble tin-hut parish chapels, muttered and murmured in every
strange tongue under the heavens, as well as in the church's
special language, Latin.

The liturgy is a 'many-splendoured thing' and it is not surprising
that it draws aesthetes and lovers of art, who might otherwise be
agnostics or members of other religious organisations, into the
Catholic Church. There was never a time in my life when I was
not accustomed to participating in these ceremonies, seeing the
flickering candles, smelling the incense, watching my parents and
elder brother and sisters go up to receive the sacrificial host on

their tongues. Later, at Stonyhurst, I saw the full magnificence of the liturgy and participated in it, first as a treble in the choir, later as a member of the altar staff. In those days the full annual cycle of the liturgy was celebrated by the Stonyhurst Jesuits with a completeness and style to be found nowhere else, except possibly at Westminster Cathedral and, of course, in St Peter's itself. We prided ourselves on the way we did things, aided by holy altar vessels of immense beauty and value, by elaborately embroidered vestments going back to the sixteenth century and by all the time in the world to get things exactly right. The solemn preparations of Advent, the mournful ceremonies of Lent, the huge drama of Holy Week, culminating in the amazing ceremonies of Holy Saturday, the longest service in the entire calendar, followed by the blaze of glory on Easter Sunday – then, in rapid succession, a whole series of splendid feasts, Ascension, Pentecost, Corpus Christi, St Peter and Paul, we did all these things with the precision and flourish which the Brigade of Guards brings to the ceremony of Trooping the Colour on Horse Guards parade-ground. There was, indeed, a martial dimension to it all, for Stonyhurst vindicated the ultra-loyalism of English Catholics by the efficiency of its Officer Cadet Corps and the number of its *alumni* who had won the Victoria Cross – portraits of their fierce uniformed figures lined the walls of our dining-hall. So during High Mass on the feast of Corpus Christi, a sovereign's guard of honour in full uniform lined up before the High Altar just before the act of consecration, and when the priest raised the host so all the congregation could see it – bread turned into the living flesh of Christ – the guard presented arms with fixed bayonets and a great stamping of boots. I was once a member of this guard of honour and participated in this ceremony, which some may find bizarre but which we took for granted and delighted in. And that evening at Benediction we saw an annual miracle when 2,000 candles on the high altar, linked by an invisible thread of guncotton, were ignited at each side, so that the flame leapt from one to another, at dazzling speed, till all were alight.

The liturgy is there to dazzle and excite, among other purposes, but I often think its chief function, in most lives, is simply to repeat itself, to function endlessly, from one day to the next, from one year to the next, in order to provide a reliable framework of normality in religious life. All this is mechanical, but then the mechanism of religious continuity is necessary to provide the security of faith. Few if any of us are saints. We are not usually called to martyrdom. Our religious life lacks the drama of persecution and extreme sacrifice, we are confronted with humdrum temptations and everyday sins, and our spirituality and enthusiasm languish accordingly. The sheer mechanical activity of the liturgy, its endless whirring and clattering, its muttering and singing and chanting, its tinkling and incensing, provides a wonderful and, if we stop to ponder a second, meaningful support and daily nourishment for our spiritual life. We lean on the liturgy and so stay spiritually awake. It baptises us into the church, it punctuates our days throughout our life, it confirms us and marries us and, eventually, it buries us. I could not do without it and I rejoice that I am part of an immense multitude of a billion believers who cannot do without it either, and who share it and participate in it along with myself. That is all the work of the church, it is one chief reason why the church exists and it is a compelling reason, for me, to belong to it. Authority, organisation and structure have their uses.

CHAPTER 11

Separate brethren, Jews and Christians

It has never seriously occurred to me that I could belong to any other church but my own. I love it, despite its faults. It is of my flesh and blood, as it were. To leave it would be irreparable loss; not to belong to it, daily deprivation. But I look at other churches, other faiths, other religious systems, and I feel no hostility. Very little envy either. In some ways I respect the Church of England. It has a magnificent liturgy in English, which it has not yet wholly abandoned. The sixteenth-century Protestants who rebelled against Rome and founded rival branches of the Christian Church had one undoubted gift, the ability to translate the old Latin services and the Vulgate of the Old and New Testaments into magnificent vernacular renderings. I love Cranmer's Prayerbook and I take immense pleasure in the solemn German of Martin Luther, set to music so marvellously in Brahms's *Requiem in German*, for example. Certainly in English there is no beating the words with which the Anglican Church solemnises a marriage or buries the dead. These services might have been scripted by Shakespeare.

Then too the Anglicans have superb hymns, and a great many of them. Only recently have Catholics in England been encouraged to sing them by their own church and they form a huge addition to the richness and enjoyment of our services. It is also true that Anglicans have a much finer tradition of pulpit oratory, they take more trouble about the content and delivery of their sermons, and they have – at any rate until recently – a much better-educated clergy. But all these are little by comparison with the loss of self-confidence displayed by the Anglican authorities in recent decades, the weak, uncertain and often contradictory voices with which its bishops speak, the hedgings and prevarications and deliberate ambiguities of its Synods, as they are swayed by this pressure-group and that, and its almost total absence of spiritual leadership.

I find that the Church of England and its overseas affiliates are at their best when seen as individual units. I have actually preached in Anglican cathedrals and churches in Australia, and found myself at home and comfortable among their keen congregations: they seem to share my vision of Christianity, and I theirs. And, in the autumn of 1994, I spent a day with the Anglican church in Washington DC, going all over its magnificent Gothic cathedral, to my mind the finest building in the entire federal capital, which is spread at its feet, and teaching the boys and girls from the attached Anglican schools – or, rather, listening to them converse with me about the glorious and not-so-glorious history of their country. It was a hugely satisfying day and I felt I had visited a corner of Christianity where the faith is held strongly and young Christian minds are lovingly cultivated and encouraged. In England I visit Anglican churches often, and sometimes attend services. I admire the beauty of the one and the decorum of the other. But I do not get the feeling, though I pray for it to come, that God is present in the grandest Anglican cathedral – Wells, say, or Lincoln or Ely – in the same way I feel he is present in the humblest Catholic chapel. What is this? Prejudice? Sectarianism? Bigotry? At all events, the feeling is very strong for me, indeed insuperable.

Then there is the huge chorus of different voices from the wider world of non-Catholic Christianity. These are changing and being added to all the time, and some of them are persuasive. In large parts of Latin America, for instance, the missionary Evangelical churches are carrying all before them in what used to be Catholic heartlands. They are very open and direct, simple and sincere. They preach the gospel and they preach the traditional morality of the Ten Commandments. They do not dabble in politics and indulge in Revolutionary Theology, as the radical wing of the Catholic Church in Latin America has done in recent decades, with lamentable results for all concerned. It is now clear that the poor of the towns and the peasants of the village do not want politics on Sunday – they can get that every other day of the week and much good it has done them, as they are painfully aware.

What they seem to want and respond to is what the Evangelicals provide – the story of salvation and what they must do, and not do, to be worthy of it. Now, belatedly, the Catholic Church in those parts is beginning to provide it too.

This immensely successful Evangelical effort in Latin America – which I believe will eventually be followed by similar efforts in black Africa, where it will be equally readily received – has its origins in the United States, both in the Protestant churches of the Bible Belt and in the freelance varieties of religion which in America cluster round individual evangelists and preachers, especially those skilled in using mass-communications. In England, this kind of religion is seen as brash, embarrassing, commercial, vulgar and materialistic. It is sneered at and feared by the educated middle classes, whether Christian, Jewish, agnostic or atheist, and so hated by the Anglican and Catholic hierarchies that they conspire together to use their considerable entrenched power to keep it off the airwaves and to prevent by law the creation of private religious radio or television stations.

I take a much more relaxed view of American popular religion, perhaps because I have studied the huge and fruitful part it has played in American history – it it impossible, in fact, to understand American history without it – and partly because I have been able to observe this kind of religion at work on the ground. Its effects on balance are immensely beneficial. The Bible Belt, so-called, is in many ways the morally healthy core of America. In the whole of the United States, I know of no more religious city than Dallas in Texas. To those who have never been there its image is indelibly etched by a ridiculous TV soap-opera, falsely portraying it as a centre of ruthless business, greed and lust. It is in fact a much God-fearing place, the centre of a district known for its churches, seminaries, religious colleges and universities, excellent Christian schools and church institutions of all kinds, flourishing mightily. It is the kind of place where all the family sit down to meals together and a grace is said before and after them, and a visiting lecturer, like myself, is requested, before a meal begins: 'Professor Johnson, will you ask a blessing of God?'

For that matter, I have also attended popular religious meetings in the United States, which are part of a long tradition going back to the early eighteenth century, beginning in camps held near the rough frontiers of the expanding country. There is very little to object to them and much to commend them to all branches of the Christian faith. These religious enthusiasts speak to the human heart and get a rich response. They have much more in common with Jesus Christ, a popular evangelist himself, than the hierarchs of Rome and Canterbury care to admit. Immense opportunities exist for this kind of direct, personal and popular religion all over the world, not least among nearly four billion Asians, and I hope that the Catholic Church, which has been evangelising Asia now for the best part of five centuries, with indifferent success, will start to learn something from these despised American preachers.

Some question whether the Christian churches, let alone the freelance evangelists, ought to penetrate the heartlands of rival faiths like Islam, Buddhism, Confucianism, Shinto and Hinduism. I think they should, indeed must. Christianity is a missionary faith, or it is nothing. We feel its message is the truth; not indeed the only truth – for elements of truth are to be found everywhere in nature and in Natural Law – but the specially revealed truth, which we have been privileged to receive and are bound in conscience to share with others. My faith is everything to me, the key to happiness in this world and the next, and I would be criminally remiss not to want and strive to give it to others if I can. I do not doubt that there are valuable elements in all these long-established faiths. We must examine and, if suitable, incorporate or imitate them. But all the Afro-Asian religions I have been able to examine, historically and doctrinally, seem to me to have serious shortcomings and some have aspects which are positively evil.

I would not be happy if I did not believe Christianity is ultimately committed to the evangelisation of all Asia, so that the vast majority of the souls who live there will eventually be baptised and educated in my faith. At the same time, we must not shut our eyes to the fact that, in parts of Africa, a war of religions is taking place at the frontiers where Islam and Christianity meet. Islam is by nature a militant religion and in the Sudan and East Africa, for instance, and in parts of West Africa, it is using state power to persecute or stamp out or forcibly convert Christian communities, tribes and nations. These efforts have to be resisted, and the power of the Christian churches mobilised to repel such Islamic invasions. We must further mobilise Christian resources to put pressure on Islamic states to practise religious toleration, as we do to Islamic communities in our midst, and to secure equality of rights for Christians. We must not hesitate to evangelise Islamic territory, not least where the theocracy holds sway. The Arab masses of North Africa and the Middle East, the Hindus of the Indian sub-continent, and the Buddhists, animalists, Shintoists and Confucians of East Asia, as well as the Muslims of Pakistan, Malaysia and Indonesia, have a right to hear the Gospel so they can freely choose to follow it. The twenty-first century must be, and I think will be, a missionary century, like the nineteenth before it.

My mind is much less clear about the relationship between Christianity and the Jews. When I wrote my *History of Christianity* in the early 1970s, I learnt a great deal about my own faith which had hitherto been obscure or quite unknown to me. In particular I was able to explore its roots in Judaism and to discover how deep and strong and intricate they were. There is virtually no belief or practice in Christianity which does not have some antecedent in the religion of ancient Israel, and the overlap between modern Christianity and modern Judaism is considerable. When I became aware of all this I determined, if I found the time and opportunity, to investigate the history of the Jews too, and I eventually did so later in the 1970s decade. The result was my *A History of the Jews*.

While preparing this book, I not only conceived an admiration for the Jewish people in history, whose spirit and resourcefulness and sheer intelligent fidelity has allowed them to survive so much persecution and suffering over so many long, hard centuries, but I acquired knowledge of and much affection for the Jewish faith and practice of religion. Jewish prayers are often moving and pregnant with illuminating thoughts. Jewish moral theology is often superior to the Christian equivalent, in my judgment. Jewish teachers have been at it twice as long, to begin with, and they have not been burdened, as Christian theologians and teachers have been, by the immensely complicated dogmatic theology of the Trinity, the Incarnation and the Eucharist, which has led to so many controversies and splits and schisms within Christianity. The Jews have escaped all that, and they have in consequence been able to devote more time and thought to moral behaviour. Indeed, that is what Judaism is really about – what a Jew should do or not do. As a result, they have acquired insights into perennial and difficult problems of morality which have been denied to Christians. In particular, the Jews have been skilful at striking a correct balance between the duties of the individual to him or herself, and his or her duties to the community. They have usually got the balance right and that is one reason, I discovered while writing my book, that the Jews have proved so resilient in such adverse situations. The individual is given great and productive freedom, and partly as a result of this, the needs of the community are fully insisted on, and can be met.

That is one reason why I welcome the reconciliation which has taken place between Christians and Jews – and particularly between the Catholic Church and the Jews – during my lifetime. I am not one of those who believe that anti-Semitism is rooted in Christianity – I know it is not, as a historical fact. But the Christian layer in the archaeological history of anti-Semitism is a particularly massive one, and for that reason alone the *rapprochement* which began with the efforts of that saintly German, Cardinal Augustine Bea, at the Second Vatican Council, is so important. In recent years Christian theologians and liturgists have been studying Judaism and discovering a surprising number of points in common. There is a significant passage in the new *Catholic Catechism* (paragraph 1096) which recognises this and is worth quoting:

A better knowledge of the Jewish people's faith and religious life as professed and lived even now can help our better understanding of certain aspects of Christian liturgy. For both Jews and Christians sacred scripture is an essential part of their respective liturgies: in their proclamations of the word of God, response to this word, prayer of intercession for the living and the dead, invocation of God's mercy. In its characteristic structure the Liturgy of the Word originates in Jewish prayer. The Liturgy of the Hours and other liturgical texts and formularies, as well as those of our most venerable prayers, including the Lord's Prayer, have parallels in Jewish prayer. The Eucharist Prayers also draw their inspiration from the Jewish tradition. The relationship between Jewish liturgy and Christian liturgy, but also their differences in content, are particularly evident in the great feasts of the liturgical year, such as Passover. Christians and Jews both celebrate the Passover. For Jews, it is the Passover of history, tending towards the future; for

Christians, it is the Passover fulfilled in the death and resurrection of Christ, though always in expectation of its definitive consummation.

In addition to this, it became apparent to me, while preparing my Jewish history, not only that Jewish moral theology has a lot to teach Christians, as I have already noted, but that many of the great Jewish rabbinical scholars and theologians have left bodies of work full of riches for Christians to explore and use. In particular the great Maimonides – wisest of all the Jewish thinkers, in my view – is someone who ought to be studied in Christian seminaries and colleges. I would like to see his *Guide to the Perplexed* widely read and anthologised, and presented and commented upon by Christian writers.

Nevertheless, when all this is admitted, the awkward fact remains that the Jewish and Christian religions are, or at any rate appear to be, mutually incompatible. They teach things which are in violent and seemingly irreconcilable conflict. If Jesus Christ was the Son of God, as Christians must and do believe, then the Jews, in refusing to acknowledge the fact, reject the truth, and God's plan for humanity, and cut themselves off from the process of religious development which the Old Testament records before it lapses into a significant silence. The warnings about the Messiah, the foreshadowings of Christ's coming in the prophecies, are ignored, and the Jewish self-criticism which is so prominent in the second half of the Old Testament is seen to be abundantly justified. If Christ is God, then the Jews forfeit their claim to be a Chosen People, a priestly elect, a light to the Gentiles, and become the stiff-necked reprobates so roundly denounced by the prophets for their blindness and disobedience and defiance of God's word. Alternatively, if the Jews are right and Jesus, far from being the Son of God, is merely a false-Messiah, one of many, then the whole of Christianity is a delusion and the two millenniums of the church are a gigantic sham. Put thus bluntly, the quarrel between the religions is awesome. There appears to be no possible basis for compromise, no overlap at all. The two teachings, at their central point – Almighty God's programme for humanity – are as incompatible as it is possible for such things to be, and reconciliation is logically ruled out.

I have often pondered on this tragedy, and discussed it not long ago with an audience of highly educated Jews at a Jewish Book Week in North London. We could see no obvious way out of the dilemma. But then, as we observed, human intelligence is limited and human ignorance is great. By contrast, the power and scope of the divine wisdom is limitless. In Chapter 11 of his great Epistle to the Romans, St Paul, Jew of the Jews and Christian of the Christians, speaks eloquently on this point: 'O the depth of the riches both of the wisdom and knowledge of God! How unsearchable are his judgments, and his ways past finding out! For who hath known the mind of the Lord? Or who hath been his counsellor?' Who are we, then, to say there is no bringing together in truth and harmony the beliefs of his Chosen People and those of the Children of Christ? It is not beyond the power of God to find a way and in his own good time to reveal it to us, Jew and Christian both, and then a deep and painful schism in the story of the spiritual development of humankind will finally be healed. It will surely be worth waiting for, this squaring by God of the Jewish–Christian circle.

CHAPTER 12

The four last things: death

The first fact of life primitive man accepted, and pondered, was death. Mankind has been thinking about it ever since, for tens of thousands of years, during which billions of our species have met their deaths and disappeared; and after all that anxious cogitation, we are not much the wiser. The new *Catholic Catechism* begins its section on death by quoting the document *Gaudium et Spes* published by the Second Vatican Council in 1965: 'It is in regard to death that man's condition is most shrouded in doubt.' It is unusual for the Catholic Church to strike such a note of uncertitude.

The church is also troubled, not to say confused, on the history of death. It teaches, through its *magisterium* – its role as the authentic interpreter of scripture and early tradition – that it was sin which brought death into the world. Originally God had intended man to live for ever, even though his nature was mortal. Adam and Eve were destined to escape bodily death. By sinning, they invoked death – invented it almost – and left it as a fearful legacy to all their progeny. Death will be with us to the end of the world: as St Paul puts it in his First Letter to the Corinthians, 'The last enemy that shall be destroyed is death.'

The Catholic Church therefore asks us to believe that God altered his plan for mankind in a fundamental respect, when his new creatures behaved more badly than he had intended. It tells us, in effect, that the almighty, all-seeing, all-foreseeing God had not expected Adam to sin, and in his surprise and anger at Adam's disobedience, revoked his edict of bodily immortality and so re-created the earth as a vale of tears. All this seems very strange. Why had God not foreseen Adam's weakness – or Eve's propensity to listen to temptation and to tempt in her turn – and made his male creature stronger? And why did God permit Satan, in serpent-guise, to upset his carefully considered plan to create a paradisal Garden of Eden with sinless and deathless inhabitants, and settle instead for a world full of sin and suffering? I cannot answer these questions. It seems to me far more likely that God knew perfectly well what he was doing when he gave Adam free will – that he knew his creatures would sin and thus invoke misery on themselves – but that he wished to create a moral drama in which sinful man would be redeemed by the passion and death of his own divine son made man. The sinless, deathless Adam and Eve in their semi-celestial garden are of little moral interest or significance. Their adoration of God, seemly though it might be, is no more valuable or edifying than the adoration of the angels, whose nature it is to adore. On the other hand, an imperfect, frail-willed man, a flawed creature, born in sin, living in suffering, exposed to all the evils and temptations of a rugged, dangerous world, who nonetheless, with the help of God's grace and mercy, and by virtue of the supreme sacrifice of his only son, manages to struggle successfully against his sinful nature and contrives in the end – just – to make himself worthy of joining God in Paradise: that is indeed a tale worth telling. But death is an indispensable element in it, a crucial function of the mechanism of salvation and redemption. If this argument is valid, the fact of death is not an accident, a modification of God's original plan, but absolutely central to his concept of creation. Death, then, is very much God's idea, and we are intended to think long and hard about it, to ponder its mysteries, and to shiver at its awesome inevitability.

Nevertheless, a large part of mankind, hating and fearing death, has always striven to wish or magic it away, to play it down, to euphemise it, to try to conceal it from themselves. The Ancient Egyptians crowded their tombs with exact replicas of all the good things of this life to persuade themselves that continuity of living and enjoyment was a fact. The dead man took with him all the things he would need precisely because death was not an end but a new phase of life, in which he would continue his pleasures, albeit now immortal. The Egyptians placed their cities of the living on the Right Bank of the Nile, their cities of the dead, their pyramids and tombs, on the Left Bank. So death was minimised to a mere crossing of the river – it was all the same land after all.

The famous Egyptian papyrus, 'The Book of the Dead', now in the British Museum, was called such only by modern Egyptologists. In fact it is not a celebration of death at all, but a denial of death, a manifesto against death, a celebration rather of immortality, of the continuity of life, but in a different place.

Many societies have striven to make death a taboo word, at any rate in polite circles. The Roman gentry circled nervously round death, circumnavigated it by periphrasis: *discessit e vita* – 'he has departed from life' – they said of a dead friend. Or they said simply *vixit*, 'he has lived'. The Arabs put it a little more grandly: 'His destiny is finished.' We refer to 'the dear departed', 'the loved ones', who have 'passed away'. In his novel *The Loved One*, about 'Hollywood burial customs', as he put it, Evelyn Waugh satirised Forest Lawn cemetery and the extraordinary ingenuity with which its proprietors avoided any mention of death or other disturbing words. They did not even use the word cemetery, not knowing that it was an example of earlier euphemism – it is Greek for 'sleeping place'. 'He is asleep', 'she fell asleep', often used of the death today, are expressions which were in common use 2,500 years ago. We too now emulate the Romans: when we hold a memorial service for the dead, we no longer call it that: it is 'a celebration for the life of' a person who is 'asleep', who has 'passed over', 'gone', 'departed this life'. Death is a topic we try to avoid. It has replaced the four-letter obscenities as the taboo-word. Fashionable novelists, who sprinkle their pages with genital and copulative expressions, and describe sexual, perverted and bestial acts of lust in lubricious detail – I do not say 'loving' detail, as love has little to do with it – are curiously reluctant to describe death, even though they spend much time in characterising the violence which leads to it. No novelist writing today is capable of depicting a deathbed scene with the sincerity it requires. Nor would they attempt to do so: it would be a turn-off for readers. The last great novelist to make a deathbed the climax of a novel was, as you would expect, Evelyn Waugh, who positively longed to look death in the face. But his death of Lord Marchmain in *Brideshead Revisited* (1945) was not well received. Many thought it a weakness in an otherwise triumphant narrative. Cyril Connolly had London drawing-rooms in fits with his cruel pastiche of what he called 'His Lordship's Expiry'.

It was a different matter in Victorian times, one of those periods in human history when death was magnified, talked about, minutely examined and, almost, relished. The death of Little Nell in Charles Dickens' *The Old Curiosity Shop* (1840) seems to have had greater public impact than any other scene in the whole of nineteenth-century literature. It was Nell's end which caused the public to buy 100,000 copies of the novel, within six months of publication, in Britain alone, and to make it, in its day, Dickens' most successful work all over the world. Edgar Allan Poe, an expert on literary deaths, found it 'excessively painful', so harrowing to the senses that he doubted the morality of publishing it. The poet Edward Fitzgerald copied out by hand not only the death-passage itself but all other parts of the book dealing with Little Nell, so that he would have 'a kind of Nelly-ad or Homeric narration'. Thomas Carlyle, who liked to think of himself as totally unsentimental, found it 'overwhelming'. Daniel O'Connell, coarse political rabble-rouser though he was, burst into tears when he finished the passage, and hurled the book out of the window. (It was a portent of change to come when, in 1895, Oscar Wilde risked outrage by remarking: 'One must have a heart of stone to read the death of Little Nell without laughing.')

The Victorians, with their death-masks, their elaborate funeral processions and carriages (the one made for the Duke of Wellington's, in 1852, was of cast-iron, weighed 20 tons and can still be seen in the crypt of St Paul's Cathedral), their mutes, wrapped knockers and mourning etiquette, looked death squarely and ceremoniously in the face. Deathbed scenes were elaborately recorded or committed to memory, and became part of family folklore, reverently told to children and grandchildren. My mother related to me numerous accounts of the deaths of her relations, great-aunts and the like, which were notable for their edifying circumstances, final sayings, last prayers and ejaculations, signs of the hand, etc. In my childhood, elderly priests, with much experience of tending the dying, had fine repertoires of these scenes. There was an extensive devotional literature on the theme. In the old days, death was a domestic, household, family affair, with the dying person upstairs in a well-attended bedroom with a fire in the grate, people downstairs walking softly and talking in whispers, straw in the street outside to muffle the noise of carriage-wheels, the neighbours alerted to the impending event and sending regular and anxious enquiries. When the moment of death came, the entire watchful household and neighbourhood suddenly sprang to life to prepare the obsequies as ostentatiously as possible. Not only were public men, like Wellington and Lincoln, buried with fitting ceremony, but private funerals were grand affairs, students of form and arbiters of fashion counting the number of coaches, the splendour of the mutes, and the caparisons of the black carriage horses. I well remember the funerals of my childhood: the endless cortèges of black-clad mourners trudging on foot behind the hearse and the carriages or limousines of the gentry, traffic at a standstill, everyone in the street stopping till the whole went by, the men raising their hats, women dabbing at their eyes with a handkerchief even if the deceased was unknown to them. Death was seen as an important event, to be publicly noted and decorously marked by a seemly display of pomp.

Alas, it is very different now. Most people die in hospital, sparsely attended, if at all, by their families; often alone, save for professionals of the caring trade. We have lost the art of great state funerals. The last one of any note was Sir Winston Churchill's, a memorable affair to be sure. But the reason for this was that the old warrior had himself planned and replanned it for many years, down to the last detail. And Sir Winston was himself a Victorian – had actually fought as a soldier of the Queen, in India and the Sudan, some time before she died – so he knew exactly what he was doing. The funeral of John F. Kennedy, on the other hand, which might have been a comparable event, was a hasty, straggling affair, much more typical of our times. State obsequies since then have been still more poverty-stricken affairs. As for private funerals, the chief ones of note are held for gangsters.

Even the Vatican has given a lower profile to death in my lifetime. Time was when the death and burial of a pope was an event, presented *urbi et orbi* for all to see, wonder at and reflect upon. The greatest living artists, like Brunelleschi and Michel-angelo, were called upon to superintend a pope's funeral, to design the catafalques and effigies and mourning decorations, and later to exercise their skills on the pontifical monument in St Peter's. Antonio Canova, for instance, ended the Baroque epoch almost at a stroke, and introduced neo-classicism, in 1783–7, with his stupendous tomb of Pope Clement XIV.

Half a century ago there was considerable fuss when a pope died. When Pius XII finally succumbed in 1958, after a pontificate of nearly twenty years – as a child I had heard the 1939 announcement of his election on Vatican Radio – I hastened to Rome to find the entire city on tiptoe. The late pope's doctor and confidant, the Marquess Galeazzi-Lisi, a prominent figure in the Byzantine court which had clustered round Pius in his last years, was determined to preserve his master for posterity. He claimed he had recovered the 'lost secret' of the 'ancient Egyptian system of embalming the body whole'. This struck me as strange, for it is well known to Egyptologists, indeed to anyone who pays a careful visit to the Ancient Egyptian gallery of a major museum, that the Egyptians never embalmed a body whole. They reverently took out the heart, entrails, etc. and placed them embalmed separately in what are known as Canopic Jars, with a different animal-god adorning each lid. However, Galeazzi-Lisi was sure of what he was doing and no one had the power, it seemed, to stop him.

So the pope was embalmed whole, and therein lay a Roman comedy–tragedy. By the time I reached Rome the thing had been done, and the pope's body was lying in state in the Vatican, with a Swiss Guard at each corner of the open coffin. But the embalming had palpably not been a success, as the *esprit de corps* and a certain green pallor in the dead pope's face attested. The guards were evidently distressed, and the Roman mob, filing past the coffin, were appalled. They were fiercely devoted to the Roncalli Pope, who was a Roman himself, and they had expected to smell the odour of sanctity, as prelude to rapid canonisation. What they got was quite different. So the plan to make the pope an immediate saint by popular acclamation, as it were, was quietly put aside. At all events, the passing of Pius XII was the last of the great papal obsequies. Popes are now buried, if not quietly at least discreetly, and there is no fuss about their monuments. Even in Rome, then, there is a tendency to sweep death under the carpet.

Yet death, whether we make much of it or little, remains a huge, uncomfortable fact. We all know we are to die. We all, at some time, give thought to death. How will we die? In agony or painlessly – suddenly or after much suffering? Will we face death well?

Will we be edifying in the way we go, or will we disappoint our friends and relations? Will anyone care, anyway? More and more fear a lonely death, and with reason. Or rather, it is not so much death people fear now – the doctors can usually make that painless and even insensible – as long periods of senility before it, while we are kept barely living by modern science, but lose our wits, our dignity and our savings, while our relatives grow increasingly impatient.

I note a growing desire among people I know not for the traditional *bona mors*, the good death after weeks of illness, with the family around, all passion and suffering spent, and the soul easing itself reluctantly but painlessly out of the emaciated body, the loved ones given a dying blessing, the suitable last words duly recorded. Instead, the aspiration is for a sudden end, unexpected, instantaneous. My old climbing-friend Simon Fraser, with whom I walked the Highland summits and ridges for twenty years, had such a longed-for death. He had mounted his horse for the annual drag of his local hunt, of which he was master, and had just taken the hounds out of the policies of his pink-granite castle, when he was seized with a rare and unexpected heart-complaint, which killed him in a second. He was dead while still firmly seated on his favourite hunter, and I have a photograph, taken a few moments before, showing him thus, the castle behind him. Everyone said, 'Oh, what a fine way to go.' But this is the very opposite of the traditional Christian sentiment. The *Roman Missal*, in its Litany of the Saints, specifically pleads: 'From a sudden and unforeseen death, deliver us, O Lord!' Few men or women are prepared for death if it comes suddenly. I have prayed all my life for a premonition of death, so that I have a chance to repent of my sins, to confess them and receive absolution. I think that most Catholics still probably share my view, and likewise pray for a timely death, not a sudden one. But I am not sure.

What is certain is that most Christian churches have specific prayers and even ceremonies preparing the sick and dying for death. In the Catholic Church, the anointing of the sick is a special sacrament, given to those who are seriously ill or preparing for a major operation. The priest anoints the sick person with holy oil and says the words: 'Through this holy anointing may the Lord in his love and mercy help you with the grace of the Holy

Spirit. May the Lord who frees you from sin save you and raise you up.' This sacrament of anointing can be given not merely to those who are obviously dying, but to all the sick. It can be repeated if the illness is prolonged or if the sick person recovers and then has a further illness. But there is, in addition, the special administration of the Eucharist as *viaticum* to those who are about to leave this life. When the human soul is *in extremis*, the Eucharist is the sacrament of passing over from death to new life, from this world to the Father. All these comforting and holy administrations are available, and when my time comes to die I hope I shall be able to receive them – that is what I understand by a fortunate death.

But death is a terrible thing, not only in its inevitability but often in its manner too. We like to think there is justice in death, just as there is certainly justice in the next life. But it is not so. The bad often die peacefully, the good in torment. Pope Honorius IV, not only a fine pastor of the church but a man of exemplary piety and kindness throughout his life, died such a prolonged and agonising death that those who saw him suffer were amazed that God should have subjected the good old man to such a final trial. Could it be, they wondered, that the purgatorial penalties for such light sins as he had committed were being imposed in this life, so he could pass more speedily to Heaven? That, at least, was their uneasy rationalisation.

Recently I was made aware of the similar case of Christina Rossetti, by a fine exhibition of her works and life at the National Portrait Gallery in London. Miss Rossetti, the sister of the better-known poet and painter Dante Gabriel Rossetti, was a lifelong Anglo-Catholic of the most devout kind, who led a life of selfless devotion to her family, to the poor and to the worship of God. Her poetry, which is at last receiving the appreciation it merits, is not predominantly religious in tone – in many ways she is the English equivalent of Emily Dickinson – but when she touches on sacred themes her spirituality is profound and moving. Indeed it has occurred to me that, had she been a Catholic instead of a member of the Church of England, the movement for her canonisation would have already been under way. However that may be, this saintly woman had the most appalling death. A letter survives, written immediately after her death by the woman who attended her, describing her sufferings and reporting that Christina was so distraught towards the end that she had to be tied to the bed. The letter is a remarkable document for, though its contents are disturbing, its tone is radiant with the love and respect which Christina evidently aroused in those who were near her. Here was a death the very reverse of a *bona mors* in the conventional sense, but one which yet had a positive spiritual impact on those witnesses to it. Among Christina's greatest admirers was the poet Swinburne, who was deeply affected by her final sufferings. Immediately after her death he recorded his feelings in a remarkable poem, written apparently while he was half-drunk but still capable of composing finely. The manuscript of this poem, in irregular writing and stained with tears and liquor, also survives.

There is, indeed, no spiritual pattern to death that the historian can discern. The courage and composure and serenity of the martyrs still astonishes me. I am particularly moved by the humble stoicism of St Peter, who felt he was unworthy to be crucified standing up, like his Master, and insisted on being put to death upside down, an amazing request in view of the fact that, to Romans, crucifixion was the most degrading of deaths anyway. On the other hand, the tranquil end of David Hume, the first confessed atheist, whose death was minutely recorded – by Boswell, of course – was also notable and caused annoyance at the time to true believers, who were accustomed to tell tales of the horrifying deaths of infidels and chronic sinners. The fact that Hume died calmly and without apparent fear was, in a curious way, a portent of the modern age. People are superstitious about the last acts or sayings of the dying and give them symbolic significance. But Famous Last Words are often apocryphal. Can Henry James really have left this life asking so characteristically: 'So it has come at last, this grey, distinguished thing?' And were Bonaparte's last words indeed: 'Tête d'armée!'? Stalin died alone, on the camp bed in his cluttered office where he lived for the sake of security, so no final words are recorded. But he was found with one arm thrust out to Heaven in a last gesture, whether of alarm or fear or defiance is not clear.

The death of Jesus Christ, prolonged and harrowing and con-tra̶d̶ictory as it was, should serve as a model for us all. I have often thought about it, particularly since I acquired a recording of Haydn's meditation, for string quartet, on *The Seven Last Words of Christ from the Cross*. This unsurpassed work of genius, to my mind on a level with the final quartets of Beethoven, forms a musical commentary to the utterances of Christ, as he hung in agony, with their striking revelations of both his humanity and his divinity, and his final utter surrender to his Father's will and his redemptive role. Haydn's music brings out the sublimity of it all, not least the uncomfortable but necessary recognition that death can be a horrific experience even for the entirely innocent and for those most ready to embrace it.

Christ's death was for a transcendental purpose, so it was positive, a beginning. That is the true Christian approach to death. One may not welcome death – few of us do, whatever we may say in advance – but we can train ourselves to accept it not as a negative event but as a positive one, an opening and an opportunity to move into a higher form of life. St Paul is most insistent on this. 'For me to live is Christ, and to die is gain.' Or again: 'The saying is sure: if we have died with him, we will also live with him.' He wrote to Philemon: 'My desire is to depart and to be with Christ.' Many holy women have made the same point. St Teresa of Avila put it thus: 'I want to see God and, in order to see him, I must die.' The great French saint, Thérèse of Lisieux, is recorded to have said in *The Last Conversations*, 'I am not dying: I am entering life.' There are some remarkable reflections on dying in the works of St Ignatius of Antioch, quoted in the new *Catholic Catechism*. He writes: 'There is living water in me, water that murmurs and says within me: Come to the Father.' And again: 'It is better for me to die in Christ Jesus than to reign over the ends of the earth. Him it is I seek, who died for us. Him it is I desire, who rose for us. I am on the point of giving birth ... Let me receive pure light; when I shall have arrived here, then shall I be a man.'

In all this writing on death, by great saints who had reflected much on the subject and approached their own death with eagerness, even with ecstasy, there is still no clear indication of what happens when death is actually accomplished and the soul quits the body. 'This grey distinguished thing', as James put it, is still a mystery, as it always has been. It is right to see death not as a precipice into the abyss but as a bridge. But a bridge to what? There are precious few clues of any kind. But I am struck by St Ignatius of Antioch's reference to 'pure light'. It is a common metaphor which creeps into references to or descriptions of the experience of death; more than a metaphor, indeed, a physical description of what is seen – the darkness of the deathbed being suddenly illuminated by a great accession of light. 'May perpetual light shine upon them' – the famous ejaculation of the Christian burial service is the summation of much apparent experience. This real rather than intuitive human knowledge of the moment of death, while fragmentary, crops up again and again, and I suspect it springs, at least in part, from those who not only came close to death but actually, in a clinical sense, were dead, then recovered. Such resuscitations are by no means rare and are not as carefully recorded as one would like. However, Professor Freddie Ayer, the philosopher, whose attitude to death I have already referred to, left a detailed description of his experience. He says that, unlike David Hume, whom he much admired, as a man as well as a confirmed atheist, he himself was not at all anxious to go when the moment came and is convinced 'that I made an effort to prolong my life'. However, having as it were crossed over the River Styx, what happened next was 'very vivid'. He wrote:

> I was confronted by a red light, exceedingly bright, and also very painful even when I turned away from it. I was aware that this light was responsible for the government of the universe. Among its ministers were two creatures who had been put in charge of space. These ministers periodically inspected space and had recently carried out an inspection. They had, however, failed to do their work properly, with the result that space, like a badly fitting jigsaw puzzle, was slightly out of joint. A further consequence was that the laws of nature had ceased to function as they should. I felt that it was up to me to put things right.

Ayer's description then continues and we need not follow him into the trackless intricacies of Newtonian and Einsteinian astrophysics, of which Freddie, I suspect, had an imperfect knowledge, but which figured in his death-experience. It occurs to me that much of it, which was very characteristic of the Freddie we knew, was in fact a dream which signified that the death-moment was past and immediately preceded his recovery of consciousness. But the red light experience is another matter. Ayer himself compared it to the description of a friend of his, who had a heart-stoppage similar to his own, and who also remembered a powerful and intense red light, together with the feeling that she must stay close to it or follow it.

A woman in her early forties recently told me of her experience as a sixteen-year-old, when she had an acute attack of a rare form of colitis and was given up for dead. Indeed, she firmly believes she was dead for a short time. She told me:

> I was in this tunnel, with a very powerful, intense light at the end, which seemed to be beckoning me, and I moved towards it up or along the tunnel. I was with my grandmother, who held my hand. I was not anxious to retrace my steps at all, but on the contrary wanted to approach the light, which was getting nearer. Then my grandmother told me I must proceed no further but must leave her, and she released my hand and told me to go back along the tunnel, which I was most reluctant to do. Some time later I began to recover consciousness, and when I became fully awake, I was told that my grandmother had died whilst I was insensible.

This woman said she had recently come across a collection, printed in America, called *Resuscitations*, which described a variety of death-experiences undergone by men and women, and children, who had been in some way restored to life. Without exception, all referred to the bright light – intense, even painful as in Ayer's experience, but never hostile. It was invariably the central fact in their memory of the experience.

Can this be the 'kindly light' which, in Newman's great poem, leads us 'amid the encircling gloom' from this life to the next? That is something we shall all discover for ourselves one day. In a way it is a comforting fact that death, the greatest of all mysteries, is also one which will be clarified for each and every one of us. Or is it a comforting fact? And is the light necessarily kindly? For one thing which we tend to forget in our present times, but which our forebears did not forget, is that death itself is not the experience we have to fear most. It is the judgment that follows death. That, too, is a matter of blinding light, and I will now try to examine it.

CHAPTER 13

Dies Irae: the Day of Wrath

It is clear, if one accepts the existence of God and the idea of the next life at all, that we are living not in a static or cyclical or repetitive process, but in a dynamic and historical one, proceeding inexorably from the beginning to the end of time. In this historical process, the Day of Judgment is the greatest of all events, the culminating event, indeed, in the whole of history. It is a day of transcendental importance for each and every one of us, for it settles what is to be our fate through all eternity. Odd, then, that we hear so little about this dread day now, we who are so loquacious about our 'rights' in this world, whose expectations are so minutely examined in the media, so endlessly debated in congresses and parliaments. Even more than death, the judgment ahead is pushed to one side, treated as though it can conveniently be forgotten. Let sleeping judgments lie, is our motto today. Even in religious circles, it is not much talked about now. It is a long time since I heard a sermon on the Last Judgment.

It was not always thus. On the north side of Venice, rather by itself and not much visited, is one of the city's greatest treasures, Sta Maria dell'Orto. It has an ancient image of the Virgin, originally in a neighbouring garden, which is said to have worked miracles, and which is now in the church. Hence its name, although the original dedication was to St Christopher, whose statue is over the central portico of the West Front. The church was first built in the twelfth century and was much frequented by sailors who lived nearby on the *Fondimenta dei Mori*, and who needed St Christopher to come to their aid at sea. But it was extensively rebuilt in the fifteenth century in the characteristic Venetian Gothic style, the traceries of the windows being rich and quaint, and the white marble decorations and statuary admirable, pretty and elegant. It is one of my favourite Venetian churches and some ten years ago I did a careful drawing of its West Front, which turned out to be a success, and which hangs near me as I write this book. The church was also the favourite, as I discovered, of Tintoretto, who lived nearby for the last twenty years of his life and is buried in it. Inside are four major works by the master, *The Worship of the Golden Calf, The Presentation of the Virgin, St Agnes Raising Licinius to Life* and *The Last Judgment.*

All these works were beautifully restored, in the years 1968– 72, by funds supplied from the United Kingdom Italian Art and Archives Restoration Fund. But it is *The Last Judgment* which stands out, as John Ruskin discovered when he first visited the church. He recorded his impressions of the painting in the second volume of *Modern Painters*, and even by Ruskin's standards, his presentation is memorable:

By Tintoretto only has this unimaginable event [the Last Judgment] been grappled with in all its Verity; not typically nor symbolically, but as they may see it who shall not sleep, but be changed. Only one traditional circumstance he has received, with Dante and Michelangelo, the Boat of the Condemned; but the impetuosity of his mind burst out even in the adoption of this image; he has not stopped at the scowling ferryman of the one, nor at the sweeping blow and demon dragging of the other, but, seized Hylas-like by the limbs, and tearing up the earth in his agony, the victim is dashed into his destruction; nor is the sluggish Lethe, nor the fiery lake, that bears the cursed vessel, but the oceans of the earth and the waters of the firmament gathered into one white, ghastly cataract; the river of the Wrath of God, roaring down into the gulf where the world has been melted with its fervent heat, choked with the ruins of nations, and the limbs of its corpses tossed out of its whirling, like waterwheels. Bat-like, out of the holes and caverns and shadows of the earth, the bones gather, and the clay heaps heave, rattling and adhering into half-kneaded anatomies, that crawl, and startle, and struggle up among the putrid weeds, with the clay clinging to their clotted hair, and their heavy eyes sealed by the earth darkness yet, like his of old who went his way unseeing to the Siloan Pool; shaking off one by one the dreams of the prison-house, hardly hearing the clangour of the trumpets of the armies of God, blinded yet more, as they awake, by the white light of the new Heaven, until the great vortex of the four winds bears up their bodies to the judgement-seat; the Firmament is all full of them, a very dust of human souls, that drifts, and floats, and falls into the interminable, inevitable light; the bright clouds are darkened with them as with thick snow, currents of atom life in the arteries of heaven, now soaring up slowly, and higher and higher still, till the eye and the thought can follow no farther, borne up, wingless, by their inward faith and by the angel power invisible, now hurled in countless drifts of horror before the breath of their condemnation.

A careful scrutiny of this amazing work of art shows that the fine passage by Ruskin is in no way hyperbolic or exaggerated, but merely puts into striking words what our eyes can see and what Tintoretto imagined into painted forms. The Last Judgment is indeed there, in all its horror and majesty.

The notion of the entire human race, past, present and to come, being summoned collectively into a gigantic scene of justice is certainly alarming as well as spectacular. It was always present, or perhaps I should say intermittently but frequently present, in the Christian mind, from the days of the early church, through the Dark and Middle Ages, into Early Modern times. Depictions of the Last Judgment were a challenge to painters and sculptors throughout, and eagerly accepted by them, relished indeed, as Tintoretto clearly relished his opportunity in Sta Maria dell'Orto. In many a *timpanum* at the entrance to a Christian church, we see Christ carved in stone, with the saved on his right and the damned on his left, and medieval man and woman were made well aware of what was coming to them – for good or ill – every time they entered the sacred edifice. Painters worked on an even greater scale, and far more explicitly. It may be, as Ruskin contended, that Tintoretto alone got the hair-raising essence of the event, but all had a try and some, at least, made the flesh creep and the spine tingle and the spirit quail. Amazing to think that we can now look at their efforts, in churches and museums, with such composure, with the interest merely of art connoisseurs and tourists!

Nor were Christians warned of the wrath to come solely in stone and paint. It so happens that the greatest of all medieval Latin poems, the *Dies Irae* (so-called from its opening words), deals with this topic, with a directness and simplicity but also with a power and authority which is overwhelming. There is no other medieval liturgical poem which comes anywhere near it. Its vigorous concision is remarkable. It reveals Latin, even the debased Latin of the monks, at its best, so that none of the translations, even those attempted by scholars and versifiers of real gifts, begins to work as well, or at all. Who wrote it? We do not know. The author was almost certainly a Franciscan of the mid-thirteenth century. When I was a boy he was said to be St Thomas of Celano, the earliest of St Francis's biographers, who also composed a description of St Francis's miracles – all in rhythmical prose. But this attribution has now been undermined, without the real author being found, in the annoying way scholars have. The poem is written in the first person, so it was probably not intended for liturgical use. But the big men of the church relished it, as well they might, and soon turned it into an important addition to the liturgy of the Mass. It was made a Sequence: that is, the passage sung or chanted or read when the priest is accompanied by thurifers and altar staff from the high altar to the pulpit, bearing the gospel of the day, so he can read it to the congregation. I believe that the *Dies Irae* was for a time said at all masses given in commemoration of the soul of a particular person, and for centuries it remained obligatory in all requiem masses. It was also mandatory on All Souls' Day, 2 November, which happens to be my birthday, so I became very attached to this poem and used to know it by heart.

The merit of the poem, it seems to me, lies not just in its wonderful directness and concision but in its balance. It does not disguise the horror and fear of the day. As it says, in the first verse, it is a Day of Wrath when the entire human race, all who have ever lived, are intended to tremble with fear, however virtuous they may have been and however sure they may think they are that they are not due to be cast aside for burning. A great judgment, a *lit de justice*, is meant to inspire awe in all those summoned to attend, whether they are put on trial or not. Thus did medieval villagers or townspeople cluster round the largest hall in the place, or take their apprehensive seats inside it, when a grand red-robed judge from Westminster Hall came on circuit to *oyer et terminer* – hear and dispose of – all outstanding litigation in the district. And thus, when I was a boy, did the entire school file into assembly, or whatever it was called, when the headmaster announced that, because of the enormities committed by certain depraved boys – whose guilt had been uncovered – he proposed to punish them publicly in front of all. We all felt foreboding and dread even though we knew that we, personally, were not going to get a thrashing. But on the Day of Judgment the fear and apprehension is not distilled in us vicariously: it is direct and personal, for all of us are to be tried, convicted or declared innocent. And all the evidence is public. The *Dies Irae* conveys this emotion brilliantly. But it is not intended just to frighten us. In its last verses the mood changes and a note of compassion and mercy intervenes, as the fearful soul begs for forgiveness and prays for eternal life. This note of hope and intercession, after the tremendous storm of wrath, is introduced with great skill and is wonderfully soothing, so that the reader emerges, as it were, purged and refreshed. The plain chant setting of this great poem – let alone the renderings by Mozart, Verdi and others – is medieval chanting at its best, so that singing the *Dies Irae* is one of the most satisfying experiences for ordinary churchgoers in the entire liturgy.

In recent years, I have begun to think about the Day of Judgment a lot, and often, and have reached certain tentative conclusions. Like Tintoretto, I do see it, or some of it, in visual terms, but I add a sound-track too, as no doubt Tintoretto would also, if it had been possible. The tremendous scenes enacted on his canvas must have generated a colossal amount of noise – earthquakes, 'cataracts and hurricanos', thunderbolts splitting rocks and entire nations disintegrating and disappearing into abysses, as well as the cries of the damned. In my vision, however, I concentrate on two things, one visual, one aural. The visual setting encompasses an almost infinite amount of space. I got the idea for this once while flying, when the giant airliner in which I was sitting, for some reason, went over 40,000 feet, a fact which was reported to us by the pilot. From the window it was possible to grasp the curvature of the earth, but what struck me most was the intense brilliance of the stratosphere, which seemed to be filled with blue-white light, like the rays of a gigantic diamond, and stretched for ever. At once I imagined this as the setting for Judgment Day, the last dawn of history, when a limitless stage is erected in the empyrean for the final confrontation between God and all mortals. The stage is pure and bright and empty, and it is at this point that sound enters. I imagine a trumpet-blast so piercing as to make the senses recoil in agony and fear, and which is so powerful that it reverberates and echoes across the entire oval of space which I glimpsed from the aircraft window. There is no hiding from the glittering space and no shielding one's ears from the trump of summons. So, slowly, the dead awake and the souls gather, but it is at this point that my vision, my imaginative projection of the Day of Wrath, falters.

What happens next, then, I can put together only from the relevant texts and others' imaginations, and I feel it is much more pedestrian. It is complicated by confusion, which no amount of theological head-scratching and holding-forth has ever quite dispersed, between the Particular Judgment and the General Judgment. Judgment Day is not a topic or issue in Judaism, so Jewish texts and commentary are unhelpful here. The idea of the judgment was first made specific by Jesus Christ himself, and it is very much a Christian doctrine. Indeed its complications are largely a Roman Catholic doctrine. So let us proceed. In St John's Gospel, Jesus is reported to have said: 'Marvel not at this: for the hour is coming, in the which all that are in the graves shall hear [my] voice. And shall come forth; they that have done good, unto the resurrection of life; and they that have done evil, unto the resurrection of damnation.' The scene is enlarged upon in St Matthew's Gospel, where Jesus says:

> When the Son of Man shall come in his glory, and all the holy angels with him, then shall he sit upon the throne of his glory. And before him shall be gathered all nations: and he shall separate them one from another, as a shepherd divideth his sheep from the goats: he shall set the sheep on the right hand, but the goats on the left. Then shall the King say unto them on his right hand, Come ye blessed of my Father, inherit the kingdom prepared for you from the foundation of the world! ... Then shall he say also unto them on the left hand, Depart from me ye cursed, into everlasting fire, prepared for the devil and his angels.

The chapter concludes: 'And these shall go away unto everlasting punishment: but the righteous into life eternal.'

Now it is clear that what Jesus Christ is talking about in both these passages is the General Judgment or the Last Judgment, which takes place at the end of the world and is immediately preceded by his Second Coming. But there is also the problem of what happens immediately to each one of us when we die. This too was alluded to by Jesus in St Luke's Gospel, when he has the Good Thief rebuke the malefactor who 'railed' against the Saviour, saying to him: 'Dost not thou fear God, seeing thou art in the same condemnation? And we indeed justly; for we receive the due reward of our deeds: but this man hath done nothing amiss. And he said unto Jesus, Lord remember me when thou comest into thy kingdom. And Jesus said unto him, Verily I say unto thee, Today thou shalt be with me in paradise.' The man was about to die and it was plain he had repented of his sins and, even in his agony, had summoned up the strength to see that Jesus was innocent and to proclaim it, and had been granted the gift of faith accordingly, so that he died in a state of grace. Hence in his case the Particular Judgment passed on him would immediately or 'today' elevate him to eternal life.

However, it might be that Jesus was granting a special grace to the man who hung crucified alongside him and said comforting words in Jesus's death-agony. It was not thought by many early theologians that this applied to the entire human race, though there is a hint that it does in the parable of Lazarus, the poor man, where both rich and poor men are immediately judged on dying. Other interpretations of the Last Judgment scenario have it that the dead lie in their graves until the Last Trump, when they are summoned to judgment, and come surging up from their sepulchres from all over the world and from throughout history, an amazing sight, which was what Tintoretto so vividly portrayed in the great painting Ruskin admired. A further possibility, which fits in neatly to the Catholic doctrine of Purgatory, is that between individual death and Last Judgement, the souls of the sinners not sufficiently wicked enough to go to Hell are taken to Purgatory, where they atone for their faults, until such time as they are expiated, when they move up to Heaven. Obviously some are in Purgatory much longer than others and may still be there when the Last Trump sounds. Equally, some have their purgatorial sentence cut as a result of prayers for the dead offered up on their behalf from earth, or indulgences which remit purgatorial punishment and which are won on their behalf by earthlings. But we are here in one of those intricate doctrinal complexities beloved of traditional Catholics like myself, but which cause offence and scandal to others, so I will leave the point. It is enough to say there is a possible gap between the Particular Judgment and the General Judgment which is filled in various ways.

This is not just a minor point of dogmatic theology either. The gap concerns everyone and is of interest to them. We want to know whether we shall know our fate immediately we die, or whether we will have to wait, and what will happen to us in the meantime. One answer, of course, and in a way it is the most logical answer, is that after death time does not exist – everything is in the immediate present, and 'time must have a stop', as Shakespeare puts it, for all. In that case the Particular Judgment and the General Judgment are simultaneous. But this is not, on the whole, the solution the theologians prefer. Some of the earlier ones, like St Justin, Tertullian and St Ambrose – the last normally a treasure-trove of good sense and orthodoxy – held that the gap was filled by the soul remaining asleep or enjoying partial suffering or happiness. The second Council of Lyons in 1274 supported the idea of a purification period. Then in 1336 in a bull called *Benedictus Deus*, Benedict XII laid down that the Particular Judgment took place immediately at death, admitting the soul either to Hell or Heaven or Purgatory. This was eventually confirmed by the Council of Florence in 1439 and, more authoritatively, by the Council of Trent in 1563, and so far as I can see has remained the agreed Catholic doctrine ever since. The new *Catholic Catechism* states: 'Each man [it says nothing about women] receives his eternal retribution in his immortal soul at the very moment of his death, in a particular judgment that refers his life to Christ: either entrance into the blessedness of heaven – through a purification or immediately – or immediate and everlasting damnation.'

According to Catholic teaching, then, Judgment Day is quite a complicated affair. Correction: it is an infinitely complicated affair, involving literally billions of people. In addition to the masses of souls involved, there is the added complication that they are divided into two main groups, each subdivided into three. The two main groups are those who have already been dealt with at their Particular Judgments, spread over thousands of years – or more: we do not know how long this world will last – and those still on earth when it comes to an end, whose Particular Judgment is telescoped into the General Judgment. Each group is further divided into those for Heaven, those for Hell and those for Purgatory. What is not immediately obvious, for instance, is whether those who have got to Heaven already will be summoned back to the judgment place to have their reward confirmed or will watch events from a sort of celestial balcony. And what of those already in Hell? Will they be driven up, screaming and swearing and smouldering, to be sentenced a second time, and then back into Hell again? Or will they watch the proceedings from afar, knowing the outcome anyway? One would like to think that those committed to Hell at the Particular Judgment and who may have been there thousands of years, in our time anyway, will finally have their perpetual sentence remitted at the Last Trump. But that is not what the church teaches. In any case, had they been destined for such a final fate, they would have been sent to Purgatory.

I have been writing about these events as though they actually take place in space, in a kind of vast amphitheatre, a sort of colossal judgmental saucer, thousands of miles across perhaps, yet such as everything can be seen in it. But the end of the world and the Second Coming mark the end of space as well as time, and it may be that all these visualisations are vain. On the other hand, a Last Judgment without some collective presence and some form of solemn tribunal, indeed some final separation of just and unjust which has to be *seen* as well as felt by each individual, would be almost a contradiction in terms and a non-event. It would lose much of its awe and terror if it could not in some way be perceived by the senses, albeit disembodied ones.

Moreover, the Last Judgment, as I understand it, is by its nature a public event, not a happening in the mind, even a happening in billions of minds. It is a final summation of history, a collective report on the human race and a general verdict on the results of God's decision to create the universe. For justice to be done, it must be seen to be done. The true nature of sin, its bottomless horror and depravity, has to be demonstrated for all to witness and appreciate, so that there remains not the smallest scintilla of doubt in any soul that sin demands retribution. Then there has to be a public and collective demonstration that God's sentencing is, indeed, just and that means the particular sins (and virtues) of each soul have to be displayed and examined, so that the verdict is seen to be inevitable in each case, and the equity of the sentence or reward endorsed by all. You may say: how can these things be? What – must we sit and watch a re-enactment of the Particular Judgment on each and every soul which has ever been attached to a body? If so, eternity has hidden terrors indeed! My answer is yes, and for two reasons. First, the entire life, including the concealed and inner life, of each man and woman must be made public, for there can be no secrets in the next life. We may forgive all or condemn all, but in any event we must know all. It may be shameful, on that day, to have all our hidden, mean and disgusting thoughts revealed to the entire human race, but that is part of their purgation and it may be that, once they are so revealed, they disappear as though they had never been, so that we enter Heaven – if we are fortunate – without a past. Second, it is essential that the collectivity of humankind must be assured of God's justice in each particular case, must bear witness to the evidence, the verdict and the consequences. All must be revealed – all.

Now I do not pretend to know how these things will actually happen. But I am satisfied they will happen. Without space or time or embodiment, all things are possible. We have to escape from the limitations of our human, worldly imaginations and put ourselves into an eternal framework in which numbers, distances, repetition, simultaneity and the perception of the senses mean absolutely nothing, at any rate in our terms. We have simply to assume that the intimate record of every human soul is made available to all on this Judgment Day and is absorbed by all, and that the judgments on all are endorsed by all.

One final point must be added, and it is a comforting one. In God's divine plan, it is not proposed that the Father himself, in his person as the Almighty Creator, infinite in all his perfections, shall himself carry out the acts of judgment. The notion of an all-perfect being, albeit he is an all-perceiving and all-understanding being, judging those who, by their nature – for which he is responsible – are imperfect and fallible and frail, somehow seems to run contrary to natural justice. So God the Father places his son, the Son of Man, in the judgment seat, and it is one who has dwelt on earth, who has undergone the limitations and weakness of a human *persona*, who has experienced the world, and who has suffered death himself, who accesses the evidence and delivers the verdicts and decides the rewards and punishments. On the Day of Judgment, it is Jesus Christ who is in charge.

This is made explicit and unambiguous in the New Testament. In Chapter 5 of St John's Gospel, when Jesus reveals the nature of his mission to the Apostles, and speaks of himself in the third person, he insists on his judicial role in words which cannot be open to any misconstruction. He says: 'For the Father judgeth no man, but hath committed all judgment unto the Son.' This is of set purpose, so that the judge be separated from the law-making Father, and reach his decision on the evidence. The text continues with Christ's frank admission: 'I can of mine own self do nothing: as I hear, I judge: and my judgment is just; because I seek not mine own will, but the will of the Father which hath sent me.'

That is clear enough. There is an element of humanity in this judgment of so many humans, for the judge is, or was, man as well as God. But in fact there may be more than this element of humanity. In another section of St John's Gospel, Jesus reminds his hearers that 'God sent not his son into the world to condemn the world; but that the world through him might be saved.' The Last Judgment is not so much delivering verdicts as confirming verdicts already reached in the heart of each individual. Jesus continues: 'And *this* [my italics] is the condemnation, that light is come into the world, and men loved darkness rather than light, because their deeds were evil. For every one that doeth evil hateth the light, neither cometh to the light, lest his deeds should be reproved. But he that doeth truth cometh to the light, that his deeds may be made manifest, that they were wrought in God.'

I say that this is a comforting doctrine, in one sense, because it suggests that, on Judgment Day, the sinners identify themselves, as indeed they have already done in this life by rejecting the light. By pursuing certain courses, while they have the choice, and exercising their free will to choose between good and evil, they are pre-empting both the Particular and the General Judgment. They are in fact condemning themselves. What makes the Last Judgment perfect judgment is the fact that, on top of everything else, it is self-judgment. And, since the punishment reflects the choice made, that too is self-imposed. But this does not make it any less dreadful.

CHAPTER 14

Does Hell exist, and what is going there like?

There has never been a time when I have not believed in the existence of Hell, though the frequency and extent to which I think about it has varied greatly. There are times when months pass without the thought of Hell so much as crossing my mind. There are other times when it looms large and baneful in my consciousness. These periods do not occur often, or last long, and they are usually ones of unhappiness and depression. I think the unconscious train of thought runs thus: 'If I am miserable now, how much worse off will I be if, by some catastrophe, I find myself in Hell, where horror is habitual, deliberate, systematic and eternal?'

In my childhood we talked often about Purgatory, which is an omnipresent, almost cheerful part of the furniture of belief in an old-fashioned Catholic household. We assumed none of us was perfect; that all, when we died, would be unfit to enter Heaven directly; but that all would get there eventually, and in the meantime would have to spend some time in Purgatory, atoning for our sins, stripping and purging ourselves of the remaining integuments of evil, and thus becoming purified and fit to enter the presence of God. So Purgatory was a virtually certain fact we had to face. We did not know how long we would be there. Among our acquaintance we counted no saints, let alone martyrs, who would see God the instant of death, and be invited to sit by his side. But we knew good, old people, usually women, who had led long-suffering lives which they had borne with stoicism and cheerfulness. My mother would say of such a one, when she died: 'Well, *she* is not long for purgatory, that is sure.' But it was never quite discussed how long the rest of us would have to be there.

What we did know, and acted upon, was the system of indulgences, some partial, some plenary, which could be secured, for ourselves and those already dead, to mitigate and shorten purgatorial pain, by prayers and good works in this world. I will not go into the mechanics of indulgences because I know nothing is more calculated to irritate and even disgust those not brought up as Catholics. Moreover, I do not think they are important. The notion of the indulgence is very old. But the cult itself is a late-medieval creation, whose abuses sprang from the need of the church to raise huge sums of money to build the great cathedrals. York Minster, for instance, which is the largest medieval cathedral in England and contains one of the most remarkable collections of medieval stained glass in the world, could not have been built without the sale of indulgences. The same is true of many other European cathedrals built or rebuilt in the fourteenth, fifteenth and early sixteenth centuries. We revere and use these vast structures now for what they are: objects of beauty and holy places which testify to the faith of men and women and the goodness and glory of God. And if it was part of God's plan that they should have been constructed, in part, with the coinage of ecclesiastical corruption, who are we to object?

However that may be, I do not believe the mechanics of indulgences now matter. What I was taught to believe, and do believe, is a much simpler doctrine: that we can all earn remission of our time in Purgatory by prayer and good works; and, more important, that our prayers and acts of goodness can help those already in Purgatory – relations, friends, unknown but deserving souls – by the workings of some celestial system of exchange. When I was a small boy, and in pain because of a fall or cut or toothache, my mother would say to me: 'Offer it up to the souls in Purgatory.' And what was meant has always seemed to me perfectly credible: that our willing acceptance of the pains which God, in his infinite wisdom, inflicts on us in this world – our submission to them without complaint or anger – carries merit in the next; and that we can use this merit either to remit our own purgatorial pain, or to buy remission for others.

Praying, helping the souls in Purgatory, has always carried with me a powerful visual image. I recall seeing an old print of a prison whose upper windows, though barred, opened to the world. The poor prisoners, who were ill-fed, perhaps starving, could lower a basket through the bars, and good folk passing in the street could put into the basket coins or bread or clothing, which would then be precariously raised and snatched through the bars. This procedure was common in medieval prisons, where there were no funds to feed the inmates, and I have always seen praying for those in Purgatory as an analogy. I do so pray, every day of my life; and when I leave this world, I hope others will pray for me.

We were, then, all pretty sure that we would spend time in Purgatory – probably a long time, though we had no idea how long. We did not believe we would go to Hell, for the simple reason that we did not feel we were wicked enough, or in a sense important enough. Hell was for those who were not just evil but evil on a large and imposing scale – Hitlers, Stalins, those featured in the newspapers as murderers, people who were famously or notoriously evil. It did not seem to me that little people, ordinary men, women and children, who failed to attract much notice and whose misdoings, though undoubtedly sinful, were of no public consequence, would find themselves in Hell. Or, if they did, I could not imagine seeing them there.

Now this is not good doctrine, as I now understand it. But the doctrine of Hell has always been uncertain, obscure and difficult to grasp, at least in some respects. To begin with, it is a doctrine with a definite history. In the New Testament it is already in full and flaming existence: an eternal place of darkness and fire, a furnace, a lake of fire, a bottomless pit, a place of outer darkness inhabited by the devil and his demons, where there is endless weeping and torment (Matthew 13:42, 50; 25:41, 45; Mark 3:29; St Paul: Romans 2:5, 2 Thessalonians 1:9; Revelations 9:1, 11; 14:10–11, 21:8 and so on). In the Old Testament, however, particularly in its earlier books, Hell as we understand it – a place where the wicked are punished eternally – did not seem to exist. The Hebrew word *Sheol* usually meant the grave, the death-pit, the place where the departed went. All went there, irrespective of merit, to the world below, where reigned gloom, darkness, decay, weariness and silence, a place remote from God. To the primitive Hebrews, the mark of happiness was life itself, the object was to enjoy it, to stay alive, and death was a defeat.

The Egyptians seem to have been the first people to develop a specific doctrine of survival after death, followed in time with the concept of an individual judgment, a literal 'weighing of souls' on a huge scale or balance, with the good enjoying eternal life and those who failed perishing in some definitive manner. It was from this idea that the Hebrews drew their notion of separate divisions in Sheol for the good and the evil. The first Hell in people's minds may have been an actual place. On the south side of Jerusalem there was a fearful valley, abominated by the Jews as a one-time centre of idolatrous worship of the god Moloch, whose wrath was appeased by the burnt offering of children (2 Chronicles 28:3, 33:6). The fires of Moloch were replaced, in the time of Josiah, by perpetually smouldering garbage dumps, which consumed the filth of Jerusalem and the bones of dead men (1 Kings 23:10–14). All but the most menial municipal workers avoided the place, but its fires could be seen by night from the city. To this horrible place, familiar to all Jerusalem, was added the equally real but more remote vision of underground fires, known to most Hebrews only by hearsay, but confirmed by many travellers' tales. These were endlessly burning seepages from the great underground reservoirs of crude oil, between the rivers Tigris and Euphrates, in what we now call Iraq.

In the post-canonical Hebrew literature, produced after the Old Testament itself, Jerusalem's abominated Valley of Himmon, as it was called, was married to the oil fires to fashion the theology of Hell, as a perpetual fiery underground, beneath the earth just as Heaven was above the skies, where the wicked were endlessly incinerated. This Hell was real as well as awful, and it appears fully developed, specific and urgent, in the teachings of Christ. Christ is quite clear that the wicked would be judged and find themselves in Hell, a place of horrific punishment, for ever. The term Himmon becomes, in the Greek transliteration of the New Testament, Gehenna (Matthew 5:22, 29, 30; 10:28; 18:9; 23:15, 33, etc.).

Hell as a developed doctrine, a fiercely detailed belief, is therefore only as old as Christianity. It acquired many visual and doctrinal accretions in the Dark and Middle Ages and was probably at its most vivid on the eve of the Reformation. But the odd thing about Hell is that man, by which of course I mean essentially European man, is tremendously imaginative and industrious in depicting Hell and elaborating its horrors, and also remarkably insouciant in carrying on living, and sinning. Late-medieval men and women were confronted everywhere with paintings and sculptures and writings presenting the tortures of Hell in the most hair-raising detail, and at one level everyone certainly believed in what they were taught and shown. But it did not seem to make much difference to what people actually did. Nor do we hear of people having nightmares about Hell or developing neuroses or pathological conditions because they feared it. In a way, Hell was tamed simply because its images became so much part of life, were so familiar to young and old, rich and poor. What would the preacher have done without Hell? More – what would the artist? Hell is the core of Dante's imaginative universe. *L'Inferno* is clearly what he most enjoyed writing, just as we most enjoy reading it; *Il Purgatorio* is less interesting; *Il Paradiso*, by comparison, tedious, unmemorable. It is the scenes of the inferno, and the conversation with those Dante and Virgil meet there, which cling to the memory.

Again, it is impossible to examine the *oeuvre* of Hieronymus Bosch without thinking: how this great artist loved Hell – and how impoverished his work would have been without it! Some forty-eight of his paintings have survived. Most of them, and all the best, deal with the question of Hell and its inhabitants. Bosch must have spent countless hours thinking about Hell and elaborating its visual images in his mind, before even putting his brush to the board. He loved Hell – it was his work, his life, his creative universe – and though he set about depicting it as a place of horror, which would produce in those who studied it revulsion and the desire to repent while there was still time, he also made it a place of beauty of colour and form, of scintillating detail and ingenuity. All nature is there, metamorphosed into evil, and the birds, though creatures of doom, sing in their trees, the fishes swim in the lake-pits, all the weird half-humans, animals and devils display extraordinary energy and delight in their death-life. His lakes of evil and exploding cities of doom and fire are so exciting, the colours so exquisite, the eye is so irresistibly drawn into the picture, to dwell there on its fascinating details, that I wonder how many errant souls were actually frightened by Bosch into a better life.

Yet we have to accept that Hell was a deterrent. Every greedy medieval merchant, however hardened in avarice, every proud and cruel Renaissance prince, who stormed cities for his glory and put his enemies to the sword and torture, every lady of fashion who flaunted her body and lent her ear to tempting voices – all these ready and repetitive sinners must have paused, from time to time, and considered that Hell was waiting for them too. Medieval paintings and sculptures of Hell were particularly careful to show the rich, the well-born and the beautiful being plunged into the pit, and prodded and taunted by demons. Thanks to Hell, and its ubiquitous presentation by artists, a mighty man would often think twice before doing something he knew to be wrong. Or, as he grew older, and the possibility of Hell grew nearer, he would set about making amends to those he had wronged. However rich or educated or sophisticated, medieval men and women could not get out of their minds that Hell might, very likely did, exist, exactly as the preachers said.

Certainly when the doctrine of Hell went into its long historical decline, from the seventeenth century onwards, those who studied the facts of crime and evil felt its waning power was significant. In England, for instance, the century following the 'Glorious Revolution' of 1688, which sanctified property as the basis of political life and introduced a long period of internal peace, also witnessed an extraordinary expansion of the number of statutory crimes carrying the death penalty, from 50 to almost 200. There was a similar development in America. This sprang from the well-founded belief among the ruling class that the idea of eternal punishment was no longer an effective deterrent. Hence, as Hell-fire died down, the gallows would have to rise from its ashes.

Some sought to keep the fires stoked up, however, believing that it is better for men and women – and children – to be scared from wickedness by the fear of Hell, than that the state should be forced to bring into existence an immense apparatus of police and prisons and courts to achieve the same effect by secular means. I have a feeling that they are right, and that belief in punishment to come is more effective in keeping most people in awe and sobriety than the clumsy, undiscriminating and frequently unjust arm of the law. However that may be, the cooling of eternal fires was (and is) a fact. It is charted in D. P. Walker's brilliant book *The Decline of Hell* (London 1964). By the closing decades of the eighteenth century, among educated people at least, the notion of

Hell-fire already evoked scepticism and even distaste; and forceful assertion of the pristine doctrine was received with uneasiness. James Boswell gives a vivid account of a discussion between Dr Samuel Johnson, then aged 75, and Dr Adams, head of Pembroke College, and others, which took place in Oxford in 1784:

> *Dr Johnson*: '... as I cannot be *sure* that I have fulfilled the conditions on which salvation is granted, I am afraid that I may be one of those who shall be damned' (looking dismally). *Dr Adams*: 'What do you mean by damned?' *Johnson* (passionately and loudly): 'Sent to Hell, Sir, and punished everlastingly.' *Dr Adams*: 'I don't believe that doctrine.' *Johnson*: 'Hold, Sir: do you believe that some will be punished at all?' *Dr Adams*: 'Being excluded from Heaven will be a punishment; yet there may be no great positive suffering.' *Johnson*: 'Well, Sir; but if you admit any degree of punishment, there is an end of your argument for infinite goodness simply considered; for infinite goodness would inflict no punishment whatever. There is not infinite goodness physically considered; morally, there is.' *Boswell*: 'But may not a man attain to such a degree of hope as not to be uneasy from the fear of death?' *Johnson*: 'A man may have such a degree of hope as to keep him quiet. You see I am not quiet, from the vehemence with which I talk; but I do not despair.' *Mrs Adams*: 'You seem, Sir, to forget the merits of our Redeemer.' *Johnson*: 'Madame, I do not forget the merits of my Redeemer; but my Redeemer has said he will set some on his right hand, and some on his left.' He was in gloomy agitation, and said: 'I'll have no more on't.'

This little snatch of discussion shows an age when many people were already pushing Hell to the backs of their minds, and discounting or minimising it when the topic was raised.

Dr Johnson was unusually courageous in seeing the necessity for eternal punishment and being willing to confront it in his own life and mind. He was not the only one. Clever and learned men have continued to regard Hell as a fact and faced its implications. Samuel Taylor Coleridge argued, for example, that Hell was a necessary consequence of free will. In his *Biographia Literaria* he asserts: 'Man cannot be a moral human being without having had the choice of good and evil, and he cannot choose good without being able to choose evil.' If man deliberately chose evil, he was unfit for the presence of God. So the doctrine of Heaven necessarily implied the existence of an alternative. Coleridge, like

Johnson, was happy to consider as probable the Catholic doctrine of Purgatory – he argued that it had a more positive effect on morality than the stark Protestant alternative of Hell/Heaven. He thought it possible that, in the event, no one would actually go to Hell and was willing to argue this from scripture. But that there could be and was such a state as Hell he was sure, because he felt he had had a horrific glimpse of it through his opium addiction. And Hell and the infinite goodness of God could co-exist, as he knew from his experiences:

> I feel, with an intensity unfathomable by words, my utter nothingness, impotence and worthlessness, in and for myself – I have learnt *what* a sin is against an infinite imperishable Being, such as is the Soul of Man – I have had more than a glimpse of what is meant by Death and utter Darkness, and the Worm that dieth not – and that all the Hell of the Reprobate is no more inconsistent with the Love of God, than the Blindness of one who has occasioned loathsome and guilty Diseases to eat out his eyes, is inconsistent with the Light of the Sun. (Letter to Joseph Cottle, 27 May 1814)

Coleridge, being a poet possessed of the most wonderful imagination, as well as an addict who had undergone hellish experiences, perceived that the reality of Hell was far more likely to resemble, perhaps in yet more fearsome form, the agonies of the addict, compounded of guilt, remorse and sheer terror, as well as physical suffering, than the somewhat mechanical penology of traditional Christian writers and preachers. He thought the Hell-fire approach unimaginative, in the deepest sense, and often ineffective. For many, its very crudeness hindered acceptance of the existence of Hell. For others, it suggested that Hell was too monstrous a place to apply to them.

But of course most ministers of religion are not poets, or even skilled versifiers. They are fairly ordinary, not particularly well-educated, earnest and anxious men, labouring in a sinful world to bring home to vast, ignorant congregations the reality of sin, the inevitability of death, and the risk of eternal punishment. So they reach for their fiery adjectives and metaphors and word-pictures. In the mid-eighteenth century, struggling against the rising waters of indifference, cynicism and the secular Enlightenment, St Alphonsus Liguori (1696–1787) set about bringing Hell firmly before people's minds again. He was a well-born lawyer who turned to religious life comparatively late, aged thirty, and went on to found the Redemptorist Congregation, which special-ised in devotional and moral theology and preaching to the masses. His own books dealt with eternal punishment in detail. Thus, in *The Eternal Truth: Preparation for Death*, he stressed the importance of fire in Hell:

> the unhappy wretch will be surrounded by fire like wood in a furnace. He will find an abyss of fire below, an abyss above, and an abyss on every side. If he touches, if he sees, if he breathes, he touches, he sees, he breathes only fire. He will be in fire like a fish in water. This fire will not only surround the damned, but it will enter into his bowels to torment him. His body will become all fire; so that the bowels within him will burn, his heart will burn in his bosom, his brains in his head, his blood in his veins, even the marrow in his bones: each reprobate will in himself become a furnace of fire.

Liguori's Redemptorists created a tradition of putting the horrors of Hell before the public. They became particularly expert at preaching Hell-fire to children. In Victorian times, a Redemptorist father called the Revd Joseph Furniss started a mission for children in 1847, preaching the need for repentance before Hell's gates closed and reinforcing his sermons with tracts. He was particularly anxious to remind children that they might die at any time, as indeed was only too true in those days, and that an unconfessed mortal sin would be fatal to their eternal chances. He was a showman. On the evening before he preached his big Hell sermon, he would encourage a large attendance by saying:

> My dear children, we are going to make a long journey tomorrow. We are all going out of the church. We are going to see something very wonderful. Be in good time, or you will be too late, and you won't be able to go – you will be left behind.

He took them, in fact, on a journey down to Hell, in the steps, as it were, of Dante. In his sermon, and in his accompanying tract, *Sight of Hell*, he placed the scene of torment in the middle of the earth. The damned are themselves fiery objects:

> The fire burns through every bone and every muscle. Every nerve is

trembling and quivering with the sharp fire. The fire rages inside the skull, it shoots through the eyes, it drops through the ears, it roars in the throat as it roars up a chimney.

Furniss's Hell was also provided with six dungeons, each with different forms of fiery torture – a burning press, a deep pit, a red-hot floor, a boiling kettle, a red-hot coffin and a red-hot oven. In the last he drew the picture of a tormented child:

> The little child is in the red-hot oven. Hear how it screams to come out; see how it turns and twists itself about in the fire. It beats its head against the roof of the oven. It stamps its little feet upon the floor ... God was very good to this little child. Very likely God saw it would get worse and worse and never repent and so it would have been punished more severely in Hell. So God in His mercy called it out of the world in early childhood.

The Redemptorists were still going strong in my youth, and still specialising in bring Hell-fire to boys. That is why I dwell on their role – they are old friends of mine. When I was at Stonyhurst, between the ages of twelve and seventeen, we had an extra weekly sermon on the evenings of the Wednesdays in Lent, filing into what was called the Boys' Chapel after supper. The sermons on the last four Wednesdays in Lent (school did not break up until Holy Saturday, the day before Easter Sunday) were eschatological, dealing in turn with Death, Judgment, Hell and Heaven. The Jesuits were a little ambivalent about eschatology, and especially about stressing the pains of Hell. They thought it necessary to warn, perhaps even to alarm, boys already capable of fearful sins, about the risks of impenitence. But they were not prepared to do such vulgar work themselves. So they called in the Redemptorists. Each year, an expert Redemptorist Hell-fire sermoniser was invited to the school to give the four eschatological sermons. This was a shrewd move. If a preacher went too far, and a boy complained to his parents that he had been frightened, and the parents complained to the school, the Jesuits could blame the Redemptorists. In fact no boy so far as I know ever complained. Considering they were an extra service, the sermons were remarkably popular. We boys thought of them as out-of-the-ordinary, unsubtle perhaps but vivid, even entertaining in the same way as a horror-movie.

Of course, we were frightened, or perhaps impressed is a better word, especially by the third sermon on Hell. That evening, special confessionals were kept open after the service, so no boy need go to bed with an unconfessed mortal sin and fear dying during the night. My last Lent at school I congratulated the Redemptorist after his Hell sermon and asked him what it felt like to deliver it. He was a grizzled veteran and visibly pleased by my praise.

> Oh, it's my job, you know. I do my best. I have heard better Hell sermons – old Father Fitzgerald you know, God rest his soul, he was a real scorcher. He made the hairs stand on your head. But I do my best. I don't consider I've succeeded unless there are at least three rows of boys waiting to make their confessions afterwards. Sometimes I get four. Two is disappointing.

These sermons were similar to those so vividly described by James Joyce in his *Portrait of the Artist as a Young Man*. I reacted to them in the same way as Joyce; initially impressed, but the images soon faded. It is exactly as Coleridge said: the stress on Hell-fire somehow persuades the hearer that Hell does not apply to him. The more vividly the mechanical tortures are described, the more remote and irrelevant Hell seems. These terrible images, implanted on the tender mind of a teenager, ought by all the laws of Freud to have left permanent scars. In my case, at least, they left nothing – no more than my reading of Mary Shelley's *Frankenstein* or Bram Stoker's *Dracula*. I was much more frightened by M. R. James's *Ghost Stories of an Antiquary*, which I recall reading one Lent at school. The subtleties of James's fear-inducing tricks, and the skilful way in which he used his profound academic knowledge of ancient documents and buildings to convey authenticity, made me shiver at the time, and I still hesitate before reading one of his stories even today. But the Hell of the Redemptorists produced no lasting impression on me.

Far more telling is the approach of John Henry Newman, in my judgment. Newman was a poet, a superb journalist, a showman, as well as a theologian of intense and sinuous subtlety. He writes like an angel; he ravishes you with his power over the language. I know of nothing which comes closer, in imagination, to the moment of death, and to the conflicting feelings of pain and hope – and apprehension – of a departing soul, than Newman's great poem, *The Dream of Gerontius*. The effect is deepened and heightened by the superb musical setting provided by Sir Edward Elgar, another Catholic, though a much more disturbed one than Newman. I imagine, or at least I hope, that my own death will have something in common with Gerontius's, and I am preparing for it with Newman's words, and Elgar's music, as guides.

Not that Newman was eager to inspire more hope and comfort than he thought wise. He was always anxious to stress, in his sermons and writings, how easy it is for educated men (not women: he knew little of them and seems rarely to have them in mind when dealing with serious topics) to be over-confident about eternity. He disapproved of crude Hell-fire sermons if only because they encouraged the sophisticated to dismiss the entire business of Hell as childish nonsense. Thus, Newman argued, they led men to imperil their souls because Hell was, and is, far from nonsense but a terrible reality and, properly presented and understood, an intensely plausible reality too. Newman was particularly concerned by the anguish of a soul who, reasonably well meaning in life, though careless and sinful – not a monster of sin but a fallible human being – dies unshriven and discovers too late that the rules which precipitate men into Hell are horribly clear and inflexible. The soul, appalled and mortified by his sudden realisation he is damned, protests. Newman described this in a powerful sermon, printed in his *Discourses to Mixed Congregations*:

Oh, what a moment for the poor soul, when it comes to itself, and finds itself suddenly before the judgment seat of Christ! Oh what a moment, when breathless with the journey and dizzy with the brightness, and overwhelmed with the strangeness of what is happening to him, and unable to realise where he is, the sinner hears the voice of the accusing spirit, bringing up all the sins of his past life, which he has forgotten or which he has explained away, which he would not allow to be sins, though he suspected that they were ... And, oh! still more terrible, still more distressing, when the Judge speaks and consigns it to the jailors, till it shall pay the endless debt which lies against it! And the poor soul struggles and wrestles in the grasp of the mighty demon which has hold of it, and whose every touch is torment. 'Oh, atrocious!' it shrieks in agony, and in anger too, as if the very keenness of its affliction were proof of its injustice. 'A second! and a third! I can bear no more! Stop, horrible fiend, give over; I am a man and not such as thou, I have not on me the smell of fire, nor the taint of the charnel house ... I know what human feelings are; I have been taught religion; I have a conscience; I have a cultivated mind; I am well versed in science and art ...

Newman's point is potent: a soul suddenly taken from his or her civilised, sophisticated existence by death and poised on the brink of the pit, or huddled with other souls in one of its grubby antechambers, is conscious first of a loss of status and dignity. The shock of being treated like countless other tarnished and damaged creatures, black, white, coloured, young, old, dirty and diseased, cursing and blaspheming or simply howling in strange tongues, the congealed, quivering mass of naked humanity, suddenly placed on a footing of total equality one with another, is profound and horrifying. The soul's realisation that it is not dreaming, that its life on earth has gone, irrevocably, and that it is now on its own, without friends, relations, possessions or claims to importance of any kind and, not least, that it is totally unfree, at the bidding of strange, unknown authorities, is still more disturbing. Many self-important people experienced a similar loss, in the turmoils of wartime Europe, when the elaborate, secure ant-hill of the pre-war world was suddenly stamped into total ruins and dust by vast armies, and the concentration camps yawned. A man first finding himself, naked, ordered about, in a concentration camp would have an inkling of what Hell is. Or, in present-day life, a man going into a centre for treatment of an addiction – drugs, alcohol, over-eating, etc. – will have a similar inkling of his insignificance and of the degradation of Hell. A duke who was treated for alcoholism in such a clinic told me:

I was quite prepared for a spartan life, and to be bossed around, but the humiliations came as a shock. It was made plain to me I was nobody, nothing, just a mess, a nuisance, someone without rights of any kind, who deserved nothing but contempt and would be lucky if he got a kind word. They kept saying, 'You're not a duke here, you know' – though in fact I had made no attempt to say I was. The first night, I cried myself to sleep, like a child in his first term at boarding school.

The addiction clinic, where the physical pains of withdrawal are combined with shame and degradation and utter loneliness, to

impose almost unbearable misery on the inmate, is a hint of Hell. But no more than a hint. In human life, the ability of those at the bottom of the heap to create tiny fragments of happiness for themselves is, fortunately, infinite. In a concentration camp, in a tent-city of displaced persons, in an addiction clinic, once the utter humiliation is accepted, and the fact of an equality of misery adjusted to, the human spirit reasserts its capacity to squeeze enjoyment out of life. Above all, friendships spring up, in the most unlikely manner, between the most incongruous people. With each friend, misery is halved; with two it is quartered – and then the positive merits of friendly co-operation in mitigating the harshness of life make themselves felt. Within a week, the crushed human plant is reviving strongly, hope is returning, the future no longer seems unbearable.

But it is here, of course, that the analogy fails, for there is no adjustment to Hell, no friendship, no co-operation, nothing but hatred. Jean-Paul Sartre, a much spoiled only child who hated the proximity of other demanding bodies even at the best of times (unless they were abjectly obedient young girls, and even then he wanted them near only until his desire was satisfied), portrayed Hell in his play *Huis clos* as 'other people'. It is not the demons who are to be feared most, but the other lost souls, with their bitter reproaches and recriminations, their increasingly hostile presence. George Eliot, perhaps optimistically, thought that human heroism and courage was so great that damned souls could cling to and comfort each other 'even in the fiery whirlwind of Hell'. Well: she may be right – who can say? But I fear not. I suspect it is of the nature of Hell that it brings out the worst in every person who is there, and that the mutual antagonisms increase with time.

Moreover, there is one more all-important aspect in which the analogy with the concentration camp or the addiction clinic fails – the positive, never-ending torment of the loss of God. All the writers on Hell, even those who stress the physical torments, like St Alphonsus Liguori, agree that the pain of loss is the central suffering of Hell, the one besides which all the others pale. It is only in Hell, irrevocably condemned to exist there for eternity, that the soul grasps the infinite goodness and beauty of God; and the realisation that it has, of its own wilful volition, rejected God, is the sharpest pain of all. It is only in Hell, too, that the soul appreciates, for the first time, the sheer enormity of evil, as a reality and as a principle, and sees how it exists as the opposite polarity to God, and so begins to understand the vertiginous nature of the choice it has made by opting for sin. This is a pain beyond mitigation, the sharpness of which must grow with time, or with the passage of what serves for time in Hell.

Yet there is a problem here, and I will try to tackle it. The soul described by Newman, the type of person we have been portraying here, finding himself in Hell, is not one who has deliberately, consciously and in full knowledge of the implications, opted against God and for evil. He is a soul who finds himself, as it were, in Hell by mistake. It is all a colossal misunderstanding! If he had known what Hell really was – if he had been sure of its awful existence – he would not have sinned at all, or at least would not have sinned so much. This sinner is a mixed-up person, ill-informed, inattentive, weak, silly, vain perhaps and shallow, but not a monster. He is not someone who, given the choice, would deliberately choose evil in preference for good. Other things being equal – and they rarely are equal when there is temptation – he is on the side of the angels. Of course, he should have listened more, and prayed more, and exerted himself more on the side of goodness, and sinned less and been less selfish and silly and weak. But surely he is not Hell-fodder, not a person or soul for whom evil and Godlessness are the natural environment?

In implying that such a soul could find itself irrevocably damned in Hell, I suspect Newman is reverting to his Protestant background, which was not without Evangelical overtones – a background which accepted an absolute choice between Heaven and Hell, and rejected Purgatory as a Romish superstition. Of course, as a Catholic, Newman fully accepted the doctrine of Purgatory, and indeed could not have written *The Dream of Gerontius* without Purgatory in mind. But so anxious was he, notably in the sermon from which I have just quoted, to stress the enormity of sin, that he was liable to slip back into his Protestant absolutes, and shovel the poor second-rate sinner into the pit, forgetting that Purgatory was made precisely for such as him.

I suspect, following this line of argument, that Hell is not for the weak, but for the strong. To become Hell-fodder, a soul must have a pronounced and ineradicable streak of arrogance, a con-viction that his or her judgment is infallible. I was taught as a child, and I still believe, that we cannot be certain that any one particular human creature has ever been sent to Hell, and that it is wrong to assert that anyone, however irredeemably wicked he or she may appear, is now in Hell. We cannot say Hitler is there, or Stalin, or Mao Tse-tung, though together they were responsible for the deaths of about 40 million people, as well as countless other crimes against God and humankind. But if anyone in particular is there, such men are likely candidates.

The first inhabitants of Hell, and still its gaolers, the 'trusties', the equivalent of the professional criminals who, in Stalin's Gulag, were allowed to bully, torture and work to death the vast numbers of helpless political prisoners, were Satan and his angels. Satan tried to set himself on a par with his creator, God himself, by demanding an equality of judgment and command. He recruited followers, rebelled, and was overwhelmed and driven to Hell by the loyal angels. His sin was the capital one of pride, an active arrogance which made him think he, like God, had the capacity and right to judge between good and evil. He himself defined justice and injustice, thus trying to seize a moral power which belongs to God alone. The crime of Satan is echoed in those who construct for themselves, in political and state terms, systems of morality which they, not God, lay down. Thus Lenin, in insisting that inhabitants of the Soviet Union must follow what he called 'the Revolutionary Conscience', as opposed to the natural con-science implanted in human beings by divine power, was guilty of this Satan-like sin. So was Hitler, when he ordered all Germans to obey 'the higher law of the Party', as opposed to the traditional moral doctrines they were taught at home and in the churches.

However, we must not suppose that totalitarian leaders alone are the archetype of Hell's denizens. The archetype, rather, is anyone who, driven by pride in their own power or skill, their own beauty or genius, their own unaided intellect, abrogates to themselves a Godlike role. The road to Hell is paved by self-apotheosis. I suspect, therefore, that men and women of out-standing intellect and gifts are peculiarly liable to the temptations which make human Hell-fodder. Those who find themselves in Hell – if anyone does – will include painters and composers and writers and philosophers as well as dictators and tyrants. A man, like Beethoven, who saw himself, through the sublimity of his work, as an intermediary between God and man, was walking close to the precipice. So was Tolstoy, whose idea of his own moral righteousness and importance led him, at times, to see himself – as a friend put it – as 'God's elder brother'. Picasso, in his old age, fancied himself as an art-god, a painter endowed not just with skill and intelligence and the mastery which comes of a lifetime's application to his art, but as a special being, capable of transmuting by his divine magic base materials like paints and canvas, bronze and stone, clay and paper, into manifestations of the numinous. Here was a case of pride, fed by many decades of universal flattery, taking a frail moral being to the very brink of eternal damnation.

Matisse was a similar case. Having completed the chapel he had designed and decorated in the South of France, he showed and explained his work to two nuns, a prioress and a simple sister whom he had known for many years. The prioress thanked him for devoting so much time and genius to the glory of God. Matisse replied: 'But I did it all for myself.' The sister, shocked, said: 'But *Maître*, when you were still at work, you told me you were doing it for Almighty God.' Matisse replied calmly: 'I am God.' Was he serious? Did he believe what he was saying? Art, no less than politics, carries with it a whiff of sulphur, the stench of the charnel-house. All men and women of exceptional will and achievement, whose work brings them close to or across the normal limits of human capacity, are at risk of the Divine Temptation. This is a form of moral madness which can all too easily become incurable, irreversible, permanent, and therefore makes those who succumb to it natural inhabitants of an anti-Heaven where they can play out their fantasies for all eternity.

Hell must be an awesome place not so much because of its fires, whether real or metaphorical, but because of its deluded occupants. St Thomas Aquinas, in his *Summa Theologica*, indicates that the blessed in Heaven derive satisfaction from the plight of the damned. This observation has shocked many people because they understand it to mean that the sufferings of Hell constitute one of the pleasures of the saved, as if happy souls parade on a sort of celestial balcony to watch the devils prodding and incinerating the damned down below. That is, in fact, exactly as some fifteenth-century Flemish and Italian painters presented the scene. But Aquinas was making a different point. He was saying that, in Heaven, the righteous see, not just through a mirror, darkly, but face to face, the two contrasting systems of good and evil: the one they inhabit and which they have chosen by their free will, and its counterpart, the system of God-denying absolute evil, equally inhabited by those who have freely chosen it and where they, the damned – and this is the point of the image – are just as at home as the blessed in Heaven. Here we come close to solving the mystery of Hell. Hell is not just other people. It is something which those who find themselves there have helped to construct. It is not so much the prison of the damned as their chosen domicile.

But if Hell is for the strong in evil, rather than the weak in flesh, we cannot be certain that we – the weak majority – are never in peril of it. Pride, which takes innumerable forms and burns strongly in the hearts of all of us, can never be entirely discounted as a possible moral detonator which can cause an explosion in our soul. St Jerome says that pride lies in wait for us, like a great beast in the desert, a mountain lion or puma, which springs on us when we least expect it and crushes our living conscience beneath its dreadful claws and fangs. Drugged by, imprisoned in, our pride we sleep-walk towards the pit. The only safeguard is perpetual watchfulness, a constant asking of ourselves the question: 'Is what I am doing my will, or God's?' We should ask this every morning and every evening, and at moments of great activity and decisiveness, and we must be content only with a strictly honest answer. If we cannot truthfully say we are doing, or trying to do, God's business, then Hell for us is not an academic question, but a dreadful possibility, even perhaps an imminent one. There can be no peace of mind for us on the subject of eternal damnation without a total submission to God's will. The point was made by Dante seven centuries ago and it remains true: the road to peace lies over the dead body of our egos.

However, we must not assume that, if we escape Hell – and perhaps all of will escape it – Heaven is at our command. The process of purgation awaits, for virtually all of us. We know, among our own acquaintance, people whom we can genuinely pronounce to be 'good' – whom we are sure will be saved if anyone is – whom we admire and perhaps seek to imitate. But are any perfect? Can we honestly say that they have no faults of character or performance but, on the contrary, are totally committed to doing what is right, in all circumstances? I know of no such person: I wish I did, because then I would be the acquaintance, even perhaps the friend, of a saint, and so possess a model for my own life. That there are such saints, living, visible, I do not doubt, but experience and history show them to be rare. All the rest of us must be purified at our entrance to the next world so that we become worthy of it, are ready for it, and are capable of enjoying its infinite blessing to the full.

Purgation of evil, purification to be fit for the sight of God – not in the abstract but in the overwhelming reality of his radiance – is thus a positive, creative process. But I have no doubt it is a painful one and a long one. Only at the moment of death and the entrance to eternity do we become fully aware of the sheer enormity of sin. In the horror and relief of that moment we will willingly submit to the ordeal of purgation, an ordeal perhaps incomparably more severe than anything we have had to suffer in this life, but redeemed by one comforting certitude: that it will end and that, when it does, we will be truly ready for God. At that stage, the knowledge we are not destined for Hell – which we will then be conscious of in all its fearful reality – will be our overwhelming comfort. But let us make no mistake about the agony of purification. Imagine being sentenced to the dark heart of the Gulag for the equivalent of hundreds, perhaps thousands, of years. That is why we must always pray for the poor souls in Purgatory, and hope that one day there will be people praying for us.

CHAPTER 15

The timeless world waiting

It may be true, as some believe, that the efforts of foolish theologians to frighten sinners by dwelling on the physical pains and unquenchable fires of Hell are counter-productive and cause the more sophisticated to lose their faith altogether. I rather doubt it, because the more sophisticated a person is, the more likely he or she will grasp that Hell-fire merely represents a failure of imagination, and that there are far more dreadful terrors with which to punish us if the supreme being is minded to do so. I believe, on the contrary, that the notion of eternal or at least inconceivably harsh punishment is if anything a buttress of faith, for human beings believe in retribution and want the wicked of this world to be dealt with adequately in the next. No one ever lost his or her faith by rejecting the idea of Hell. And Hell is still, albeit to a more limited extent than in the old days, a deterrent to sinners. I know of one beautiful and fashionable lady who is prevented from deceiving her husband and taking lovers almost entirely because she fears she will be sent to Hell if she does.

No; it is far more likely, in my opinion, that faith is eroded or diminished – perhaps even fatally undermined – by our lamentable failure to make the rewards of Heaven seem real and worth having. Heaven, as presented by the Judeo-Christian tradition, lacks genuine incentive. Indeed, it lacks definition of any kind. It is the great hole in theology. Even St Paul, usually so brilliant a writer, so wonderfully adept at getting us excited about the facts and mysteries of faith, fails us here, and falls into flatulence: 'no eye has seen, nor ear heard, nor the heart of man conceived, what God has prepared for those that love him'. That is no better, you may think, than Lear's imprecise threat: 'I shall do such things – as yet I know not – as 'twill be the terror of the earth.' Heaven is a case of words fail us. And not just words, ideas too. Where Milton confessed himself at a loss, who can expect to do better? Certainly not T. S. Eliot, a fine poet of strong imagination, who admitted he did not know how to make Heaven interesting.

The danger is that inability to conjure up some convincing and appealing notion of Heaven ends by casting doubt on its very existence. The pagans seem to have had no such difficulty. We are all familiar with Olympus – the mountain itself, the marble ante-chambers and throne-rooms and gardens and pools of this sporting-place of the gods. We know all about Valhalla too, how it was built and what happened to it. But these are just lath-and-plaster things, stage-scenery. Heaven is difficult to describe precisely because it is real, rather than a twopence-coloured projection of our childish imaginations. It was St Cyprian, I think, who coined the phrase 'the Beatific Vision', and summed up the delights of Heaven as the final unveiling of the invisible: 'How great will be your glory and happiness', he wrote, 'to be allowed to see God, to be honoured with sharing the joy of salvation and eternal light with Christ your Lord and God ... to delight in the joy of immortality in the Kingdom of Heaven with the righteous and God's friends.' But that does not get us very far either. The new *Catholic Catechism*, normally so impressive, has no fresh ideas. Its definition is: 'Heaven is the ultimate end and fulfilment of the deepest human longings, the state of supreme, definitive happiness.' A little desperate, it falls back on quoting St Cyprian and, worse, dragging up that tired old bull of Pope Benedict XII, *Benedictus Deus*, which begins with the off-putting formula: 'By virtue of our apostolic authority, we define the following', and then produces something which reads as though it was drafted by a celestial lawyer, and tells us nothing at all. Finally, the *Catechism* admits that 'This mystery of blessed communion with God' is 'beyond all understanding and description'. But if we cannot describe it and, even if we could, cannot understand it, how do we know we want it? It is all rather like the investment opportunity offered during the eighteenth-century South Sea Bubble, whose promoter invited the public to subscribe immediately to 'Something Wonderful, the Nature of which shall Shortly Be Revealed'.

It may be that, when we think of horrors, our imaginations are sharp and precise, but that when asked to describe what we want most of all, we become vague and dream-like and vaporous. There is something disturbingly imprecise even about the word 'Heaven' itself. I am not referring to the Hellenistic nonsense of the seven heavens, though many in the early church, including St Paul, seemed to have swallowed it for want of anything better. What I mean, rather, is that the church did not seem to be sure whether the word meant the sky, which we can more or less see, or something beyond and above the sky, which is invisible. God is often presented as being 'above Heaven' and St Paul, in his letter to the Ephesians, tells us that Christ, since his Ascension, reigns supreme with the Father 'far above all heavens'.

In fact if we look closely at the ancient texts in both the Old and New Testaments, references to Heaven are more about moving into it or down from it, rather than actually being there, or what it consists of. The Jews and early Christians could visualise the dynamics of transferring from this world to the next, but what was actually there when you got to it was beyond them. At the risk of appearing blasphemous, it is all rather like Jack and the Beanstalk: the beanstalk itself is real and vivid, but what is at the top of it is much less precise, or interesting. So these writers, and the artists who followed their scripts, concentrated more on the actual process of getting up to Heaven or down from it, than on the place. Their starting-point was what happened to Elijah, when he was swept up to Heaven in a whirlwind, and what happened to Jesus Christ, when he ascended to Heaven under his own power. The ancients were anxious to distinguish clearly between these two events. St Bede, in his commentary on the Acts of the Apostles, insists that Elijah merely went up into the sky, while Christ went much further, into Heaven itself. This squares with a Jewish legend that Elijah did not go exactly to Heaven, but to somewhere in its close vicinity. St Gregory the Great also takes this line, but adds that Elijah was not self-propelled, and the birds and the airstream which carried him could not get beyond a certain point, whereas Christ, being a living autogyro, could ascend as far as he wished.

From the earliest times right up to the end of the sixteenth century, artists were fascinated by the act of ascension, for obvious visual reasons, and allowed it to divert their attention from Heaven itself. They went to considerable pains to recreate the actual experiences of the Apostles, who saw Christ levitate himself up into the heavens and out of sight. But whereas early Christian artists from the oriental tradition, mainly in Syria and Palestine, take a static view, presenting the Ascension as already accomplished, with Christ seated passively in Heaven and the Apostles worshipping him from below, in the more dynamic Western tradition, Christ tends to move upwards, with the Apostles following his ascent with their eyes.

In a famous essay published in 1943, *The Image of the Disappearing Christ*, the art historian Meyer Shapiro drew attention to a remarkable artistic innovation which appeared in England around the year 1000. In this novel presentation, only the legs or feet of Christ were represented, the rest of his body disappearing into the clouds. The artist obviously wanted to show Christ from the angle of vision of the Apostles at the precise moment when he began to disappear – the visual heart of the miracle, as it were. Shapiro describes this English artistic invention as 'astonishingly precocious', since it is a step forward from the illusionism of the ancient world and 'goes beyond the most advanced naturalistic classical representation of ascension and disappearance'. It foreshadows the artistic innovations of the Renaissance, introduced by masters like Mantegna. Shapiro traced the source of this innovation to a tenth-century text, in Old English, called the *Blickling Homilies*, which includes a sermon on the Ascension. The key passage, in translation, reads:

> The cloud [as described in the Acts of the Apostles] did not make its appearance there, because our Lord had need of the cloud's aid at the Ascension; nor did the cloud raise him up, but he took the cloud before him, since he hath all creatures in his hand, and by his divine power and by his eternal wisdom, according to his will, he orders and disposes all things. And he, in the cloud, disappeared from their sight and ascended into Heaven, as a sign that from thence in like manner he will on Doomsday again come to earth in a cloud, with hosts of angels.

The writer, and following him the English artists of the early eleventh century, were clearly anxious to make a point which to them was important, and we may well think it important too when we understand it. Unlike earlier writers, both Jewish and Christian, and their attendant artists, who presented the heroes of these ascents as travelling *on* clouds, which thus became a species of vehicle on whose support and propulsion they are dependent, this novel presentation depicts Christ, who is all-powerful and independent of nature, ascending *through* clouds. He may, in this and other depictions of his ascending to Heaven and descending to judge, carry the cloud around with him, as a visual aid, but he does not need it in any way – he is 'above the clouds' both literally and figuratively.

These Dark Age English writers and artists were, in fact, struggling to cope with the theological truth that Heaven is both everywhere and nowhere. They had to think of Heaven as 'above' – where else could they put it, seeking as they were to give it definite existence in the minds of their congregations? – but they knew it was not material even in the sense that an insubstantial cloud was material. I have noticed that Michelangelo, in his presentation of the divine reality in the wall and vault of the Sistine Chapel, similarly fights shy of giving Heaven visible substance, and he makes it clear that Christ is not in any way anchored in or dependent upon physical objects or scenery. There is in fact no heavenly scenery. Christ is shown in the act of descending from Heaven (not revealed) in order to carry out judgment, and it is almost as if the artist is relieved he can present him thus, as it spares him the duty of depicting a place which he knows is beyond the powers of his imagination. The reader may wonder why I dwell on such points. But it is important to remember that these artists – in Michelangelo's case one of the very greatest of artists – devoted an enormous amount of time and effort to thinking about these things, much more than we would dream of doing. They racked their brains to make every episode in the whole story of the Old and New Testaments as vivid and real as they could achieve. That was their job, and though they were conscious of their skills and anxious to demonstrate them for the sake of their art and reputations, the spiritual urge to do God's work through their brushes was also strong. So they felt they had to get it right or, if that was beyond them, avoid the problem by concentrating on other aspects where they could tell the truth. Hence Michelangelo, who was so solid and three-dimensional in all his forms when he knew exactly what he was doing, becomes vague and insubstantial the nearer he gets to Heaven.

What of the artists who did try to come to grips with Paradise?

They are few in number, and the closer we examine their work, the less we find. We have already noted the reluctance of Hieronymus Bosch, who so lovingly and so often depicted Hell, to get involved with Heaven. We know very little about Bosch. We do not know when he was born, who his teachers were, or his friends and patrons, or what led him to create the extraordinary kind of art in which he delighted. So we can only speculate on why he preferred Hell to Heaven. But one reason, surely, was that he discovered by experiment, as many other artists have done, that it is less difficult and much more satisfying to depict suffering than ecstasy. We have all suffered. Few of us have experienced ecstasy. Suffering has a human face, but ecstasy, especially at its most intense, is superhuman or even non-human.

Yet Bosch, like all artists, loved contrasts, and he knew that he could make his Hell more real by depicting opposites or alternatives. In this great triptych in the Prado of Madrid, known variously as *The Garden of Delights* or the *Millennium*, he gets as close to Paradise as he feels able. The right panel is Hell, but the central one, twice its size, shows the Earthly Paradise in enormous detail, and the left-hand one actually takes us right into the Garden of Eden, whose scenery and inhabitants are presented as a background to the figure of Christ presenting the newly created Eve to Adam. The whole of this masterpiece was subjected to intense scrutiny over decades by the Berlin art historian Wilhelm Fraenger, who produced evidence that its symbolism and iconography, and its most vivid episodes, reflected Bosch's membership of a sectarian group known as the Community of the Free Spirit, which flourished on the eve of the Reformation. That need not concern us. What also emerges from this huge and rich painting is Bosch's inability, try as he may, to depict perfection, or even unalloyed happiness. In the Garden of Eden, Christ radiates serenity, Eve is submissive and humble, and Bosch has succeeded in making Adam appear quite innocent. But even in Eden we are shown some vicious encounters between predatory animals. Some unpleasant specimens, especially of savage bird-life, are seen disporting in a circular pond at the bottom of the panel, and engaging in beak-to-beak battles over fish. From the pool formed by the Fountain of Life, disgusting reptilian creatures are plodding ashore to begin a career of uncleanly depredations. The distant scenery, which seems to be coming to vicious life too, is not reassuring at all.

When we move to the central millenarian panel, Bosch provides us with innumerable examples of pleasures being enjoyed, usually of the grosser sort however, and the depravities and excesses make an early appearance, leading in turn to the production of monstrous forms of a life-threatening kind, and a growing air of hysteria. Like most artists, I imagine that Bosch worked from left to right, laying down his design thus, then painting it in accordingly, and one feels his enthusiasm for the project increasing as he moves towards the inferno on the right. The topography of the right-hand side of the central panel is marked by a disagreeable-looking owl sitting on the head of a multi-limbed human, by some sinister creeping shellfish, of giant size, making their appearance and, above all, by what appears to be a gigantic floating bomb or mine, with detonators sticking out, which has drifted ashore in the top right-hand corner. When Bosch finally reaches the right-hand panel and Hell, he is hard put to it to create contrasting horrors, but he works with a will and succeeds in producing some of his most spine-tingling effects, including a revolting amorous pig dressed as an abbess, a musical Hell in which the harps, bagpipes, viols and so forth have become instruments of torture and execution, and, not least, at the top of the panel, a vivid scene of the entire world in flames as a result of what appears to have been a thermo-nuclear explosion – the evil bomb in the central panel having, presumably, gone off. In short, Heaven seems very far away.

However, I never expected much help from Bosch. What is more disappointing is that artists whom we feel are much closer by temperament to the beatific vision also seem unable to get to grips with Heaven as a fact. William Blake, more so perhaps than any medieval or Renaissance or Baroque artist, was fond of depicting God the Father, who makes innumerable appearances throughout Blake's *oeuvre*. But the Father is always shown doing things – gesturing to Job, throwing out Satan, presenting his Son, and so forth, never in repose in his own habitat. Heaven itself is missing, or touched upon only in the most fragmentary and tantalising way. This is curious, for Blake was accustomed, as he claimed, to seeing visions of all kinds, of kings and famous men and women in history, as well as sacred personages, and then setting them down in line and colour. Why, then, did he have no proper vision of Heaven, so that he could show it to us with his matchless pencil? We do not know. But the fact is I have examined all 1,193 plates in Martin Butler's comprehensive catalogue of William Blake's works and I am none the wiser about his ideas on Heaven.

Caspar David Friedrich, whom one would have thought of as a likely visionary source for the heavenly landscape, also lets us down. His immensities and solitudes, enthralling though they are, are worldly or perhaps other-worldly, but not heavenly. They are mystic, but sad, not ecstatic. He attempts a vision of Christianity, with a mystic cathedral ascending into Heaven, but that is not the same thing. John Martin is the only considerable painter of the romantic epoch who rises to the challenge, not once but twice. Both in *The Plains of Heaven* and *The Celestial City and River of Bliss* he tackles the problem of depicting the topography of Heaven head-on and on the largest possible scale to permit the maximum detail. *The Celestial City*, which is privately owned but was exhibited in a St James's gallery in 1975, where I was able to examine it, is nearly six-and-a-half feet long by four feet high. *The Plains of Heaven* is even bigger, being ten feet by six, but is unfortunately in the Tate Gallery and therefore rarely if ever on display, space having to be found for piles of bricks, rubbish-sculpture and other important masterpieces of modern art. The two paintings are similar: vast landscapes ending in low mountains and bordered by forests of cedars and similar trees, with misty clouds and tranquil lakes and pools occupying the saucers thus formed. Fairy-like figures rest gracefully on the edges of these waters, and in *The Celestial City* a flying angel transports a newly arrived human to join the heavenly throng. All this is decorous and even pleasing, but it is not imaginative and, in the end, is unhelpful. Martin's visions of God's wrath and of Babylonian cities being riven by lightning or consumed by fire or engulfed by rising floods are much more exciting. But what can you expect? Any Hollywood director will tell you that it is the disaster movies which are box-office. Whoever in his or her sense invested money in an epic about Heaven?

The difficulty, I expect, is that our imaginations are inhibited not merely by the limitations of space, from which we cannot escape, but by the less obvious but even more severe limitations of time. If we sit down to think about Heaven, one obvious approach is to say to ourselves: 'When was I most happy? When did I experience the most complete and intense feelings of delight? Cannot I conceive of an experience where these feelings are enormously enhanced and prolonged indefinitely? That will give me some inkling of Heaven.' Not long ago I heard a simple Carmelite friar preach a sermon on Heaven in which he adopted this technique, laboriously going through the most agreeable sensual pleasures he had experienced, all delightfully innocent, to be sure – swallowing a fresh mango, looking out over the plains of Tuscany from a Florentine tower, listening to Mozart's *Don Giovanni* – and then multiplying them. But all these delights, however intense, are fleeting or terminate themselves by their very nature. They are time-bound. Less fastidious people than the friar would instance sexual orgasm as the most intense pleasure to be had on earth. Might not that be, enormously enhanced, an indication of the kind of voluptuous enjoyment we experience in Heaven? But a sexual orgasm, by definition, is a happening, an episode: it has a beginning and an end. However prolonged, it is not a state.

Our recollections of happiness are glimpses. They have much to do with our age, our state of mind, our expectations, our innocence even. I have a perfect visual memory of one such moment, part real, part reconstruction. It is Paris, at a warm, clear spring noontime in the early 1950s. I am twenty-one or so, and with my newly acquired red-haired Breton mistress. We are on the Left Bank and have just sat down at a table at the Café des Deux Magots, on the corner of the Place Saint-Germain-des-Prés, on the terrace outside, with the old church opposite. At a neighbouring table, Jean-Paul Sartre has just ventured out from his nearby apartment, and has sat down and ordered himself a glass of whisky. Soon he is joined by Simone de Beauvoir and, miraculously, by his former friend Albert Camus, now reconciled, and not yet killed in a car crash. André Malraux, with his exquisite daughter Florence, gestures defiantly from another table. At a third, François Mauriac sits in front of an austere *Infusion de menthe*, composing his weekly *Bloc-notes* for the back page of *L'Express*. Juliette Greco is there, looking as if she will burst into song at any moment, so beautiful is the weather, but actually settling down to a long, cool *pastis*. And suddenly there is a flurry, as the young Brigitte Bardot, still a schoolgirl, though a precocious one, scampers in swinging her satchel and twirling the elastic of her panama hat on one rosy finger ... So it goes on, perfect in retrospect – no waiting or overcrowding, no anger or argument, no drunkenness or *ennui*, no hangovers, sex in anticipation but not in its gross actuality, elevated or at any rate sophisticated conversation, a magic moment indefinitely prolonged. But how could such a tableau be prolonged? It is destroyed by time as surely as any other sensual or even intellectual pleasure. And not only does all human pleasure fade, it tends to bring retribution too. What can be more innocent than the happy laughter of children? What can be more inevitable, as the laughter rises to fever-pitch, than that there will be, as the old nannies said, tears before bedtime?

It is only when we escape from time, as well as space, that we can possibly begin to imagine what Heaven will be like. When astronauts are being trained for trips into space, one of the things they have to learn is to cope with weightlessness. Coping with timelessness is far more difficult. In fact we would not know how to start. The very word 'start' is time-bound. We and our bodies are more thoroughly prisoners of time than we are held captive by space. We can move now at will on this earth – and will soon move about space with comparative freedom – but we cannot get out of the time dimension at all. Even when we have the peculiar experience of flying West and appearing to gain hours – or even if we cross the Pacific capturing a whole extra day – it is always taken away from us in the end. It it an illusion that we can escape from time, even for an instant, in this world. Yet that is precisely the first thing we do when we enter the next, and therein lies the huge difference and the chief obstacle to imagining it. No satiation, no culmination, no climax, no boredom, no repetition, no expectation or recollection, no delay or waiting, no sense of time passing, nothing impending or imminent or changing – just one timeless instant of total ecstasy.

Well, that is the best I can do and it is not enough. I am not so sure, on reflection, that we should try to imagine the pleasures of Heaven at all. In all probability, the essence of Heaven lies not in receiving pleasure but in giving it. Just as God created the universe from and for love, so Heaven is its culminating fulfilment and is the place of love, where love is given in its plenitude. God gives us all his love and for the first time we are in a position to receive it fully and undiluted. But, at the same time, purged of all imperfections and human limitation, we can reciprocate that love with something of his own power and intensity. We are become vessels of love, and in that instant of loving reciprocation we acquire the ecstasy which is timeless and eternal.

Let me add a footnote to this clumsy analysis. We may not be able to imagine eternal life. But we can pray that, in some way, we can become worthy of it, ready for it, capable of experiencing it. I have said little about prayer in this survey so far. But in the many perplexities of dogmatic and moral theology, some of which I have tried to sort out, prayer is the invariable solace. It does not necessarily solve problems, but it always makes them easier to bear. It rarely dispels the darkness, but it creates a small corner of light on the gloomiest occasions. It is the one thing I have found in life which never fails completely, and it is time to say something about it.

CHAPTER 16

Talking to the God we do not know and cannot prove exists

This is the most important chapter in my book. We may not be able to begin to understand God. We may not even be able to believe in him. We may be confused by the mysteries, contradictions and improbabilities of faith, and unable to unravel them in our minds. But we can all pray. It is the one resource that can never be taken away from us except by the total collapse of our minds. We may be impotent, penniless, in prison, bound hand and foot, stricken in all our limbs, unable to move, blindfold and gagged. But we can still pray. It is the last weapon of the weak, the starving, the helpless, the puzzled, the unsure.

Yet, in its own way, it is the most powerful weapon of all. What is prayer? When we pray to God there are things, each of huge importance, implicit in our action. First, there is the acknowledgment that God, albeit all-powerful and creator of the universe, is not an impersonal force or source of energy or colossal agent of nature, but is an actual being, who can be addressed in a meaningful way. Prayer is directed to a personal God, who receives it and listens to it – and who may answer it. Second, prayer reflects the fact that our relationship with this personal, receptive God, who hears what we have to say, is itself direct and personal, not mediated by a hierarchy or filtered through an institution or relayed by an interpreter, but one-to-one, always. It is an amazing thought that, of all the powerful people in the universe, protected by banks of security guards and secretaries and personal assistants and scrambler telephones and ex-directory numbers and protocol, the one who is master of them all is totally, instantly and invariably accessible. Just occasionally, when one is struggling to get through to a high functionary or at least to make sure a request is put to him or her, the protective screen, as it were, breaks down and the great personage picks up the phone him or herself: 'Yes – what is it?' It happened to me once with a prime minister. But with God it happens all the time. Many years ago, I was discussing Papal Infallibility with a Jesuit. 'I see,' said I, 'you mean that the Pope has a private line to God?' 'No,' said this Jesuit, 'we all have a private line to God.'

In one respect this is indeed true. The conversation may be one-way. We may speak and God may choose not to answer at the time; or his answer may be incomprehensible to us, ambiguous, enigmatic. But we can be certain that he hears. This is one reason I say that prayer is the resource of all. If someone says to me, 'I don't believe in God – so how can I pray to him?', I reply, 'That does not follow at all. You may not believe in God, but that does not prevent God believing in you. God's existence is independent of your believing in him.' So it makes very good sense for the unbeliever to pray for faith, just as it makes sense for the believer to pray for more faith, as I constantly do. In a way, the prayer for faith is the purest form of prayer. 'Lord, I believe; help thou mine unbelief.' Moreover, it is well to remember that those without faith, but who nevertheless pray for it, are praying for the greatest gift of all. Faith in God is the most precious possession any of us can have, especially if it is strong and healthy and exuberant. With faith all things are possible, but without it all other possessions are ultimately meaningless. So to pray for faith is the most ambitious of all prayers – you are asking God to give you the key to everything else. It makes sense, then, that those who should pray hardest are precisely the agnostics and atheists and doubters. Thus I encourage them, usually not to much purpose. But sometimes one listens.

So God hears all of us. But he may not answer. Then we must pray again. Persistence in prayer is of the essence of supplication. Primitive human beings soon discovered this and it was characteristic of the first civilisations. All the earliest prayers and litanies from the Ancient Near East are repetitive and designed to be said often. I suppose men and women learned very early that their own rulers and great people had to be petitioned again and again before they responded. So they were prepared to accept that prayer might be a long-term undertaking. When the Ancient Egyptians transferred the dead from the right bank of the Nile, the land of the living, to the left bank, where the dead were buried in their

tombs and pyramids, they set up prayer temples immediately
bordering the river. If the dead man was important enough, these
tomb-temples were served by resident priests. In any event services
were conducted at dawn and dusk, and prayers were said on behalf
of the dead man. These activities were endowed and in some cases
went on for hundreds of years, the same prayers being recited
daily, until some kind of misfortune, usually the collapse of that
particular epoch and the dissolution of the kingdom into chaos –
known in Egyptian history as an Intermediate Period – broke
the continuity of prayer, never to be resumed. In Europe similar
Christian endowments from the Middle Ages persisted for long
periods too, until Reformation, revolution, war or pillage frus-
trated the intentions of the pious. Often the endowments continue to be enjoyed, but the intentions and prayers are neglected.
In Oxford and Cambridge, atheist dons fill their bellies with
the good things the munificence of the college founders make
possible, while saying no corresponding prayers for their ben-
efactors' souls. But sometimes the practice survives all vicissitudes:
King Henry VI of England was not a fortunate monarch in his
own time, but the scholars of Eton College continue to pray for
the man responsible for their foundation, half a millennium after
his death. That is persistence in prayer.

We all know that it sometimes works too. When I was a small
boy, in the 1930s, all the Catholics of England, and I think in
most countries of the world, said some prayers every Sunday, after
Mass, for 'the Conversion of Russia', by which was meant the
overthrow of the Soviet Communist regime and the return to the
free practice of religion there. Nothing happened, year after year,
and decade after decade. I never had any doubt that these prayers
would eventually be answered, just as I had no doubt, at a purely
secular level of conviction, that the odious and evil Soviet regime
would eventually be destroyed, or destroy itself. And so it happened in dramatic form at the end of the 1980s, and nearly three-
quarters of a century of prayer were eventually answered. You may
say: the Soviet Union would have collapsed anyway. But we do
not know that, and we certainly do not know that it would have
collapsed so soon.

The world of antiquity understood the value of repetition and
persistence in prayer. Every request is a form of prayer, if it be

made decently and honourably, and the first prayer recorded in the Old Testament is the prayer of Abraham to God to spare Sodom and Gomorrah. Abraham asks God to spare the Cities of the Plain if enough righteous men are found there, and the prayer is notable for its persistence and repetition – Abraham first sets the viable figure at fifty, then forty-five, then forty, then twenty, and finally ten. This first prayer was not a formal prayer, but was made on the spur of the moment in response to God's angry intimation that he had punitive plans for the cities. But it had many of the characteristics of a set prayer and that is why the authors of Genesis put it down as they did.

However, among the Ancient Hebrews prayers soon attained permanent form and became, as it were, universal prayers as opposed to particular ones, though they continued to have nuggets of particular history buried in them. The best of them were the form of musical poetry known as psalmody, the psalms employing the Ancient Hebrew poetic device known as parallelism, though they are not strictly speaking in metre, or if they are we have not yet identified it. Parallelism is well suited to prayer because it involves an element of repetition. It is of the kind of speech-protocol suitable when addressing a great personage. Thus, synonymous parallelism simply repeats the same thought in slightly different words – 'Hear my crying O God: Give ear unto my prayer.' In antithetical parallelism, the first 'member' is contrasted with the second: 'A merry heart doth good like a medicine: But a broken spirit drieth the bones.' Then there is synthetic parallelism, in which the first member is developed by a second, similar thought, or a third. Thus: 'The kings of the earth stand up: And the rulers take counsel together: Against the Lord and against his Anointed.' There are further variations of this device, identified by scholars as climactic, introverted, stair-like and emblematic parallelisms, but all of them have the prayer-like characteristic of repetition.

I am going into this detail because the psalms are so important – and beautiful. They are perfect prayers. Considering the oldest of them were probably written well over 3,000 years ago, it is remarkable how many still resonate so powerfully, how many echoes they still find in our hearts, so that we can say or sing them to God in all sincerity, although the circumstances which

originally drew them from anguished Hebrew breasts have long
since passed away. There are human permanences of hope and
despair, sorrow and anger, love, laughter and tears in these ancient
prayers which will endure as long as our race.

There are 150 psalms, divided into five groups. Internal evidence
of different groupings indicates that these 150 were selected from
a larger, probably much larger, number. They are the best, or were
thought to be the best. Those who compiled the Hebrew Masoretic
Text of the Old Testament evidently believed that they were all
composed by King David. So did St Ambrose and St Augustine,
great theologians and scholars and judicious men not easily taken
in by pious nonsense. On the other hand, St Jerome, a closer
student of the Bible than either, refused to believe it and so, many
centuries later, did Jean Calvin, who was a keen man for the
psalms and made them the centrepiece, almost, of his approved
liturgy. It seems evident now that they were composed by a
number of authors at different dates. But some are clearly very
ancient and could have been written under the first monarchs of
Israel and even by David himself. He was a most remarkable man
by any standards, not only a great leader and warrior, but an
introspective, imaginative and thoughtful individual who lived
on his nerves as well as by his wits and courage: quite likely a
poet, in fact, and certainly a musician, as we are told explicitly by
that part of the Old Testament which is most reliable for factual
accuracy and detail. David believed in public performance and
participated in it, and religious poetry set to music was exactly
what he liked.

There is, too, an element of state policy in some of the psalms
which suggest to me a kingly hand. And the psalmist's zeal for the
right often found expression in a passionate desire to see God's
vengeance inflicted on the wicked, who are as like as not enemies
of state. These Imprecatory Psalms, as they are termed (58, 68, 69,
109, 137, etc.) are distantly reminiscent of the Ancient Egyptian
Execration Texts, repetitive and rhythmic cursing-prayers for
invoking the wrath of various gods on Pharaoh's enemies (and
later, in vulgar use, by individuals against personal enemies) and
which reek of paganism at its most distasteful. The Imprecatory
Psalms are potent and gamey stuff too, and when the somewhat
mealy-mouthed Anglican bishops prepared the revised *Book of*

Common Prayer in the 1920s, they omitted from public recitation these and similar psalms whose tone of hatred and revenge they considered inconsistent with the spirit of Christianity. This may have been one reason why members of the House of Commons, who took a more robust view of things, rejected the measure in 1928.

The book of Psalms as it has come down to us is a liturgical work for regular, public performance. These prayers are meant to be chanted or sung by an entire congregation, with or without music, and there is little doubt that collectively they formed the official hymn book of the Second Temple, erected after the return of the Jews from Babylonian exile. They were rather like the *Book of Common Prayer* or the *Stonyhurst Canzionale* which I used at school. When, at the Reformation, the psalms were translated into English and put to music, and roared out by congregations of many thousands at St Paul's Cross, immediately outside St Paul's Cathedral in London, the effect may not have been very different from what took place at the Temple in Jerusalem in the second half of the first millennium BC.

But the transcendent merit of the psalms is that they lend themselves to private, solitary prayer as well as to public performance. Jesus Christ seems to have recited the psalms to himself and he certainly employed ideas from them in his discourses (e.g. the metaphor from Psalm 118 of 'the stone which the builders rejected'). He quoted the psalms (22 and 31) even on the Cross. And it is hard to think of any great man of the early Christian Church, from St Paul on – or, for that matter, any great rabbi – who did not make continual and extensive use of the psalms. St Augustine worked out in his lengthy commentary on the psalms that the Christian message is prefigured in almost every one. St Jerome and St Ambrose, and many other doctors and teachers, recommended Christians to use the psalms constantly. And they did. When I was a boy, every priest of the Roman Catholic Church who said the Divine Office from his breviary dutifully got through all the psalms once a week. (This has now been changed: I do not know why – perhaps because priests are thought to be too busy doing others things, like preaching the 'social gospel', etc.) The Anglican liturgy goes through the cycle once a month. Devotion to the psalms cuts across every barrier of religious temperament and affiliation. It was one thing people as diverse as monkish Benedictines and fastidious Puritans, Luther and Francis Xavier, Wesley and Newman, had in common – they loved and continually recited the psalms.

Even more striking was the fact that, over the centuries, the psalms were the daily prayer-fodder of secular men and women as well as ecclesiastics. Warlike knights usually had a little psalter tucked away among their gear. It slowly became dog-eared as they used it on campaign. Kings and queens had their personal psalters, very elaborate ones by the leading miniaturists for public display, and much smaller ones, still richly decorated though, for their personal use. These books too, where they survive, often show the marks of continual use. It seems to me a pity that this habit of reciting the psalms to oneself has lapsed among most people. They still have a huge amount to offer us all, and I am sure that many today, of all ages, both sexes, all kinds of temperament, including those who find regular religious worship distasteful and personal prayer difficult, would be astonished, if they looked into the psalms, by their relevance and riches. They are, as one poet put it, 'The pastoral heart of England' – and of other lands too.

The psalms, being both public and private, transcend the fundamental division of prayer. In the ancient world, I imagine virtually all prayer was public. The ancients did not like or understand the need for privacy. There was something subversive about private acts. Even in private, men prayed aloud. They read aloud, always. Silent reading seems to have been unknown in the classical world and came into use only in the second half of the fourth century AD. When St Augustine first met St Ambrose, he was struck by the fact that the great Bishop of Milan read to himself: 'His eyes scanned the page, and his mind penetrated its meaning, but his voice and tongue were silent.' Ambrose certainly prayed silently too. But he saw the point of public prayer better than anyone else in those times. It was St Ambrose, in the splendid new basilica he completed in Milan in 386, who created the prototype medieval cathedral worship, with daily Mass, regular prayers at morning and evening and sometimes at other periods of the day, and special ceremonies to commemorate the saints according to a strict calendar. To combat Arians and other heretics, and the lingering paganism of the dying classical world, he deliberately dramatised the cathedral services, clothing the priests in splendid vestments, introducing the antiphonal singing of the psalms and new-fangled metrical hymns. For this singing he employed professional choristers, but he also trained the congregation. He was fighting the Arians with their own weapons, for Arius had been a great writer of propaganda hymns – popular monotheist ditties for guilds of tradesmen, holy marching songs for soldiers, vast numbers of whom had become Arians, and sacred sea-shanties for sailors. So Ambrose wrote his own hymns for trinitarian Christianity and he had a knack for it. He was the first to put Christian prayers into hymn form, turning them into memorable iambic diameters in four-line stanzas of eight syllables to the line, which could easily be set to music and taught to the congregation. Four are still in use.

Thus St Ambrose began the long and fruitful tradition of Christian liturgical music, with not only the psalms and hymns but, even more important, the principal prayers of the Mass – Kyrie, Confiteor, Gloria, Sequence, Credo, Sanctus, Benedictus and Agnus Dei – set to music and sung by choir or congregation or both. It is impossible to think of Western music without it. First through plain-chant, then through polyphony, finally through orchestrated settings of the Mass for full choir, these prayers became the texts used by most of the greatest composers, from Byrd and Palestrina and Purcell, through Bach and Mozart and Beethoven, then on to Verdi and finally, in our own day, to Britten, to develop musical forms. It is broadly true to say, from King David's day to this, that prayer created music and music was, until the rise of secular opera, a form of prayer, or its handmaiden. Some held and hold, of course, that prayer and music can be at variance. The Puritans of the sixteenth century argued that elaborate music was a form of vanity which destroyed prayer, that polyphony in particular was an obstacle to sincere prayer. They insisted there could not be more than one note on each syllable of a musical setting of a prayer. This was not what St Ambrose had believed. He argued that the length and complexity of a musical setting, and not least its volume, were important elements in public prayer. He specifically approved of harmonics and wrote: 'From the singing of men, women, virgins and children, there is a harmonious volume of sound, like the waves of the ocean.' He thought the volume frightened the devil, while the harmonics and the beauty of the melodic line were pleasing to God. Over the centuries most people have tended to agree with St Ambrose rather than the Puritans. The grand musical settings can indeed help us to pray and give us spiritual insights that we might not be able to obtain in any other way. Who has not been uplifted by Bach's B-minor Mass or his settings for the Passion? Who does not feel that the requiem masses composed by Mozart and Verdi enable us to think of the dead, and their relationship with God, more profoundly but also more positively than before we heard the memorial prayers in these sublime settings?

The word 'uplift' is a key one in prayer. The great eighth-century Greek-speaking theologian, St John of Damascus, distinguishes between public and vocal prayer, what he calls 'the decent beseeching of Him', and private silent prayer, which he calls 'the ascent of the mind to God' (*ascensus intellectus in Deum*). By mind, incidentally, St John did not mean the reason (*ratio*), but the faculty of spiritual vision. An alternative way of putting it is expressed in the phrase *sursum corda*, 'let us lift up the heart'. It is as though the person praying, silently and internally, not opening his or her mouth, nevertheless almost physically, as it were, sends up unspoken words to God. And the words must be tied to their thoughts – a point made, in his wicked despair, by Claudius, the bad king in *Hamlet*, who is observed praying in his chapel by the would-be-vengeful Prince:

> My words fly up, my thoughts remain below
> Words without thoughts never to Heaven go.

This practice of private prayer, of uplifting thoughts to Heaven, is not as old as public communion with God, but it is ancient nonetheless. It was already practised in Jesus Christ's day, and perhaps he learned it from his holy mother, Mary, who as a young virgin utters a prayer of acceptance the moment she is told by the Angel Gabriel that she is to bear the Son of God: 'Behold the handmaid of the Lord; be it unto me according to thy word.' Later, when she visits her cousin Elizabeth, Mary breaks into that exultant prayer we now know as the *Magnificat*, beginning 'My soul doth magnify the Lord, and my spirit hath rejoiced in God my saviour.' This spontaneous expression of Mary's joy in her state, with its radical notions of exalting the humble and over-throwing the mighty – so prophetic of the coming message of Christianity – may seem strange coming from the lips of a young virgin. But it has echoes of the psalms too, and we must assume that Mary was brought up in a household where the psalms were frequently, perhaps daily, recited, and had entered its common, everyday language. At all events, these private prayers of Mary, addressed to herself or to a single member of her family, were the precursors of the private prayers which Jesus addressed to God on a number of occasions, notably when he went into the desert to pray for his mission and again, at the end of it, when he prayed alone in the Garden of Gethsemane for strength to endure his coming Passion.

In the sixth chapter of St Matthew's Gospel, we find Jesus recommending to his disciples that they should avoid ostentatious religiosity. They should give to charity privately – 'do not sound a trumpet before thee' – and, when praying, they should not 'be as the hypocrites are: for they love to pray standing in the synagogues and in the corners of the streets, that they may be seen of men'. Instead they should pray privately: 'But thou, when thou prayest, enter into thy closet, and when thou hast shut thy door, pray to thy Father which is in secret.' Jesus then gave his disciples the text of what we now call the Lord's Prayer, and it is clear that he intended this as a private prayer in the first instance, though it is also perfectly adapted to public services.

Private prayer, then, is an essential part of Christianity, in accordance with the wishes of its founder. Jesus Christ gave his disciples the pattern of an ideal prayer, and it has been said daily by all Christians, whatever their sectarian leanings, ever since – it is one of the most important things they all have in common (though they argue a bit about one or two of the phrases). But Jesus did not insist that all private prayer must follow patterns. Prayer can take all kinds of shapes, from a simple ejaculation to an elaborately composed address, with every possible variation in between. But a complete prayer, or group of prayers forming a whole for daily recital, ought to contain four distinct elements. I have seen these set down in various different ways, but this is the way I would describe them.

First there must be praise and thanksgiving. A prayer begins with an act of adoration, of recognition of God's goodness and omnipotence and of one's love for and service to him. This is an act of abasement and humility, to be done without reserve because what we are doing is not so much saluting a mighty personage as paying reverence to the principle and embodiment of goodness and love. In this salutation we also acknowledge and render thanks for blessings already received, and there should be no difficulty about this because we all have things to be grateful for – many more things, as a rule, than we are aware of until we begin to list them.

Then follows confession and repentance. We have to acknowledge, having just thanked God for his gifts, that we have made him a poor return, and sinned both against him and our neighbours. We have to admit this, repent it, and promise to amend. Now all prayers should contain this element of confession. It is quite essential, in my view, that we dwell upon our failings with great sincerity. That is extremely difficult to do – but it does work. In my experience the specific recognition of faults does in practice help me to correct them. Hence, in the evening, when I can face it – and I cannot always or even very often – I conduct an examination of conscience just before I go to bed. A really good, practising Christian does it every night without fail. Systematically going through the day which has passed, and fearlessly picking out the faults and admitting them, is such an unpleasant and sobering experience that it does act as a deterrent, however slight, against recidivism. It works for a lot of people. It works for me. In fact I believe it works for everyone, if done honestly and relentlessly. It is one of the most valuable religious practices I know of. Of course, I do not mean that every prayer should contain this examination – that is a nightly ritual. But every prayer should contain a confessional element.

The third element deals with our intentions. This is the creative aspect of prayer. A religious life does not merely consist of the avoidance of sin and the performance of worthy acts as and when the opportunity offers. It ought to have more shape than that, a purpose or pattern one sets for oneself. We must intend to conduct ourselves in a certain way, to give a religious dimension to our normal, professional or worldly activities, to try and order our lives so that opportunities to do God's will do not merely pop up or not, as the case may be, but are systematically sought and found. The intentional aspect of prayer is a form of dedication, a commitment to positive virtue, both spiritual and practical. We ought to be specific and concrete, set ourselves goals and determine how they will be achieved.

Finally, and leading from this, come the requests, for ourselves and for others. We need help from God in carrying through our intentions, especially our efforts to improve ourselves and avoid sin. This is one of the most ancient practices of the Judeo-Christian tradition. The First Book of Kings, in the Old Testament, shows us Solomon, having just succeeded to the throne, asking God for the strength and wisdom to discharge his duties properly – 'Give therefore thy servant an understanding heart to judge thy people, that I may discern between good and bad; for who is able to judge this thy so great a people?' We are further told that 'the speech pleased the Lord', and because Solomon had been unselfish and asked not for long life or riches but for wisdom to help others, the Lord answered, 'Lo! I have given thee a wise and an understanding heart.'

Now it is interesting that this kind of request was unknown among even the civilised pagans, such as the Stoics, who in some other respects were close to our religious tradition. Cicero, in his *De Natura Deorum*, says it is quite proper to pray to Jupiter for good fortune, since that is in the gift of the gods, but he adds that 'no one has ever referred to God the acquisition of virtue', since that is in man's own power. So it is, indeed, but man often fails to acquire it nonetheless, and it seems logical and natural to ask God for assistance. So Christians have always agreed and, even more so than the ancient Hebrews, they have prayed to God for holiness, insisting that true holiness is impossible without prayer.

So we pray for help in improving ourselves. No day is complete without a prayer for better conduct: we stand so much in need of it. But after this come specific requests for ourselves and for others. These cover everything. There is nothing so large – the salvation of the world – and nothing so small – the health of a favourite dog or the victory of a football team – that is above or beneath personal prayer. When Abraham was petitioning God over Sodom, he feared that God would become angry after his third or fourth request. But God is never angry in response to prayer, or even wearisome in the face of exigent requests from those who, however rewarded, never return a word of thanks for favours received. God does not have these human failings, and the numbers, complexity and variety of our requests leave him undismayed. But, of course, he does not necessarily grant our prayers immediately or at all. Why? There is no fathoming the mysteries of God's bounty. And why does he give us some things we ask for but not others? There again, there is no answer. The only thing we can be absolutely certain of is that God has good reasons for all his decisions. They are all taken with our ultimate interests in mind, difficult though this may be for us to perceive at present. God, quite literally, knows best, and we must be content with this thought. But there is nothing to stop us petitioning. No prayer, however reiterated, however banal or commonplace, however self-centred indeed, is unwelcome to God. The most selfish prayers, in a way, are the most sincere – as Dr Johnson observed, 'No man is a hypocrite in his pleasures.'

I now come to certain aspects of prayer which some non-Catholics find particularly irritating or even scandalous. So they are welcome to skip this passage. On the other hand, reading it may remove their misunderstandings. It is possible to pray not just directly to God, but in addition to those near to God in Heaven: the Virgin Mary and the saints. We are praying to these once-human, now everlastingly blessed beings not because they have power as such, but because they have the opportunity to intercede with God on our behalf. Now it may be asked: if everyone has a direct line to God, why is it necessary to use these inter-mediaries? Or is there a hierarchy of access to God rather like in a worldly court, such as the court of Louis XIV as described by Saint-Simon in his *Memoirs*? This set out at length who had the *grandes entrées* or the *petites entrées*, or whatever, for purposes of putting requests to the Roi Soleil personally, as he drew on his shirt or his boots.

I am not sure that I have a good answer to these questions, other than the unsatisfying one that a great many people, more pious and wiser than I am, have thought it worth their while to pray in this manner. I pray directly to God, and I pray through the saints. Some saints stand exceptionally high in God's regard, as is only right – his mother highest of all. And some saints are identified with particular activities. Like millions of other Catholics I pray to St Anthony to find me things I have lost or mislaid – that is, to intercede with God to make things turn up. I pray to St Christopher before a journey, especially if it is long or hazardous. I pray to St George for courage and to St Thomas Aquinas and my namesake St Bede for wisdom and guidance in thinking out difficult matters. There are all kinds of useful saints for ailments, but those I do not bother because I am seldom or never ill – though I have prayed, occasionally, to St Blaise, who is believed to help cure sore throats.

It does not matter to me if a saint has been struck off the official calendar because of doubts about his or her historical existence, like St George, because God is not interested in historical facts in this instance, but rather the image of holiness which has been created in the minds of the faithful by long tradition of pious supplication – that is good enough for him. Equally, I do not mind if the persons I pray to have never been in the calendar. Thus I sometimes pray to Jane Austen for help in literary matters, regarding her as a saintly woman who lived a life of exemplary virtue and industry, culminating in a painful death borne with stoic courage and faith in Christ – and so well worthy of being canonised. And I pray to Dr Johnson too, another good and exemplary person, because his problems often seem so similar to my own. Some readers may laugh at this. But I do not mind. Many religious practices are ridiculous in the eye of the beholder. But they make sense to the participant and, if they do, we may be sure they are acceptable to God. Dr Johnson himself referred to the case of the writer Christopher Smart, who scandalised people by getting on his knees in the street in order to pray. Dr Johnson thought this quite all right and would sometimes get down alongside him: 'I would as lief pray with Kit Smart as with anyone else.' Francis Thompson, another odd fellow, and a Christian writer of great power, also did strange things in public and raised eyebrows. But no matter; we can be pretty sure that he is in Heaven now.

We must not despise any aids to prayer if we think we need them. Catholics have been criticised for making use of images. This is an old argument, which went on among the Ancient Israelites before Christianity even existed as a faith, and it will go on to the end of time. This is surely a matter where there is no rule valid for all men and women. Few people can now be so ignorant as to believe that Catholics, for instance, actually worship the statues and holy pictures in their churches and houses. But temperaments vary. Some find a statue conducive to holy prayer. Others find it an obstacle, even blasphemous. I have numerous holy objects in my study where I write my books and articles. I have, for instance, a little cross of mother-of-pearl which I bought in Jerusalem when I paid my first visit to the Church of the Holy Sepulchre. It was blessed for me there, and when I came home I gave it to my mother, who valued it. On her deathbed she returned it to me, with her blessing, and now it hangs near where I write. I also have a fine reproduction of a painting by Raphael of the Virgin Mary and the Infant Jesus, the original of which is in Florence and known as *La Madonna del Gran' Ducco*. It radiates holy serenity and simplicity and I am very fond of it: it rests to the left on my typewriter.

On the right is a very different object, a large eighteenth-century crucifix, finely carved in wood and painted, which once stood on the refectory wall of a Spanish convent of nuns. It was looted in the Spanish Civil War and found its way to England, and I bought it some years ago for a modest price in London. It is immensely realistic as to Christ's sufferings: some would say gruesome. But that is the Spanish manner and I think it right to be reminded forcibly of the sufferings Christ underwent for our sakes. So I was very pleased to buy it and originally intended to hang it in the hall of our London house, to gratify Catholic visitors, and administer a salutory shock to Protestant ones and agnostics. But this my wife Marigold would not allow, for all kinds of reasons, including the conclusive one that 'It would frighten the grandchildren.' So now it hangs in my study instead, and I see that my wife was perfectly correct. This is the right place for it. I kiss Our Lord's poor feet, nailed to the cross and bleeding, before I begin my work each day, thus acknowledging the debt we owe him, and I can do so in the privacy of my study without arousing derision or scandal. As for the grandchildren, they are occasionally allowed in to glimpse it, and find the experience enjoyable, if not exactly elevating.

So let us not despise these aids to prayer, be they statues or pictures, rosary beads, little crosses or medals to wear round the neck, and all the other *impedimenta* of old-style Christianity. But equally, let us not criticise those who conscientiously reject such aids and preserve complete austerity in the way they address God. I can see there is a lot to be said for the stripped-down forms of Christianity, where no concessions are made to human frailty and each man or woman must present themselves alone and unaided in front of the creator and pray nakedly. There are some moods in which I feel this may be the best and purest form of prayer. I once stayed in a remote Scottish Highland community called Applecross, on the far side of a huge range of high mountains on the West Coast of Scotland. It is accessible only by sea or a perilous mountain road, and the form of Presbyterianism practised there is ultra-austere. Even in this small community there are different divisions of the Calvinist Church, and separate chapels, and each year when Easter approaches, the only time at which Communion is taken, the elders of the most austere chapel decide which of the congregation is worthy to receive it there. If judged unworthy, a man or woman must then retreat to the next most austere chapel, and attend and take Communion there. I asked what happened if a sinner gradually dropped through all the grades and was finally found unworthy to take Communion even in the fifth or lowest. My informant scratched his head and eventually answered: 'I suppose there would be nothing but for him to become a *Roman Caathlic.'*

Well, I am a Roman Catholic and I need these things. I like the ancient stone crucifixes you find by the wayside in the Celtic fringes of the British Isles, and in Brittany and Galicia too, and the wooden ones set up high in the Alps and Pyrenees. I like the many special devotions which are a feature of ancient churches all over Europe, and especially in Rome itself – the *scala sancta* or holy staircase, which one ascends on one's knees, and the like. Pilgrimages appeal to me, and great shrines like Lourdes and Lisieux and Fátima, which I once despised as the mumbo-jumbo side of Christianity, now seem to me useful and holy. I do not share Erasmus's distaste for relics, though I do not have any particular devotion to them either, and I can see why they are important to some people. I can tolerate, in my old age, all forms of religious devotion or practices which seem to come from God or are acceptable to him, or are not obviously fraudulent or super-stitious or pagan. I have become broad-minded. I see that people find their own way to worship, and their own aids in praying – so let them. But I am less tolerant than I was towards those who, themselves without faith or reverence, use the media to sneer at and defile the things that others hold dear – the story of the Crucifixion, the image of the Mother of God, the life of holy nuns and the simple faith of the poor in spirit. I feel myself increasingly militant towards these mockers and pollutors, not at all inclined to turn the other cheek. But I may be mistaken. Militancy is often misguided, and prayer is better. When Mother Theresa, holiest of living nuns, was monstrously and mendaciously abused in a television programme in 1994, she merely remarked that she would pray for those who made it.

Prayer is always an answer even if it is not invariably the complete answer. There are countless prayers to be said, accumulated over thousands of years during which the Judeo-Christian tradition has shaped itself. They exist for all occasions, all temperaments. I have said little in this book about mysticism, because I am not a mystic and feel no inclination that way, and therefore am ill-equipped to write about it. But it occupies a distinctive place in religious experience, especially in Christianity, and everyone at some time ought to explore its riches, beginning perhaps with St John of the Cross and his pupil, St Teresa. You cannot know there is not a mystic in you until you have made the attempt to discover it. But the other resources of written prayer and sacred devotions are almost limitless and I will not list them. I am constantly discovering new prayers, often to be found in fusty old books and missals and manuals of devotion which have been out of use for hundreds of years.

One should also make use of spontaneous prayer, doing privately what the Quakers do so impressively in public. A prayer written by the dictates of one's own heart must be especially dear to God. The practice of spontaneous prayer is an important one and not difficult to acquire. I also try my hand, from time to time, at written prayers. I was led to this by reading Dr Johnson's. He composed and wrote down prayers all his life, and they have two notable characteristics. First, they are humble. There is no vainglorious striving for literary effect in them. On the contrary, he was content to follow the liturgical forms. But within them he produced evidence of much careful thought, of anxious and close inquiry into his shortcomings, and of great anguish at his apparent inability to overcome them. In other words, they were true prayers, sent directly to God with tearful sincerity, genuine remorse and a huge desire to improve – together with grateful acknowledgment of God's many mercies. Since I got to know these prayers, I have written a number myself, for a variety of occasions, public and private, for my own use and for the use of others. I give some examples in an appendix.

Dr Johnson's prayers are notable for their persistence. That is a salient merit of prayer. But another is routine. I have already noted that one must not despise the more mechanical sides of religion. They are particularly important in prayer. One should habituate oneself to praying every day, at certain times. Prayer in the morning is essential, to dedicate one's day, and so is prayer in the evening, to review it. There are other times when prayers are particularly appropriate: at meals, for instance; before beginning a particular task, and when it is finished; before anticipated pleasures, so that they be innocent or lawful; and after them, in gratitude. I like to go to church every morning. It is a habit I acquired from my mother, who went to church every day of her adult life, without fail, except when prevented by illness or other unavoidable duties. I have done it most of my adult life too, even in periods when my faith has been feeble or virtually non-existent, and my mode of life particularly unsatisfactory, as it still is in so many ways. In my case there is no particular merit in going to church daily. I like to do so, and miss it when it is impossible.

I have a great fancy for visiting cathedrals if they are nearby. I used to go to the Catholic Cathedral of Gibraltar, when I was serving in the army, and again to the Catholic Cathedral in Washington DC, when I was a visiting professor at a think-tank there. Neither was impressive, but both became very holy places for me. When I lived in Paris, in the early 1950s, I used to walk to my office in the rue St Georges, and call in at Notre-Dame de Lorette, a dark, rather dingy church at the bottom of the rue Pigalle, known as the Church of the Prostitutes, and much frequented by dancers, strip-tease artists, waitresses and plain whores, decently dressed of course and, when attending church in the morning, an exemplary type of Christian. When I worked at the *New Statesman* in Lincoln's Inn Fields, I went every morning before work to a noble classical church on Kingsway, which has a particularly fine rood-screen high above the main altar and an atmosphere peculiarly conducive, I found, to private, silent prayer. Now I go to the church of St Mary and the Angels, near my house in Bayswater, a fine nineteenth-century church which was for many years the headquarters of the great Cardinal Manning, where he kept all his papers. I do not often attend Mass there, which is a bit late for me, but I invariably say my morning prayers there, kneeling near a statue of St Anne and Our Lady. My mother had a particular devotion to St Anne, Our Lady's mother, after whom she was named, and I too often pray for the intercession of that gracious lady. It is good to go to church, at the beginning of each day, to step out of a world full of hurry and perplexity and material problems, into the quiet, timeless, tranquillity of a house built for prayer and worship, where the values have nothing whatever to do with the world outside.

In the end, that is what the love and worship of God is all about: to turn our minds, and if possible our bodies too, away from earthliness to perfection, from doubt to certitude, from the self to goodness, and from the flesh to the spirit. This act of turning is something we should do every day of our lives, and as often as we can in each day, so that in the end it becomes second nature and we cease to need to turn, but become one with the great spirit in whom alone we find peace and our destiny.

Prayers for various occasions

Morning prayer

Almighty and eternal God, I thank you for having created the world, for having created me and put me on it, and for giving me family, friends and a job to do. I thank you especially for giving all of us the gift of free will.

I am sorry that I have used it to sin against you in thought, word and deed, through my own most grievous fault. I am sorry that I have sinned against you with my body, my mind and my spirit.

I am particularly sorry because of the many blessings you have bestowed upon me. You gave me the best of parents, William and Anne, to whom I owe everything. You gave me the best of wives, Marigold, without whom I would have long since died an ignominious death. You gave me a good elder brother, Tom, and two good elder sisters, Clare and Elfride, who were kind to me in my youth, and helped me.

You have given me four good children, Daniel, Cosmo, Luke and Sophie, and two good daughters-in-law, Sarah and Cathy, and five good grandchildren, Sam, Emily, Tycho, Edith and Leo.

You have given me good health, which I have often abused, and talent, which I hope I have not abused, and the opportunity to exercise it. You have enabled me to earn a decent income, and to have two fine houses, and a comfortable life for my family, and savings and the ability to help others.

For all these blessings, and for many others, I thank you. I am ashamed that I have responded so ungratefully and meanly, with so many sins, grievous and petty, repeated so many times, despite so many promises of amendment. I beg of you to look not on my sins but on the faith of your church, and to listen to the prayers of those who love me. Please give me the intelligence and wisdom to avoid sin, and the occasions of sin, and bless me with the fortitude of mind to put all my faults behind me, once and for all.

Almighty God, grant your assistance in my efforts to make a positive contribution to the well-being of others, especially the poor, the sick, the friendless and the unhappy. Open my eyes to those who are in need, give me wisdom to see how I can best help them, and grant me the strength, patience and tact to provide that help today and at all times when it is most needed. Teach me to fight the battle against self which is the most difficult of all conflicts, and the one most worth winning.

And, finally Almighty God, grant that this day I may perform some act which will be worthy of my better self, which will be of benefit to some cause dear to your heart, or help one of your creatures in distress, and thus be to your honour and satisfaction. Amen.

Evening prayer

Almighty God, at the end of another day you have been pleased to grant me, I thank you for all the blessings I have enjoyed during it, and I earnestly pray that my own actions, or non-actions, will pass your close scrutiny. (*Here follows an examination of conscience.*) Lord, you see that I have sinned. You know that I recognise my sins – they are old friends, or rather enemies – and that I deplore them. Please grant me the strength not to repeat them yet again.

Please grant me the blessing of a tranquil night, so that I may arise refreshed to do my work in your name, and to perform such services as you assign me. And if you should summon me to account during the night, extend to me that mercy and forbearance which I do not merit but which is in your loving and forgiving nature, so that I may join you in your kingdom of truth, justice, love, goodness and beauty. Amen.

Prayer in sickness

You have thought fit, O Lord, to visit me with this affliction of body. If it continue, your will be done. Give me strength and patience to endure it. Let me offer up any pain and distress for the sake of those whose sufferings are much greater than mine. If my pain grows worse, may I have the fortitude of mind to submit to your will, in the comforting knowledge that you, in your mercy, will not place on me a greater burden than I can bear. In your own good time, give me relief and restore me to health, so that I may continue to serve you. Or, if it be your will to call me to judgment, teach me to compose myself for death, to recall my sins and repent them, and to leave this life in faith and hope.

Prayer for sleep

Lord, I have struggled this day to do your will and to perform the tasks which you, in your infinite wisdom, have set me. In your mercy and care for us all, grant me now the rest my body requires, that I may rise tomorrow morning rested and ready to do your work and mine in the day ahead. Spare me uneasy dreams and nightmares, and allow me that sweet repose which composes the mind, restores the body and makes us eager to do your service.

Prayer to banish worry

Gracious and sovereign Lord, who has power over all things, enter my mind and calm it. I have thought carefully over the problem which faces me. I have considered it in the light of your teaching and of the duties and responsibilities you have given me. I have prayed anxiously to you for guidance. In the light of all this, I have taken what I honestly believe to be the right decision, and done all in my power to make it effective. I pray you, O Lord, to reassure me that I have done right and then to help me to compose my mind, banish doubts and backward glances, and turn afresh to the new tasks which you will set me.

Prayer for a journey

Lord, bless this journey I am about to undertake. Grant me speedy and safe passage to my destination. May my voyage not be in vain, but in your service and for your honour and glory, as well as for my own lawful purposes. Let my work on this enterprise be fruitful. And, when it is completed, let my return to my family and home be sure and swift, so that I may render thanks to you from my own blessed hearth, among those I love. Amen.

Prayer on behalf of a dying woman who has nobly endured great suffering

Lord Jesus, you who suffered grievously unto death but who never lacked the courage to bear it and sanctify it, have pity on your faithful servant. Like you she has suffered much and endured much. Like you she has borne it all without complaint or recrimination. Like you she has shown courage unto death. Help her in her agony, make her final moments peaceable and secure, and ease her into her eternal reward. Make her endurance and fortitude an example to us all, so that when we, too, are called to suffer and to face death, we may do so in the same spirit of cheerfulness, and with the same confidence in the mercy and love of Almighty God our Father.

We thank you, Lord Jesus, for showing us, in so exemplary a manner, how a Christian soul can turn pain into blessings and a final illness into a triumph over adversity. Following in your own footsteps, our dear friend, by her steadfastness and magnanimity, has won her victory over death itself and so earned her safe passage into your heavenly kingdom. We bless you and thank you for this special mercy, and we implore you to help us show the same valour when our own time comes.

Prayer for a friend who has suffered a grievous reverse

O Lord, have mercy on and pity my friend who has just heard the bad news. You know how anxious he was for this blessing. You know how hard he worked for it and how he and his family were counting on it. Have pity on their disappointment. Give him strength to accept this blow to his hopes, let him not be discouraged or despair, but grant him the magnanimity to set to work afresh to rebuild his fortunes. And please give me the wit and wisdom to comfort him in his dismay, to encourage him in his efforts and to render him all practical help in my power. Amen.

Prayer to be said by a Princess beset by troubles

Almighty and eternal God, who rules over all the states and kingdoms of the world, have mercy and pity on me, called as I am to serve in a high place. Give me guidance and counsel, so that I may do what is right, and avoid what is wrong. Give me the strength of purpose, and the courage, to follow that wise counsel, even in the face of angry opposition and ridicule. Teach me to recognise and discount the foolish or vicious advice of those who wish to exploit my position, or to mislead me and draw me into evil courses.

Lord God, give me strength and prudence in educating my children, so that they may serve you faithfully in the positions to which you have been pleased to call them. Help me to teach them to follow your commandments, to love our country and to serve it dutifully. Enable me to mingle my love for them with a proper regard for their welfare and judicious upbringing. Give me the power to persuade them to adopt lifelong habits of unselfishness, self-discipline and industry.

Almighty God, be at my side always to assist me in my per-plexities. Forgive me my past faults and foolish errors. Help me to devote myself, mind, body and soul, with all my strength and with all my talents, to the service of your people, and especially to the people of my own country, most of all the sick, the unfor-tunate, the deprived, the fearful, the abandoned and the shamed. Be pleased to guide, inform, empower and render successful my efforts.

In your mercy and goodness, Almighty God, give me calmness, fortitude, a clear mind and a secure conscience in performing all the tasks you set me, so that I may do your bidding to the best of my ability, and ultimately deserve to share in your heavenly kingdom, through Jesus Christ our Lord, Amen.

A prayer for success

O Lord, I have many blessings for which to thank you. Now, in your goodness and mercy I ask for another. You know what a great store I have set on this project. I believe my wishes for its completion are worthy and innocent. If it be your will, allow my hopes to be realised. Let this thing come to pass. When it does so, may I refrain from exultation but, with a humble and contrite heart, render you grateful thanks for your bounty. Amen.

A prayer for forgiveness

Almighty God, I have sinned. You know what I have done. I have wronged you and one of your creatures. The wrong I did was wilful. I plead in extenuation that I was hasty and did not work out in advance the full consequences of my act. But that is no excuse. I am no longer a young man. I have experience of these things. The fact is, I was selfish and thoughtless. Please God, you see that I am now sorrowful and full of remorse. Accept my humble act of contrition. Assist me to make wise and tactful restitution. Give me strength to guard against any repetition of the offence. And, by forgiving me this sin, encourage me to serve you more positively and earnestly in future. Amen.

Index